The Oberon System

The Oberon System

User Guide and Programmer's Manual

Martin Reiser

IBM Zürich Research Laboratory
Säumerstrasse 4
8803 Rüschlikon

and

Institut für Computersysteme
ETH Zentrum
8092 Zürich

 ACM Press

New York, New York

 Addison-Wesley Publishing Company

Wokingham, England · Reading, Massachusetts · Menlo Park, California
New York · Don Mills, Ontario · Amsterdam · Bonn
Sydney · Singapore · Tokyo · Madrid · San Juan

Cover designed by Hybert Design and Type, Maidenhead incorporating an illustration of Oberon, Uranus' outermost satellite, courtesy of NASA, and printed by The Riverside Printing Co. (Reading) Ltd.
Typeset by CRB Typesetting Services, Ely, Cambs.
Printed in Great Britain by The Bath Press, Avon.

First printed 1991.

British Library Cataloguing in Publication Data
Reiser, Martin
   The Oberon system : user guide and programmer's manual.
   1. Computers. Operating systems
   I. Title
   005.43

   ISBN 0-201-54422-9

Library of Congress Cataloging in Publication Data
Reiser, Martin.
   The Oberon system : user guide and programmer's manual / Martin Reiser.
     p. cm.
   Includes bibliographical references and index.
   ISBN 0-201-54422-9
   1. Operating systems (Computers) 2. Oberon. I. Title.
QA76.76.063R45   1991
005.4'46--dc20   90-26629
                                             CIP

Preface

The progress in computing hardware power continues unabated. Processors double their speed every two to three years and the sizes of memory and storage devices do the same.

But what is happening on the software front? The designs of the basic operating systems which we are using are quite dated and a major international theme is standardization. New designs and architectures are hardly ever attempted. Rather, layer upon layer of code are added without regard to size or efficiency. The hope is that the progress in hardware will cure all software ills. However, a critical observer may observe that software manages to outgrow hardware in size and sluggishness. Says Niklaus Wirth, one of the authors of Oberon: 'In times when the overwhelming trend is to standardize languages, operating systems, communication protocols, interfaces, and documentation methods, often long before they have proven their merits, it is important to point out that it is still possible to depart from the bandwagon trail, although traveling may require endurance and cause some headache.'[1]

Jürg Gutknecht and Niklaus Wirth have had the courage to depart from the 'bandwagon trail' and to build a system from scratch – hardware and software. The result is the *Ceres* family of workstations and the *Oberon* operating system. To implement the Oberon system a new language has been designed which simplifies Modula-2 and adds constructs for object-oriented programming. This language, too, has been christened Oberon.

The result of only a few years effort by two University professors is first-rate and a tribute to the merits of the small programming team striving for the most efficient solution at every step.

---

[1] Wirth N. (1989). 'Designing a System from Scratch,' *Structured Programming*, **1**, 10–18.

Features of Oberon are as follows. It

- is fully graphics-based utilizing a bitmapped large display;
- is based on object oriented programming concepts implementing viewers as well as texts and other documents as abstract data types;
- uses dynamic loading;
- has a lightning-fast one-pass compiler which gives the user almost the illusion of an interpreter;
- is very fast with respect to display refreshes and performs these refreshes with a minimum of screen flicker. It is the most responsive system by far known to the author. This responsiveness substantially improves user productivity;
- features a novel user interface, the *tool viewer* which is a blend of menus and command lines;
- abolishes modes to the greatest extent known to the author.

In summary, Oberon is a state-of-the-art system in terms of functionality. And now comes the most stunning feat: *Oberon fits into less than 200 kBytes of memory*! Oberon is an existence proof that the trend towards memory wasting software can be halted and the machine resources brought back to the user's needs – not the system's.

This book is the Oberon system reference book. It describes the novel user interface and the architecture and functions of the display system. It also contains a programming guide which discusses how the Oberon system is programmed and used.

A typical reader would have an Oberon system and would use the book as a reference. However, care has been taken to write the book in a manner which also serves the curious who would like to learn about Oberon. As a minimum prerequisite, the reader should have a knowledge of Modula-2 and have read the Oberon language report.

The book provides a complete documentation of the *standard editor, compiler, file system* and the so-called *outer core*, the data structures and procedures with which the applications programmer interfaces. The modules of the *inner core* (for example, module loader, disk drive, storage management) are not normally available. No attempt is made to discuss implementation details of the abstract data types or general design issues and trade-offs.[2]

---

[2] A good introduction into these aspects is provided by N. Wirth and J. Gutknecht in 'The Oberon System,' *Software – Practice and Experience*, **19**(9), Sept 89, pp. 857–93 and in their forthcoming book *The Oberon Project* to be published by Addison-Wesley.

Following the 'Overview' given in Chapter 1, the book is organized into three parts as described below.

Part I: User's guide

This part describes the system as perceived from the user sitting at the workstation. The human interface is explained following the important example of the *standard system editor* which is part of every Oberon system. The basic system commands exported by command modules *Edit*, *System*, *Backup*, *Net*, *Compiler* and *Miscellaneous* are documented.

A user at a workstation may go through the first two chapters, 2 and 3, sequentially. The material is logically organized such that he or she may try the examples in the manner of a tutorial.

Chapter 2 is also a reference to the Oberon human interface style and should be studied by the designer of viewer classes.

Part II: Reference

The first chapter in this part introduces details of the multitasking architecture, the concept of the Oberon objects *Frame* and *Viewer* and the principles behind the object-oriented design used for late binding of applications to the central loop component.

Then, a chapter is dedicated to each of the major modules. First, a concise description and a summary in the style of the definition module of Modula-2 is provided. Then, the definitions and functions of the module are described on the level of a reference manual. Most of the modules export one or several abstract data types and care is taken to introduce their concepts.

Part II is structured in such a way that the topics are developed in a readable manner. This means that definitions and procedures are not listed alphabetically but in an order which follows the logical concepts. The reader who simply wants an introduction to these concepts can quickly scan the detailed procedure descriptions. The user who uses the book as a reference will find individual procedures through the index.

The minimum prerequisite is familiarity with Modula-2 and some knowledge of the Oberon language as provided in the original papers by Wirth.

Part III: Programming guide

Oberon programmers fall broadly into two classes:

(1) Those who simply create commands which perform either traditional computations or work on existing abstract documents such as text.

(2) Those who produce new interactive applications which require a viewer and a handler.

The first two chapters in this part cater to both types of programmers. In Chapter 18, 'Programming commands,' it is shown how to deal with texts and files and how to produce polymorphic commands. Special treatment is given to the long running command which performs tasks such as numerically intensive computations or system simulations.

Chapter 19, 'Programming viewers and frames,' gives an in-depth discussion of the handler's structure and how it reacts to messages. A complete coverage of the system messages is provided. Programming of the display screen is also a feature of this chapter.

In Appendix A, a complete example of a non-trivial viewer class is provided. Design issues are explored and the source program text is carefully discussed. Appendices B and C describe the keyboard and ASCII characters and MS/DOS files respectively.

Part III is only of interest to the actual user of an Oberon system and requires a good working knowledge of the Oberon language.

Acknowledgements

This text could only have been written with the help of Niklaus Wirth, Jürg Gutknecht, Peter Mössenböck, Regis Crelier, Robert Griesemer, Urs Hiestand, Cuno Pfister, Karl Rege, Ralph Sommerer and Josef Templ. Their patience and contributions are deeply acknowledged.

Peter Mössenböck and Cuno Pfister went through a careful reading of the entire manuscript. Their corrections and suggestions led to substantial improvements. Needless to say that the hours of work which they invested in this book deserve special thanks.

Jürg Gutknecht made valuable suggestions with respect to the example of the viewer class 'note viewers.'

Martin Reiser
Zurich, October 1990

Contents

Trademark notice
Apple™ and Macintosh™ are registered trademarks of Apple Computer, Inc.
DECsystem™ is a trademark of Digital Equipment Corporation
IBM PS/2™ is a trademark of International Business Machines Corporation
PC–DOS™ and MS-DOS™ are trademarks of MicroSoft Corporation
SUN Sparcstation™ is a trademark of Sun Microsystems Incorporated

1 Overview

1.1 Historical notes

Professor Niklaus Wirth has a long-standing interest in compilers, programming languages and personal workstations. He achieved a first breakthrough with the programming language Pascal, conceived shortly after his appointment to ETH in 1968.[1] An electrical engineer by training, he chose a unique approach of designing languages in parallel with the development of hardware.

A first product was the Lilith personal computer, a design based on the AMD 2901 chip set from Advanced Micro Devices. The aim was to explore the potential of a stack-based machine running Pascal programs. During the project, limitations of Pascal as a system programming language became apparent. This led to the programming language Modula and later Modula-2 with the clear goal to be able to support the software of the Lilith workstation.

The successor of Lilith was Ceres-1,[2] a more conventional design based on the NS32032 microprocessor which was chosen as the best commercially available chip with regard to supporting a stack-based, separately compilable language such as Modula. Ceres features a high-resolution display and uses the mouse and keyboard as input devices. A color display is optional. A hard disk serves as store for non-volatile data and a diskette drive is used for back-up purposes. The first operating system running on Ceres-1 was Medos. It was implemented in Modula-2. Ceres-1 was soon followed by Ceres-2 using the faster NS32532 chip. Lately, Ceres-3 was completed, a diskless version featuring a NS32GX32 processor.

In late 1985 Wirth and Gutknecht started to design a system from scratch with the goal of achieving *extensibility* and *flexibility*. The

---

[1] Eidgenössische Technische Hochschule or Swiss Federal Institute of Technology.
[2] Designed by H. Eberle and N. Wirth.

project was whimsically christened Oberon by Wirth who was fascinated by the accuracy and reliability of the space probe Voyager which passed the moon Oberon of planet Uranus at the time of conception of the new project.

The sizeable effort of designing a new system was to bring insights in language and system design utilizing *concepts of object-oriented programming*. Thus, Oberon is really three things:

(1) The name of the project.

(2) A new programming language, the heir of Modula-2, which introduces *type extensions*.

(3) An operating system for a personal workstation.

Guiding principle

> *Make it as simple as possible, but not simpler.*
>
> A. Einstein

Wirth put this quote at the beginning of his paper 'The Programming Language Oberon.'[3] In our opinion, it furnishes an ideal summary of the design approach – both for the language and the operating system. Wirth and Gutknecht state:

> 'In the design of both hardware and software for the Oberon system we followed a guiding principle, namely to strive for clarity and simplicity. This is not only wise in view of the tiny team and the desire to achieve a workable system within the time bounds of human patience, but simply indispensable for producing *any* system with a claim to reliability. Clarity and simplicity is best achieved through a regular and purpose-tuned structure. This in turn is possible if the underlying model of operation is well understood, reasonably simple and free of conflicting premises.'

The Oberon language

The topic of the Oberon programming language is not the object of this book (we refer the reader to *The Oberon Language: Steps beyond Pascal and Modula*).[4] The following two quotes from Wirth put the new programming language into its proper context: as an evolution of Modula-2:

> 'Initially, it was planned to express the system in Modula, as that language supports the notion of modular design quite

---

[3] Wirth N. (1988). *Software – Practice and Experience*, **18**(7), 671–90.

[4] Reiser M. and Wirth N. Addison-Wesley Publishing Company, Inc., to be published.

effectively and with conscientiously chosen interfaces. In fact, an operating system should be no more than a set of basic modules, and the design of an application must be considered as a goal-oriented extension of that basic set: programming is always extending a given system.

Whereas modern languages, such as Modula, support the notion of extensibility in the procedural realm, the notion is less well established in the domain of data types. In particular, Modula does not allow the definition of new data types as extensions of other, programmer-defined types in an adequate manner. An additional feature was called for, thereby giving rise to an *extension* of Modula.'

'It soon became clear that the rule to concentrate on the essential and to eliminate the inessential should not only be applied to the design of the new system, but equally stringently to the language in which the system is formulated. The application of the principle thus led from Modula to a new language. However, the adjective "new" has to be understood in proper context: *Oberon evolved from Modula by very few additions and several subtractions.*[5] In relying on evolution rather than revolution we remain in the tradition of a long development that led from ALGOL to Pascal, then to Modula-2 and eventually to Oberon.'

Owing to the type extension facility, Oberon allows programming in an object-oriented style. Following the designer's philosophy, it achieves this with a minimum of constructs. There are no explicit constructs, class, method and message. This is by design, as the quote from Wirth documents:

'It is impossible explicitly to acknowledge all contributions of ideas that ultimately simmered down to what is now Oberon. Most came from the use or study of existing languages, such as Modula-2, Ada, Smalltalk and Cedar, *which often taught us how not to do it.*'[6]

We shall subsequently introduce features of Oberon from the point of view of the user interface, the language and the system architecture.

---

[5]   Italics added by the author.
[6]   Wirth N. (1988). From Modula to Oberon. *Software – Practice and Experience*, **18**(7), 662–70. Italics added by the author.

1.2   The Oberon user interface

A user, looking at the screen of a typical computer terminal or personal computer, sees, most of the time, lines of text. He or she has mastered the concept of the cursor, a point where text can be entered or deleted.

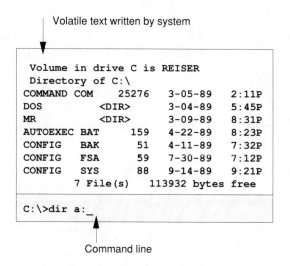

Volatile text written by system

```
Volume in drive C is REISER
Directory of C:\
COMMAND COM      25276    3-05-89    2:11P
DOS              <DIR>     3-04-89    5:45P
MR               <DIR>     3-09-89    8:31P
AUTOEXEC BAT       159     4-22-89    8:23P
CONFIG   BAK        51     4-11-89    7:32P
CONFIG   FSA        59     7-30-89    7:12P
CONFIG   SYS        88     9-14-89    9:21P
         7 File(s)    113932 bytes free

C:\>dir a:_
```

Command line

The modality of text

However, in a display as the one above, the user will quickly learn that text is not text. The list of files in our example is written by the system. It is a *volatile* text in the sense that it cannot be saved, printed or edited. Text can only be entered in the bottom line in which case it is a command. This user has discovered that text is *modal*: it is either a system message or editable text or a command.

Menus and dialog boxes

Later generations of software introduced menus: commands are displayed in lists, ready for execution by pointing. However, menus are distinct from editable texts. If a menu command requests parameters, a so-called dialog box is opened. A new mode is entered. The user must complete the box before he or she is allowed to continue.

The Oberon user interface departs radically from the standard models. The concepts of the command line and of menus are absent. Instead, there is simply one kind of text which behaves as an intelligent person not yet spoiled by so-called 'computer literacy' would expect: it can be changed, edited, printed and stored.

> *Text is a text, nothing more, nothing less.*

We shall explore the consequences of this throughout the remainder of this book.

1.2.1   Oberon display

Oberon is designed to support a human user working with a display and using the mouse and keyboard as input devices. A conscious choice was made to use a reasonably large monitor.[7] A typical Oberon display looks as follows:

Track

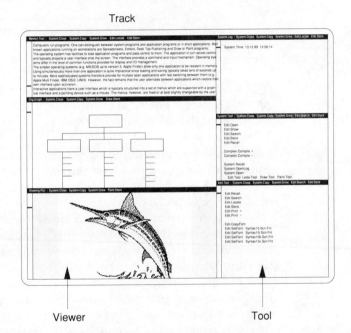

Viewer   Tool

Viewer and track   The screen is tiled into non-overlapping windows termed *viewers*. Viewers are stacked in two piles called *tracks*. Each viewer displays a document being processed by the user. Documents may be texts, graphics or pictures.

While the display shown appears familiar there is a fundamental difference of deep significance: *the modality of texts has been abolished.* What looks like menus in the title bars of the viewers is text too, no different from the editable text of the main viewer area.

---

[7] On Ceres 1024 times 800 pixels.

1.2.2   Command execution

Commands are simply typed into a text viewer and then executed by pointing at them with the mouse cursor and clicking one of the mouse keys. A command may be embedded anywhere in a text.

The command line was natural in teletype-based systems of the 1960s. Today, it is a relict whose usefulness is passed.

Command output

If a command produces output to the screen (such as the directory command shown earlier) a new text viewer is opened with the command's output text. Again, this text may be edited, stored or printed. Oberon commands produce *non-volatile* output.

> *Tools: the Bridge between 'remember and type' and 'point and click.'*

As a result of the abolition of the modality of text display and of the command line, a powerful unification of the 'remember and type' and the 'point and click' metaphors ensues.

Tool

Commands are entered into a text viewer (using the standard Oberon editor) and then executed with the mouse. It is therefore quite natural to prepare a set of frequently used commands in a text which is stored on disk. Such a text is called a *tool*.

When displayed, a tool is quite similar to a menu. A set of commands is listed and the user simply executes them with the mouse. However, if the commands request parameter input, there is no need for complex (modal) input or dialog boxes. We deal with an editable text and the parameter can be easily entered, thus recovering the flexibility of the 'remember and type' environment. In fact, Oberon tools blend almost ideally between the two worlds which, to date, both had their critics and adherents.

It is a common experience in science that principles powerful enough to unify different domains of thought transcend into novel territory. This expectation is not in vain in the case of Oberon.

Distribution of system releases is a common problem. Two things are required: a distribution medium and a sequence of commands to install the new release. It is the second requirement which is both tedious and error prone. In Oberon, a simple memorandum, which details the sequence of commands, becomes executable. The commands are simply clicked at, one after another, to install the release. The following is an electronic mail message which can be executed to actualize the system from a file server:

Simply
execute by
clicking with
the mouse

```
Submission: 14.07.89
Originator: Wirth
Recipient: CS.all
Subject: New Oberon Release


To actualize your Oberon system to the new release, execute the following
steps:


Net.ReceiveFile Pluto
    Ceres.Boot  Cursors.Bbj  Diskette.Obj  Display.Obj  Edit.Obj  Files.Sym
    Fonts.Obj  C2.Input.Obj  Mailer.Obj  Net.Obj  Oberon.Obj  Oberon.Sym
    Printer.Obj  Reals.Obj  C2.SCC.Obj  System.Obj  TextFrames.Obj
    TextFrames.Sym  TextViewers.Obj  TextViewers.Sym  Texts.Obj
    Texts.Sym  Viewers.Obj  Viewers.Sym  Viewers.Obj  Viewers.Sym
C2.V24.Obj~

...
```

An Oberon
command to
load the files
of the new
release

1.3   The Oberon system architecture

From the rich set of innovations, only a few can be highlighted in this
overview.

1.3.1   Object-oriented design

The notions of layering and data abstraction are now well understood.
It is the use of the type extension facility which adds an element of
novelty to the Oberon architecture.

Objects – more precisely active objects – are instances of abstract
data types represented by records with a procedure variable called the
object's *handler*. The parameters for the handler are the fields of a
record variable called a *message*. Filling the fields of the message and
calling the handler is termed sending a message to the object.

In contrast to traditional object orientation, Oberon does not
emulate the concept of class and method.

**Instance-
centered objects**

Oberon explores an object-oriented design which may be properly
termed *instance centered*. The binding of procedures to the object is
further delayed and done at run-time. We speak of *installation of
a handler* in an object. In the Oberon paradigm, messages (or
parameter blocks for handlers) are defined by the user, not the module
where the object is defined. Further discussion of instance-centered

object-oriented design is beyond the scope of this overview and we refer the reader to Part II.

1.3.2   Modules, commands and abstract data types

Traditional systems have facilities to run programs. Once loaded and started, the program receives control. It then runs, typically for a long time, until it is halted and the operating system starts a new program. When a program terminates, it releases all its resources, in particular the memory it occupied.

Command, dynamic loading

Oberon parts with the traditional notion of a program. The code unit, which can be executed from the user interface, is called a *command*.

A command is a parameterless procedure exported by a module written in the programming language Oberon. Since efficiency in command activation is of the essence, the command modules need to be memory resident. However, it is not practical to load all modules when the system is booting. Therefore, modules are *dynamically loaded* on demand. Once loaded, the module remains in memory.

Abstract data types

The module often implements one or several abstract data types. The fact that, once loaded, modules stay memory resident has an important consequence: instances of the abstract data types may now exist throughout the entire session: *commands may operate on and communicate through instances of abstract data types*. The abstract type *text* is an important example.

1.3.3   Command interpreter, multitasking

Every system needs a command interpreter. If a traditional system is completely idle, control is in a loop of the *system command interpreter* which waits for input. Such input may be a command to load an interactive application. Once loaded, control passes to the *application command interpreter* of the program which has its own polling loop. The user can either issue system commands or the commands understood by the application.

Clearly, a system which runs several windows with different applications needs some level of multitasking. In the known designs, this requires interruption of programs and saving of state information.

In Oberon, all commands are on the same level, waiting to be executed. A novel architecture is required which has the following key features:

- There is only one loop – *the event loop* – which is encapsulated in a system module.
- The indivisible unit of operation is the procedure call.

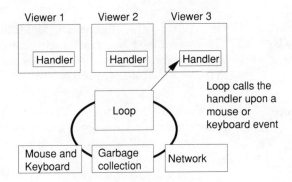

A look at the Oberon display shows many coexisting viewers, each dedicated to a specific task such as text editing, drawing, drafting etc. The viewers are embodied as active objects.

When nothing happens, control is in the event loop which constantly polls device drivers. When an event is sensed, a message that identifies that event is sent to the handler of the affected viewer. The handler determines the action to be performed as a consequence of a mouse or keyboard event. It is also the display manager drawing screen output. On completion of the call to the handler, control reverts to the loop.

The important consequence of this design is that the chain of normal procedure calls is never interrupted. There is no state information which needs to be saved for multitasking. There are no hidden states and the single process of the loop may simultaneously work on several user tasks without the complications ensuing from true multitasking.

1.3.4 Memory management, garbage collection

Oberon uses the memory management units of modern microprocessors to map modules (program segments) into memory. Modules are loaded on demand and remain memory resident once loaded.

The computer's memory is divided into a *stack* for the local variables of procedures and a *heap*. Garbage collection is used to keep the heap's size constraint. The introduction of a garbage collector is not only for convenience, *but also to achieve system reliability*. In fact, the human programmer should not be trusted to allocate free space in a consistently correct manner.

1.3.5   Abstract documents, the example of texts

Viewers typically work on documents which are displayed within their perimeter. Such documents are texts, graphics, pictures etc.

Text as an abstract data type

We have already highlighted the fact that texts play a very special role in Oberon. A text is an instance of an abstract data type which is exported by module Texts. It provides the notion of a sequence of bytes with their associated properties.

Text as an object

Texts are also active objects. When one of the procedures changes the underlying data, a message is broadcast to all visible viewers advertising this change. If a viewer does display the changed text, it will subsequently update its display. *Thus, changing the document and updating the display are strictly separated*. We may say that a text displays itself after it was changed.

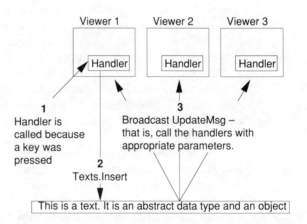

1.3.6   Extensibility

Extensibility of the Oberon system is an important design goal. It may mean:

- adding commands which are executed from texts and which operate on existing abstract documents (for example, texts);
- adding new viewer classes composed of: (a) an abstract document, (b) a viewer with its handler and (c) a set of commands to be executed from texts, including an Open command which creates an instance of the viewer.

Adding simple commands
Commands operating on documents – instances of an abstract data type – may be easily added at any time. *The ban of hidden states ensures that such commands never interfere with the viewers handling the document.* All that the programmer has to do is to create an object module containing the command. The dynamic loading system allows use of the module without prior linkage editor runs.

Adding viewer classes
The most powerful extension is the addition of a viewer class. The architecture of the Oberon system is such that both abstract documents and new viewer types may be added without any installation procedures or recompilation of system code. That this is possible in the strongly typed environment is in fact a significant success of the object-oriented design.

1.4   Summary of innovations

Oberon is the result of a research project. In this overview, we have introduced the most salient features. Throughout the book, the concepts will be refined on the level of a system reference. Let us state the conclusions drawn by the creators of Oberon:[8]

'The Oberon system deviates from conventional operating systems in several respects:

(1) The notion of program is absent; instead of a program activation, the procedure call is the unit of action specified by the computer's operator.

(2) Each procedure call (command) is an atomic action in the dialog between the operator and the computer: the switch from one task to another occurs between the user's commands rather than between two arbitrary machine instructions.

(3) Commands take their input from texts and other kinds of documents rather than from the keyboard. Instead of writing directly on to the screen, commands generate non-volatile output in the form of (displayed) data structures.

---

[8] Wirth N. and Gutknecht J. (1989). The Oberon system. *Software – Practice and Experience*, **19**(9), 890.

(4) The interface between two consecutive actions consists of abstract data structures (texts, graphics) in main store rather than of files on disk. When displayed in viewers, they are editable.

(5) Oberon provides distributed command interpretation. Viewers are regarded as rectangular areas on the screen which are capable of interpreting commands individually. To that purpose, the object-oriented programming paradigm is used. A message is sent to a viewer whenever an input event refers to it.

(6) Oberon features a simple and extremely efficient file system. The disk directory is organized as a B-tree. A clear distinction is made between a file and aggregates to access it, which are called riders.

(7) Modules are loaded under Oberon only when they are actually used. Delayed loading is important because packages may statically consist of dozens of modules, of which only a few are used for any specific application. Delayed loading is controlled by page faults, which are caused by the virtual address mechanism.

(8) A garbage collector is built into the Oberon kernel. Instead of running as a separate process, the garbage collector is explicitly activated between commands under the precondition of an empty stack. This precondition simplifies and accelerates the algorithm significantly.

(9) The system and the user packages are implemented in a language offering data type extension and polymorphic operations with guaranteed type safety. Full type safety is mandatory for a system relying on automatic storage retrieval.

(10) An Oberon system implementation can be extended (possibly years later) by declaring new data types which are extensions of existing, imported types. Objects of extended types are compatible with objects of their base type, and therefore can be integrated into existing data structures.

(11) In the Oberon system there is no real difference between users and programmers. Having a powerful module basis at their disposal, users can extend the system or adapt it to their needs by programming new tools.'

The progress in speed and memory capability of computing machinery continues unabated. In contrast, the software that we use is usually of dated origin and adapts only slowly. One layer of code is put on to another one resulting in systems of enormous size. Thus it is quite common that the operating system of a workstation will consume 1 MB and a word processor and a spreadsheet program will require 4 MB of memory and the whole thing will perform quite sluggishly on today's generation of fast workstations.

But Oberon yields an *existence proof* that this need not be so and that there is no software barrier which cannot be surpassed. The whole system is specified by 15000 lines of source text and the compiled code consists of 150 kB! Therefore, care not to waste resources does pay off. Oberon is a sophisticated system and provides equivalent, if not superior, functionality when compared with well-known commercial operating systems.

1.5 System version, implementations and applications

The premise of Oberon is that of an open system which invites the user to change functionality and add new functions. In fact, it is the hope that the distinction between user and programmer will become more and more blurred. A consequence of this is that two systems will rarely be exactly the same.

Version number The version number of the system described in this book is 1.2.

Applications Several projects adding functionality through new viewer classes are underway at the Institut für Computersysteme:

- A variety of program editors which are extensions of the basic Oberon editor described in this manual.
- Two graphics editors *Graph* and *Oil* allowing line drawings controlled by the mouse.
- A document editor *Leda* which provides advanced text processing and page layout functions in a WYSIWYG fashion.
- A paint program *Paint* manipulating bitmaps.

Object Oberon *Object Oberon* is a small extension of the Oberon language, introducing the concepts of class and message from object-oriented programming. It was developed by P. Mössenböck and J. Templ. These authors also changed the functionality of the viewer class – in fact creating a different family of Oberon systems which share the modules Oberon and those below Oberon with standard Oberon.

Implementations   Oberon has been run for some years on Ceres, the experimental work-station built at the Institut für Computersysteme. Implementations for SUN Sparcstation and Apple Macintosh computers are publicly available. Work on other machines (DECsystem 3100, IBM PS/2 and IBM RISC System/6000) is in various stages of completion.

Part I

User's guide

2 The Oberon user interface and the standard system editor

This chapter provides:

- A guide for the user on how to use Oberon. Using an Oberon workstation, the reader can use the material as a tutorial of the standard system functions, in particular the editor.
- A guide for the programmer of applications, called viewer classes. The 'look and feel' which distinguishes Oberon from established user interfaces is discussed.

A simple model of Oberon is given in the following figure:

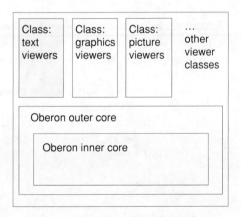

The operating system and the applications are structured as a hierarchy of modules which fall into the following broad classes:

- *Viewer class:* supplants the traditional application (for example, an editor, a draw program, a paint program etc.)

- *Outer core:* system functions managing the display, keyboard and mouse.
- *Inner core:* basic operating system functions (such as file system, storage management, loader, compiler etc.).

The facilities of the outer core provide the basis on which applications are written. As far as the appearance of the Oberon user interface is concerned, the outer core defines a display composed of rectangular, non-overlapping windows, the viewers, which exhaustively tile the screen.

Within such a viewer, the programmer has a great deal of freedom. A variety of interfaces are possible – from 'remember and type' to 'point and click.' The graphical capability of an Oberon workstation imposes no restrictions on visual layout and controls. An Oberon viewer class may look like an IBM PC with MS/DOS, like an Apple Macintosh or, of course, like an Oberon system.

However, experience over recent years indicates that systems benefit a great deal if they communicate with the user in a unified style. A successful example is the Macintosh which achieved a great uniformity across programs of many vendors thanks to the *Human Interface Guide* published by Apple.[1] For Oberon, such a style evolved and is documented in the remaining sections of this chapter which is, at the same time, an introduction to the standard editor, which is used as a key example for the Oberon interface style.

EBNF notation   To describe the syntax of commands, an extended Backus–Naur formalism (EBNF) is used. Brackets [and] denote optionality of the enclosed terms. Braces { and } denote its repetition, possibly 0 times. Parentheses (and) group terms in the usual manner. A choice is indicated by the vertical bar. For example A | B means A or B.

Syntactic entities (non-terminal symbols) are denoted by English words set in italics. Symbols of the language vocabulary (terminal symbols) are set in roman font or enclosed in double quote marks. In the syntax of commands, the following symbols occur frequently:

$$" \sim " \mid "*" \mid "\uparrow" \mid "=>" \mid "/d" \mid "/s" \mid """"$$

To improve legibility, the quote marks are omitted for the above special symbols.

For example consider the EBNF statment:

System.Free { *moduleName* [*] } ($\sim$ | $\uparrow$)

---

[1] Addison-Wesley Publishing Company, Inc., 1987.

The command name *System.Free* is followed by a list of *moduleName*. Each *moduleName* is optionally postfixed by an asterisk. The list, which may be empty, is terminated either by '~' or '↑'. The following are valid alternatives

System.Free Texts Viewers* ~
System.Free MyCmd ↑
System.Free ↑

2.1   Tiled display

One of the intrinsic concepts of the Oberon system is the *viewer*, a rectangular area on the display. Viewers provide a *port to an underlying application* which is typically an editor operating on text, picture or graphics data objects. Viewers are non-overlapping and tile the display area completely.

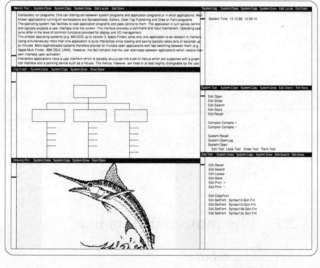

User track   System track

The figure shows six viewers of apparently different kinds. Four viewers display text. Using the mouse and keyboard, the texts can be edited. These viewers are called *text viewers*.

One viewer shows a line drawing. When the mouse is in its boundary, boxes and lines can be drawn with the mouse. This is a *graphics viewer*.

The bottom left viewer renders a raster image. When the mouse is in its perimeter, individual picture elements may be set or erased. This viewer is a *picture viewer*.

Viewer class

We may visualize a command interpreter behind each viewer. The Oberon system routes mouse events to the interpreter belonging to the viewer containing the mouse cursor. Typed characters are directed at a designated viewer – the *focus*. Thus, the semantics of the mouse and keyboard is defined by the type of the viewer. We call an individual viewer on the display an *instance of its viewer class*. Thus, in our example we have four instances of text viewers, one instance of a graphics viewer and one instance of a picture viewer.

Tracks

The viewers are allocated in *tracks*. The Oberon display knows two tracks: a wide *user track* and a narrow *system track*. This terminology suggests that the user track is the preferred place to edit documents whereas the system track serves predominantly as a control area where commands are invoked and status information is reported.

Tool viewers and the system log

In Oberon, *everything happens in viewers*. In particular, all the system control functions are performed in standard text viewers rather than in special control areas such as a command line or menu bar. Viewers specialized for command execution are termed *tool viewers*.

User control

Only the tracks are fixed. Within the tracks, placement and size of the viewers are under the control of the user. Viewers can be opened and closed. Their relative position can be changed. Their size can be increased to that of a whole track or even the whole display. The distinction between system track and user track is only one about preferred usage – any viewer may be placed anywhere.

2.2   The mouse and its use

2.2.1   The mouse

Oberon is controlled with a *three-key mouse*. Physical movement of the mouse translates into movement of a mouse cursor on the plane of the display. This cursor has the following shape:

The focus of the cursor (its tip) designates the object on which commands issued through the mouse keys will operate.

Oberon supports other cursor shapes as well. The arrow, however, is the most prevalent one and programmers of viewer classes should use it for standard pointing actions. Special cursors may *indicate modes*; for example, a 'grabber hand' to grab and shift a document plane or a 'cross-hair' to precisely place points on the Cartesian plane of a graphics program.

The three mouse keys are used to *issue commands whose meaning is defined by the class of the viewer which contains the cursor*. They have the following basic assignments:

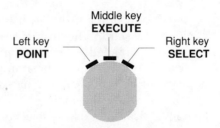

- Left key: place or track an insertion point.
- Middle key: execute a command pointed at by the mouse cursor.
- Right key: track the selection.

A detailed explanation is given in later sections.

Mouse actions   The following mouse actions are of importance:

- *Pressing:* holding a key down while the mouse is stationary.
- *Dragging:* holding a key down while the mouse moves.
- *Clicking:* pushing the key while the mouse is stationary and releasing the key, usually in quick succession.
- *Interclicking:* clicking one of the keys while the mouse is dragged on another one. Also, clicking a key while another one is pressed.

Dragging is typically linked to tracking operations on the display. For example, dragging with the right key tracks the selection. Interclicking with one of the other two keys is a standard way to issue mouse-based commands which relate to the actual tracking operation. An example is to delete the selection just being tracked.

2.2.2   Selection

A convenient way to designate the operands of commands is through mouse-based selection. A selected object is prepared prior to execution by a subsequent command. To the user, it conveys a familiar noun–verb syntax: 'Hey you (the selection), do this (the command.)'[2]

Objects are selected through clicking or dragging the right mouse key. On the display, *selected objects are visually characterized*, typically rendered in reverse video.

Removal of the selection

All selections may be removed with the ESC key (all other markings are removed too.)

Selection in text viewers

A stretch of text in a text viewer is selected by first moving the mouse cursor to the start of the desired selection. The right key is pressed and the mouse dragged. On the display, the selected area is shown in reverse video and adjusted continuously as the mouse is moved. This adjustment is termed *tracking of the selection*. The selection process is completed when the mouse key is released. Pressing the right key again will clear the existing selection and start a new one.

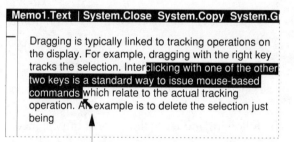

The leading edge of the selection follows the mouse

2.2.3   Insertion point and focus viewer

The viewer which receives typed characters must be explicitly designated.

The caret

This leads to the concept of the *insertion point* as the focus, where typed characters or a copied text selection appear in the document. On the

---

[2] *Human Interface Guidelines: The Apple Desktop Interface*, Addison-Wesley Publishing Company, Inc., 1987.

display, the insertion point is made visible with a symbol – the *caret*. The viewer with the caret is called the *focus viewer*. The focus viewer is unique.

In text viewers, the caret looks as follows:

Caret focus

The caret is set in place (or tracked to its destination) through clicking or dragging the left mouse key.

Removal of the caret

The caret is made invisible with the ESC key (all other markings are removed too.)

Setting the caret in text viewers

In text viewers, the caret is set by moving the mouse cursor to the insertion point and clicking the left mouse key. If the mouse is dragged on the left key, the caret is tracked; that means it jumps from character to character trying to follow the cursor. On release of the key, the caret is set in place.

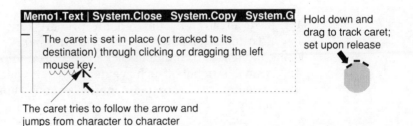

Memo1.Text | System.Close   System.Copy   System.G

The caret is set in place (or tracked to its destination) through clicking or dragging the left mouse key.

Hold down and drag to track caret; set upon release

The caret tries to follow the arrow and jumps from character to character

2.2.4   Mark and marked viewer

Some commands require a point on the display surface as one of their parameters. Such a point is set up by placing the mouse cursor and pressing the SETUP key (observe the mnemonics.)

The point is made visible by a star-shaped pattern called the *pointer*:

Pointer focus
at center

If a pointer is set, an attempt to place another one will erase the old star-shaped pattern. The pointer is unique.

Marked viewer

Besides designating a point, for example as the place where a viewer should open, the pointer is also used to *mark a viewer*. We say a viewer is marked if it contains the pointer anywhere in its frame boundary. Marked viewers are frequently the object of commands such as 'close the marked viewer' or 'print the marked viewer.'

Removal of the pointer

The pointer is made invisible with the ESC key (all other markings are removed too.) Note that the viewer, which displayed the pointer before ESC was pressed, remains the marked viewer. Commands operating on the marked viewer often remove the pointer. Again, a viewer remains marked even if the pointer is invisible.

Caution: The pointer is fixed to the screen, not to the viewer. Therefore, when viewers are opened, closed or replaced, the marked viewer may change, since after the display modification another viewer may contain the pointer. It is good practice to set the pointer explicitly prior to invoking a command operating on the marked viewer.

2.2.5   Mouse editing commands

We have already encountered the primary functions of the mouse keys. To initiate further actions with the mouse, key combinations using interclicks or multiple click events need to be defined. There is only a small number of such events, however, which a typical user can master with ease. Complex mouse events should be introduced judiciously.

Standard interclick commands

Oberon utilizes interclicking as a highly efficient way of using the mouse for editing operations. The following standard commands should be provided by all viewer classes operating on text documents.

Delete the selection

Copy selection to the caret location

Drag with the right key to track the selection

Copy most recent selection

Copy attributes from the caret location to the selection

Drag with the left key to track the caret

While tracking the caret (dragging on the left key)

- Interclicking the middle key copies the most recent selection to the place where the caret will be set on release of the left key.
- Interclicking the right key will copy the attributes of the character to the right of the caret to the most recent selection.

While tracking the selection (dragging on the right key)

- Interclicking the left key will delete the selection being tracked on release of the right key.
- Interclicking the middle key will copy the selection being tracked to the caret location on release of the right key.

Note: In many cases, these commands can be generalized to graphics and picture editors. *When natural, they should be provided.* For example, graphics objects are also selected with the right key and deleted with a left interclick. On the other hand, there are situations where the standard assignments do not apply. For example, when pointing to a graphics plane one cannot execute a command. Thus, the middle key is freed to perform another function. It is good practice, however, to limit deviations from the standard assignments. This makes the user comfortable and helps to avoid errors.

Undoing an interclick command

If a key is interclicked erroneously while the mouse is still being dragged, that command is *cancelled if all keys are pressed simultaneously*.

2.2.6 Executing commands from texts: the abolition of the command line

A distinguishing feature of Oberon is the unification of text input and command input. This unification is the end of the ubiquitous 'command line.' A text is taken literally: a sequence of characters. If this sequence is to be interpreted as a command, it is not necessary for the characters to be in a special place.

Command execution in text viewers

Text viewers are the standard place to invoke commands. In such a viewer, anywhere in the editable text, a command and its parameters may by entered and executed by pointing at the command's name with the mouse cursor and clicking the middle mouse key. While the middle key remains pressed, the word pointed at with the mouse cursor is underlined. On release of the key, Oberon tries to execute the command. If the mouse is dragged on the middle key, then words are tracked; that is, each new word pointed at is underlined.

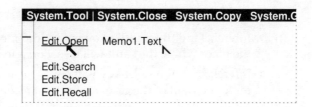

Click

In our example, the user has typed the name of the text to be opened ('Memo1.Text') and is about to execute the command *Edit.Open*. Note that the command is underlined, meaning that the middle mouse key is still pressed. The command is executed on release of the key.

Unloading a module prior to execution

If the left key is interclicked while the middle key is pressed or while words are being tracked (dragging on the middle key), the module containing the executed command is unloaded and a new copy of that module is loaded. This is useful while debugging Oberon procedures.

2.3 The keyboard

In Oberon, the principal role of the keyboard is to enter text. The caret must be visible in one of the viewers. When a character is keyed, it is inserted at the point of the caret and the caret moves one place to the right. The delete key (DEL) is used to erase the character to the left of the caret and move the caret one place to the left.

There is a small number of commands keys, as follows:

- SETUP: set the pointer at the place of the mouse cursor.
- ESC: remove all markings in all viewers; that is, all selections, the star-shaped pointer and the caret.
- PF1: display white letters on black background.
- PF2: display off (to conserve the device.)
- PF3: display black letters on white background.
- CTRL–SHIFT–DEL: interrupt a running command.

The control key (CTRL) is used to produce special language characters such as:

CTRL–a:	ä	CTRL–SHIFT–A:	Ä
CTRL–u:	ü	CTRL–SHIFT–U:	Ü
CTRL–o:	ö	CTRL–SHIFT–O:	Ö

2.4   The viewer

2.4.1   The initial display, opening a new viewer

The initial display after booting looks as follows:

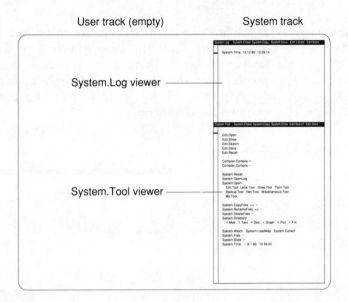

User track (empty)   System track

System.Log viewer

System.Tool viewer

Two viewers are on display named *System.Log* and *System.Tool*. Both the system log and the system tool are text viewers, which means that the user can edit their contents.

System log   In the system log (that is the viewer named *System.Log*) commands report progress, completion and error information. Initially, time and date is visible.

System tool   The system tool (that is the viewer named *System.Tool*) contains a set of often used commands to be activated with the mouse.

Opening a viewer   An instance of a viewer is created and displayed by executing the *Open* command belonging to the desired viewer class. The open command typically has a single parameter which designates the name of the viewer. If a file with the same name exists, the contents of the viewer are initialized from that file. Otherwise, an empty document is created.

Placement of new viewer

Normally, when an open command is issued, Oberon makes a reasonable guess as to where to place the viewer on the display. The user, however, can indicate where the viewer should open by means of the pointer. Regardless of where Oberon would have opened the viewer, it will open in the track of the star-shaped pointer and its top edge will be at the height of the pointer.

Opening of text viewers

There are two commands for opening text viewers – *Edit.Open* and *System.Open*. With *Edit.Open*, the text viewer will open in the user track; with *System.Open*, it will appear in the system track (unless the pointer overrides Oberon's preference.) *Edit.Open* is the first entry of the system tool. To open a text viewer, the user just types its name and executes the command.

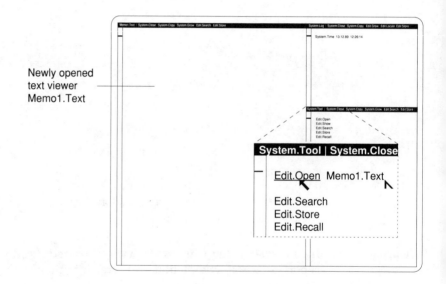

Newly opened
text viewer
Memo1.Text

2.4.2   Layout

Basic properties

Oberon viewers are rectangular areas on the display. As a minimum, a viewer has:

- A thin line outlining the frame.
- A *title bar* with a viewer name. The title bar is highlighted in reverse video.

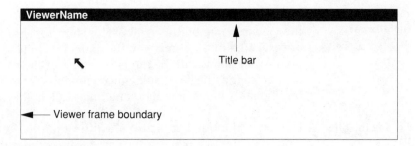

Optional
properties

Additional properties are:

- A set of commands adjacent to the viewer name.
- A *vertical scroll bar* located on the left.
- A *horizontal scroll bar* located at the top.

An important example are text viewers which look as follows:

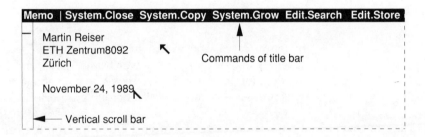

The text displayed below the title bar is called the *main text* (in contrast to the text of the title bar which is also called *menu text*.)

Picture viewers furnish an example with both vertical and horizontal scroll bars:

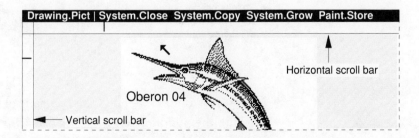

Name

The name identifies the viewer. In many cases, it corresponds to a file name designating the disk file where the data is stored.

Commands in the title bar

Normally, a list of commands appears in the title bar, separated from the viewer name by the symbol '|'. They appear for convenience and are executed in the same way as commands in text viewers; that is, by pointing at them with the mouse cursor and clicking the middle mouse key. Since the title bar displaying commands looks like the menu bar of traditional systems, it is also sometimes called 'the menu.'

Editing the title bar

However, the title bar is also a text (in the sense of text viewers.) All editing operations work in the same way as those in the main editable text – new commands may be added, the name may be changed, stretches of text may be selected, deleted and copied. The only restriction is that, in order to set the caret, the mouse has to point at the very bottom of the area rendered in reverse video, otherwise the viewer will be repositioned (see later.) Also, a changed title bar cannot be saved to disk. When the viewer is reopened, the standard commands are again displayed.

2.4.3   Scrolling

In many cases, the extent of the document (in its two-dimensional space) is bigger than the viewer frame. Thus, the user needs to move the document relative to the viewer to gain access to invisible portions. This process is called *scrolling*. Scrolling is performed with the mouse.

The scroll bar of text viewers

Text viewers have a standard Oberon scroll bar on the left. To scroll, the mouse cursor points into the scroll bar.

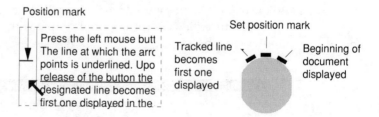

Then:

- Clicking the right key *scrolls to the beginning* of the text.
- Clicking the middle key *sets the position mark* at the point of the mouse cursor. The document is repositioned such that the character which appears on top has the same relative position in the document as the position mark in the scroll bar.

- Clicking the left key *moves the respective line to the top*. Dragging on the left key tracks lines (lines are underlined.) On release, the last line will appear on top.

The following interclick events are also defined:

- Interclicking the left key while pressing the middle key *scrolls to the end* of the document.
- Interclicking the right key while pressing the middle key *scrolls to the beginning* of the document.

Scroll bars in other document types, such as graphics or pictures, work analogously.

2.4.4 Placement of viewers

The user has control over viewer placement:

- At the time of the open command with the pointer (see Section 2.4.1);
- on the display with the mouse.

Move the viewer in its track If the mouse cursor is in the upper part of the title bar, pressing the left key will remove the reverse video to tell the user that a tracking mode has been entered. Dragging the mouse will determine the new top position in the track. On release of the left mouse key, the top edge of the viewer will move to the height of the mouse cursor and the viewer contents will be redrawn. The range of movement is restricted as shown in the following figure:

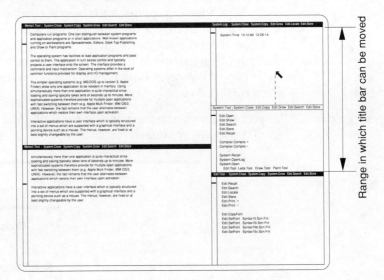

Move the viewer across tracks   If the middle mouse key is interclicked while dragging the title bar, the restriction is not observed. The viewer may be placed anywhere on the display. In particular, a viewer may be relocated across track boundaries.

2.4.5   Growing, copying and closing viewers

Creating an overlay track   Executing the command *System.Grow* will enlarge the viewer to the size of the whole track. In fact, a new track is laid over the existing track. The enlarged viewer exhausts the area of that new track as shown in the following figure:

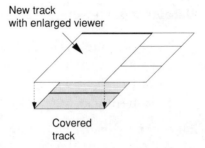

New track
with enlarged viewer

Covered
track

　　　New viewers may be opened and closed in the overlay track in the usual manner. If the last viewer in the overlay closes, the covered track is restored. If the viewer already exhausts the track, it will be enlarged to the size of the entire display. Thus, executing *System.Grow* twice will enlarge any viewer to screen size.

　　　Note: Viewers opened with *System.Grow* show the *same document* as the viewer from which *System.Grow* was executed. Any changes made in the original viewer will be visible in the enlarged viewer. Similarly, changes made in the enlarged viewer are preserved when that enlarged viewer is closed. Hence, it is not necessary to save to disk when closing an overlay.

Opening a copy of an existing viewer   A second viewer showing the same data (text or graphics) may be opened with the command *System.Copy*:

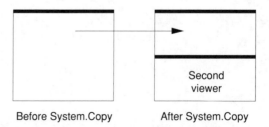

Second
viewer

Before System.Copy　　　　After System.Copy

If enough space is available, the viewer opened with *System.Copy* will take up half the area of the original viewer. It provides a second view of the *same document*. The clone viewers *may be scrolled independently*. Any changes in one viewer are reflected in the other one. No data is lost if one of the copy viewers is closed.

Closing a viewer   A viewer is closed with the command *System.Close*. It disappears from the display and the adjacent viewer (on top) claims the closed viewer's area. The document is *not saved* to disk on execution of *System.Close*. An erroneously closed viewer can be recovered through *System.Recall*.

2.4.6   The commands of the title bar

The text displayed in the title bar of a viewer is an instance of the same abstract data type as the text edited in text viewers. Thus, any word representing a valid command can be executed in the usual way – even the viewer's name.

Thus, the commands shown in the title bar are like a little local tool affording convenient access to frequently used functions. The text displayed in the title bar is written by the command which opens the viewer. Those commands deemed most useful are provided. Using the editor, the user may change or add commands.

As a general rule, *commands in the title bar operate on their viewer*. Some commands are polymorphic; that is, they discriminate between whether they are executed from an editable text or from the title bar. *Edit.Store* is an example. It has no parameter in the title bar and stores its viewer on disk. If launched from a tool, *Edit.Store* requests a name as parameter and stores the marked viewer under that name.

Standard title bar commands   As a general rule, the command *System.Close* should always be displayed after the viewer name. In most cases, *System.Copy* and *System.Grow* follow in that order.

Other title bar commands   Most viewer classes have a *Store* command which saves the document to disk. The store command, such as *Edit.Store*, is also normally shown in the title bar. Other commands may be added for additional convenience. For example:

- In text viewers, the command *Edit.Search* is included.
- In the viewer *System.Log*, the command *Edit.Locate* replaces *Edit.Search*. It is used to locate the point in a program text where the compiler reports an error.

- The viewer *Mailbox.Text* is opened by the command *Net.Mailbox* of the net tool. It is a viewer of the class text viewers which specializes in reading mail from the mail server. Besides *System.Close*, the specialized commands *Net.ReceiveMail* and *Net.DeleteMail* appear in the title bar.

```
 Mailbox.Text | System.Close  Net.ReceiveMail  Net.DeleteMail

  4 21.11.89  17:34:16  Wirth  1125
  3 20.11.89  14:57:20  Hiestand  1780
  1 17.11.89  16:29:44  Wirth  3521
```

2.5   Commands

An Oberon command is a parameterless procedure in a module written in the programming language Oberon. It follows its naming convention, viz:

> *Mod.Proc*

where *Mod* is the module name and *Proc* is the name of a parameterless procedure exported by that module. For example, *Edit.Open* denotes the procedure *Open* from the module *Edit*.

Command module

Typically, the programs comprising a viewer class are structured into different modules, one of which is specifically dedicated to providing commands. Consequently, this module is also called the *command module*. For example, *Edit* is the command module of the text viewer class. It is good practice to use suggestive names for the command modules such as *Edit*, *Paint*, *Graph* and so on.

2.5.1   Standard syntax

Most commands require *parameters*. It is important not to confuse the parameter of commands with the (formal) parameters of procedures written in the programming language Oberon. The parameters of commands have different sources such as:

- Text following the command name.
- Text contained in the selection.
- The viewer from which the command was executed.
- The viewer designated with the star-shaped pointer.

No parameter   Some commands do not require parameters. The objects on which they operate are implicitly defined. For example, the command *Edit.Recall*, which inserts the most recently deleted piece of text at the caret location, takes an internal buffer as implied parameter and inserts it at the point of the caret. Commands which appear in the title bar usually take their viewer as implied parameter. For example, *System.Close*, executed from the title bar, needs no parameters and closes its viewer.

Single name or   Several commands expect a single word after the command's name. A
word   word is a string of characters not containing blanks. The word is normally a file name or a template defined by its own syntax. If a name is expected, any special symbol terminates the name. For example, the following figure shows three instances of 'Edit.Open Test.Mod', the third one being embedded in a text.

```
Edit.Open  Test.Mod
...
Edit.Open   Test.Mod~
...
this is  Edit.Open  Test.Mod   the third version
```

List of names   Some commands take a list of names as parameters. The list may be of variable length. It is separated from the command name by one or several blanks and items in the list are blank delimited. The list is terminated by a special symbol, typically '~'. For example, executing *Compiler.Compile* in the following text will compile files M1.Mod to M5.Mod:

```
Compiler.Compile  M1.Mod  M2.Mod  M3.Mod
    M4.Mod  M5.Mod~
    ...
```

The marked   Other commands operate on the marked viewer (the viewer which
viewer   contains the star-shaped pointer.) They do this either implicitly (for example, *System.Close* executed from a text viewer) or they expect an asterisk after the command name (for example, *Compiler.Compile*.) For example, assume that the viewer with name *Test.Mod* contains a program text. Let this viewer be marked. Then executing 'Compiler.Compile*' will compile *Test.Mod*. This is equivalent to issuing 'Compiler.Compile Test.Mod~'.

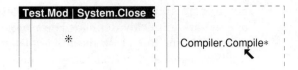

The selection as operand

The command acts on the selected object. For example, *Edit.CopyFont* changes the font of the selected text to match the font found at the location of the pointer.

The selection contains names

As a general rule, *Oberon commands consider the selection as an alternative place to find their parameters.* To refer to the selection, the symbol '↑' appears after the command name or after a list of parameters.

In the case of a command which expects a single parameter, the symbol '↑' may substitute for that parameter. This means that the name or template is contained in the selection.

If the command expects a list of parameters, then that list may be terminated with '↑' rather than '~'. In this case, the command looks for *exactly one more* parameter in the selection. This option is typically used with the empty list.

For example, the command *Compiler.Compile* is followed by the character '↑'. The name in the selection, here 'Test.Mod', is compiled.

Note: The code used for the upward pointing arrow '↑' is 5EX. It differs from the ASCII character 5EX which is the caret ' ^ '.

There is a second convention used to refer to the selection. The command restricts the parameter search to the text line on which the command name appears. If that line is empty, the scan continues to the selection. *Edit.Open* and *System.Open* show that behavior, although they accept '↑' as an alternative. We recommend referring to the selection explicitly by means of '↑'.

2.5.2   Complex syntax

Commands may process the text following the command name or designated by the selection. Thus, the parameters provided in that text may be of arbitrarily complex syntax. A single name or a list of names are just the simplest cases. The following examples illustrate this.

The command *System.RenameFiles* processes a list of name pairs which are indicated as follows:

```
System.RenameFiles Memo1.Text => Memo2.Text ~
```

The arrow composed of the character '=' immediately followed by '>' indicates that the file 'Memo1.Text' is being renamed to 'Memo2.Text' and not the other way around.

Often, a set of attributes is set with a single command. The attributes with their values can be conveniently symbolized with an '=' sign. The following is a hypothetical example of a command *Write.Page* which defines the page format for a document editor:

```
Write.Page
    Width = 21 Height = 29.7
    Margins: Left = 3 Right = 2.5 Top = 4 Bottom = 5~
```

2.5.3   Polymorphic commands

Some commands discriminate between several of the described parameter sources according to the environment from where they are executed. Such commands are called *polymorphic*.

We have already come across the example of *Edit.Store* which behaves differently depending on whether it is executed from the command line or from the title bar.

Another example is *Edit.Open* which takes a name typed on the same line as the command text and, if none is found, extends the search to the selection.

2.6   Tool viewers

2.6.1   The tool viewer as an alternative to the menu

A text viewer which displays a set of commands is called a *tool viewer*, a novel concept which is a blend of the two paradigms 'remember and type' and 'point and click.' 'Remember and type' interfaces feature the well-known command line. The usual embodiment of 'point and click' is through (pull-down) menus.

    To explain the new concept, let us look at the text viewer named *System.Tool*, which is automatically opened after the system is turned on.

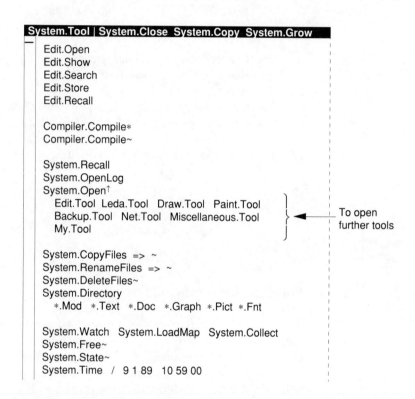

Like a menu, the system tool viewer presents a set of commands ready for execution with the mouse. However, since the tool is simply a text viewer, parameters can be typed prior to execution. Therefore, there is no need for (modal) dialog boxes. An example was given earlier on page 28 (text viewer *Memo1.Text* was opened from the system tool.)

    An Oberon system usually has a variety of tools. These tools are opened with the command *System.Open*, which means that they will be displayed in the system track (unless overridden with the pointer.)

    The standard system tool has a section for opening further tools. Since space is at a premium in tool viewers, an elegant way to economize space, based on the polymorphic nature of *System.Open*, is used:

```
┌─────────────────────────────────────────────────┐
│  System.Open ↑                                    │
│     Edit.Tool  Leda.Tool  Draw.Tool  Paint.Tool   │
│     Backup.Tool  Net.Tool  Miscellaneous.Tool     │
│     My.Tool                                       │
│                                                   │
└─────────────────────────────────────────────────┘
```

The command *System.Open* appears on its own line, optionally followed by '↑'. Below this line, several tool names are listed. To open a tool, the user simply selects its name and clicks at *System.Open*. It suffices to select the first character.

A variety of tools are prepared on the standard release disk (or release file server.) These encompass:

- *Edit.Tool*: text viewers.
- *Leda.Tool*: text document editor *Leda*.
- *Draw.Tool*: line graphics.
- *Paint.Tool*: pixel drawings.
- *Backup.Tool*: diskettes.
- *Net.Tool*: network and mail server.
- *Miscellaneous.Tool*: miscellaneous commands.
- *My.Tool*: place holder for a user-supplied tool.

Except for *My.Tool* the names of these tools correspond to the names of command modules. *Leda*, *Draw* and *Paint* are viewer classes which are not described in this book.

2.6.2   Conventions for listing commands in tool viewers

It is possible to infer what kind of parameters apply from the way the commands are listed in a tool:

Mod.Cmd	The command has implied parameters (for example, *Edit.Recall*), takes the selection as parameter (for example, *Edit.CopyFont*) or admits a single typed name (for example, *Edit.Open.*)
Mod.Cmd~	The command expects a list of names (for example, *System.Free.*) Before executing, enter the list before the termination character '~'.
Mod.Cmd∗	The command takes the marked viewer as a parameter. Mark a viewer before executing the command.

| *Mod.Cmd* ↑ | The command is referred to the selection. |
| *!Mod.Cmd* | This is a protected or dangerous command (for example, *Diskette.Format*.) The exclamation mark prevents inadvertent execution. To use the command, insert a blank between the exclamation mark and the command name. *Caution:* Remove the separating blank again after usage. Otherwise, the protection is lost. |

If commands expect more complex syntax, this should be indicated. For example, *System.RenameFiles* is listed as:

```
System.RenameFiles  =>  ~
```

The arrow composed of '=' and '>' indicates pairs of names; the terminating symbol '~' reminds that a list of such pairs is accepted. The command *Write.Page*, discussed in an earlier example, would be listed in the tool viewer exactly as it is expected, with suitable default values already filled in:

```
Write.Page
    Width = 21 Height = 29.7
    Margins: Left = 3 Right = 2.5 Top = 4 Bottom = 5~
```

2.6.3   Customizing tools

The malleability of texts affords an ease of customizing the system controls which is unknown in other systems. Using the system editor, any tool can be modified quickly. Contrast this to menus which are mostly frozen or only adaptable, if at all, with expert system knowledge. The standard tools of the Oberon distribution disk (or distribution file server) should be considered only a starting point.

Customizing the system tool

The system tool is special in the sense that it appears on the start-up display. *It should provide a convenient starting environment.*

Clearly, commands which are not likely to be useful should be removed. Similarly, irrelevant tools should be deleted from the block of names listed after *System.Open*.

If a user works predominantly on a single task, the respective commands should be added at the beginning of the system tool. This allows immediate productivity after booting.

User tools   If the user's tasks are more varied, the number of commands may become too large to conveniently fit into the system tool. In this case, several user tools provide an efficient solution. The name of these tools should be included in the list after the line *System.Open* in the system tool. In this way, the user tools can be conveniently opened. The entry 'My.Tool' is a placeholder for such a user tool.

Tools are task centered   Efficient tools are *task centered*. In fact, the efficiency of the Oberon user interface can only be fully utilized if tools are customized. Task centered means that all the commands used in performing a user's work are found in the same tool and thus can be accessed efficiently.

In the following example, commands from modules *System*, *Edit*, *Compiler* and *M* are all listed in the same tool. That this is possible pays tribute to the fact that Oberon applications are implemented as families of cooperating commands rather than monolithic application programs.

The user tool shown serves a programmer who is in the process of testing procedures *TestProc1* and *TestProc2* in module *M*. It affords easy editing, compiling and execution. The network is accessible to print listings.

```
My.Tool | System.Close  System.Cop

      System.SetUser
      Edit.Open OberonErrors.Text
      Edit.Print Pluto*

      Edit.Open M.Mod
      Edit.Show M.TestProc1
      Edit.Show M.TestProc2

      Compiler.Compile*
      Compiler.Compile*/s

      System.Free M~
      M.TestProc1
      M.TestProc2
```

Guidelines for customizing tools   Tools can be structured in many ways. The user is in fact encouraged to experiment until an environment is found which best supports his or her needs. The following hints may help in achieving this goal:

- Keep tools small enough to fit into about one-quarter of the system track height.

- Design task-centered tools.
- Generate many tools specialized for different tasks.
- Use meaningful names for your tools.
- Follow the naming convention for command entries.
- Make the system tool an efficient starting point (since it will be displayed automatically.) Often, it is most convenient to add the commands currently used at the top of the system tool.

Note: The user should not forget to save a tool text after it has been modified using *Edit.Store* from the title bar.

2.7   Naming

Oberon provides structured names to identify objects such as files, servers and viewers. The syntax of names is:

Name = NamePart { "." NamePart }
NamePart = Letter { Letter | Digit }

Examples are: Pluto, Test.Mod, Mail.Text, Syntax10.Scn.Fnt.

File names   The name of files can be structured with a period. There are no mandatory rules to be followed but it is advisable to use suffices to distinguish the type of the file. Often, file names have two name parts:

FileName.FileType

Some frequently used types are:

- *Mod*: Oberon modules (source program text).
- *Text*: text files created with the standard editor.
- *Doc*: text documents.
- *Graph*: graphics documents.
- *Pict*: picture files (bitmaps).
- *Obj*: Oberon modules (object files).
- *Sym*: symbol files.

Note: Structured file names together with the 'wild card' character '*' in the *System.Directory* command provide functions similar to those afforded by hierarchical directories.

Viewer names   In the case of document viewers, the viewer name and the file name are identical. The Open command constructs the correspondence.

If a command opens a viewer for the purpose of text output, the name of this viewer is identical to the command's name. For example, the command *System.State* opens a viewer named 'System.State' which displays state data.

2.8 Design for user satisfaction

2.8.1 Commands have visible consequences

One of the basic tenets of the Oberon system is that *commands have visible consequences*. This assures the user that things are going well.

For some commands, especially editing commands, visibility is a natural consequence of their action. The result of other commands, however, is not directly visible. Take *Edit.Print* for example. It does not change the data, takes some time to execute and is not guaranteed to succeed. Such commands need additional visual feedback.

The system log Commands without a natural visible consequence do report their outcome in the system log. Like all text displays, the system log is an ordinary text viewer. The system log is part of the initial display after booting.

Output viewers Only progress, completion or error reports appear in the system log. If a command produces text output, it should open a new text viewer with an appropriate name. For example, the command *System.State* opens a text viewer with name 'System.State' in which the state information is revealed.

Busy viewer If a command has an execution time which is noticeable by the user, it displays the busy viewer arrow in the lower left corner.

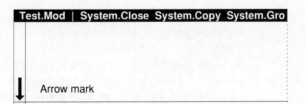

2.8.2 Recovery of erroneously deleted data

Any data lost through inadvertent use of a command should be recoverable. However, Oberon viewer classes typically leave it to the user to find out when data should be recovered. *This means that modal warning messages are avoided.*

Edit.Recall   If a selection is deleted in a text viewer, then the command *Edit.Recall* will recover the deleted stretch of text and reinsert it at the place of the caret.

System.Recall   If a viewer is erroneously closed before saving to disk, data may be permanently lost. The last viewer to be closed can be reopened using the command *System.Recall*.

Back-up files   If the contents of a viewer are saved and if a file with the viewer's name already exists, then the old file is kept under a modified file name. For example, if text viewer *Memo.Text* is saved with the command *Edit.Store*, then the previous version is still available under file name *Memo.Bak*.

2.8.3   What Oberon viewer classes avoid

In the preceding sections, we went through the 'look and feel' which Oberon viewer classes *do* provide. We shall conclude with a list of things they *avoid*.

Modes   Oberon commands and viewer classes go to great lengths to avoid unnecessary, unnatural or invisible modes. Modes are not a hindrance per se. Some modes are a natural consequence of the task at hand. For example, the modality of the scroll bar is both visible and natural. However, other modes lead to confusion and error or to user frustration. These modes must be avoided. Two examples should clarify what we mean by harmful modes.

Unnatural modes   A word-processing program moves the insertion point with the arrow keys (in addition to the mouse.) It also furnishes an 'outline mode.' There is nothing to criticize about this, the mode is visible and unquestionably of great utility. However, when in outline mode, the arrow keys move the headings rather than the insertion point. A user who has acquired the skill of using the arrow keys automatically will be regularly disturbed when changing text in outline mode. It is not the outline mode which is the problem, it is the invisible modality of the arrow keys which is open for criticism.

Modal messages   Other programs go to excesses to restrict users 'for their own good.' User conformance is enforced with modal message boxes: 'Do you really want to do that?' In most cases, the user does indeed want to do what he or she has told the system and is predictably non-plussed by the need to make the nagging messages disappear with mouse clicks or key actions.

Pretentious controls and graphics

Oberon gave proof that the unification of text input and command input in text viewers is a powerful concept capable of supplanting the command line and most 'pull-down' menus and complex dialog boxes. Oberon viewer classes should use this concept whenever it is adequate.

3 Using the standard editor

Like most operating systems, Oberon has a standard system editor – the viewer class text viewers. The reader has already gained a good understanding of text viewers from Chapter 2.

This chapter gives an exhaustive description of the functions and commands of the system editor. Besides the mouse-based actions with which we are already familiar, the editor has a set of commands, exported by command module *Edit*, to:

- search for the occurrence of a pattern;
- place the caret after the nth character in the text;
- recover deleted text;
- change fonts;
- print texts.

A text viewer *Edit.Tool* lists the commands from module *Edit*. On the Oberon distribution disk (or distribution file server), the edit tool looks as follows:

```
Edit.Tool | System.Close System.Co
    Edit.Recall
    Edit.Search
    Edit.Locate
    Edit.Store
    Edit.Print *
    Edit.Print ~

    Edit.CopyFont
    System.SetFont Syntax10.Scn.Fnt
    System.SetFont Syntax10i.Scn.Fnt
    System.SetFont Syntax10b.Scn.Fnt
    System.SetFont Syntax10x.Scn.Fnt
```

Of course, the user may change the tool or edit commands into other tools (for more details see Section 2.6.3.)

3.1 Mouse and keyboard

The system editor implements all the mouse commands listed in Chapter 2. These are summarized in Tables 3.1, 3.2 and 3.3.

Table 3.1 Cursor in text area: edit and execute commands.

	Primary key		
Interclick	Left	Middle	Right
None	Track caret	Track word, execute	Track selection
Left	—	Execute, load module	Delete selection
Middle	Copy selection to caret location	—	Copy selection to caret location
Right	Copy attribute at caret location to selection	—	—

Table 3.2 Cursor in scroll bar: scroll up and down.

	Primary key		
Interclick	Left	Middle	Right
None	Track line, scroll down	Set position mark, scroll to arbitrary point	Scroll to top
Left	—	Scroll to bottom	Delete selection
Right	—	Scroll to top	—

Table 3.3 Cursor in title bar: select and execute commands.

	Primary key		
Interclick	Left	Middle	Right
None	Track title bar, move viewer in track	Track word, execute	Track selection
Left	—	Execute, load module	—
Middle	Track title bar, reposition viewer[1]	—	—

Selecting a line The text from the mouse cursor to the left edge of the viewer is selected if the left mouse key is pressed two times without moving the mouse. It is not necessary for the two clicks to be in quick succession.

[1] Possibly across tracks.

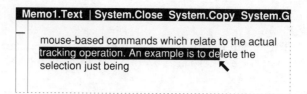

Click right
key twice

Line breaks

It is necessary to use the RETURN key to break lines. Oberon text viewers do not wrap words at the right margin.

3.2 Multiple views and the large selection

Two viewers showing the same text can be helpful when editing large documents. A second view of the same text is opened with the command *System.Copy* in the title bar.

Opening second viewer

Execution of *System.Copy* opens a new viewer with the same name. Normally, the new viewer is adjacent to the original one, whose frame is divided equally between the two clones.

The two viewers may be scrolled independently but *show the same text*. Changes in one viewer are immediately displayed in the other one, if the stretch of text being changed is visible there.

System.Copy may be executed more than once leading to a number of viewers displaying the same text.

Viewer opened
with Edit.Copy
showing second
view of text of
Memo1.Text

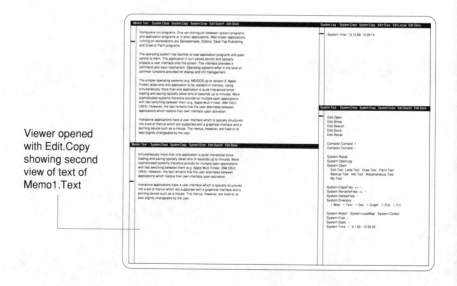

Closing second viewer

Any one of the twin viewers may be closed using the command *System.Close*. There is no need to previously store the text on disk (using *Edit.Store*) since a viewer remains on the display through which that text can be accessed.

Large selection

If a large document has to be selected, it may not fit into the viewer's frame. In this case, a second viewer must be opened adjacent to the original one using *System.Copy*. The text in the second viewer is scrolled such that the end of the desired selection becomes visible. The large selection can now be made as follows:

(1) Select the beginning of the desired large selection in the first viewer. An arbitrary piece of the beginning may be selected – just one character is sufficient.

(2) Select the end of the desired large selection in the second viewer. As before, an arbitrarily large piece of the end may be selected. Interclick commands can be given while selecting the tail piece. They operate on the whole large selection.

Now the entire text, including the invisible portion between the beginning of the first and the end of the second subselection, is selected.
Note: The entire large selection is not highlighted in reverse video. Only the two subselections are.

3.3   Closing viewers and saving to disk

Text which was generated or modified in a text viewer must be saved to disk if a permanent copy is required.

Storing to disk

The command *Edit.Store* is displayed in the title bar and can be conveniently activated with the mouse. The text will be stored in a file which has the same name as the viewer from which *Edit.Store* was executed. If the text is a new one, a new file with the viewer's name will be created on disk. The next *Edit.Open* with that name as parameter will load the file.

Store under different name

To store a text under a name which is different from the viewer's title:

(1) The command *Edit.Store* is used from a tool. In this case, it expects the new name as a parameter and stores the marked viewer.

(2) The viewer's name is changed using the editor prior to executing *Edit.Store* from the title bar.

Closing viewer   If *System.Close* is executed, the viewer is removed from the display. If the closed viewer covers the whole track and if that track is an overlay (generated with *System.Grow*), the underlying track is recovered. Otherwise, its upper viewer is enlarged to use the freed space.

Note: Always save before executing *System.Close* (unless one of multiple views is closed.) Otherwise, data may be lost.

Closing multiple views   If the *same* text is viewed through several viewers created with *System.Copy* or *System.Grow*, changes are not lost when a viewer is closed until the last viewer displaying the text is closed. The text may be saved to disk from any one of the multiple viewers.

Caution: The same text can be displayed in two viewers if *Edit.Open* is issued twice. In this case, these are *independent* instances which may have different modifications. Only one of them can be saved under the viewer's name.

Undo closing   An erroneously closed viewer can be reopened with the command *System.Recall*.

Caution: Only the last viewer which was closed can be recovered.

3.4   Command module Edit

Open   Edit.Open (*name* | ↑)

Open a text viewer *name*. If '↑' follows *Edit.Open*, the name is found in the selection.

Note: If the name is in the selection, only part of it needs to be selected (see discussion of *System.Open*.) The selection is also searched if the text line is empty after the command name.

The viewer is automatically placed in the user track, unless the pointer is set. In this case, the viewer opens with its upper edge at the place of the pointer. This means that if the pointer is placed in the system track, the viewer will open there.

If a text with the given name has previously been stored, it is initialized from disk and shown in the newly opened viewer. If the text is a new one, new text is created; consequently, the viewer is empty.

Show   Edit.Show (*module.txt* | ↑)

A viewer displaying file '*module*.Mod' is opened and the first occurrence of the string *txt* is positioned near the top of that viewer. *Edit.Show* is typically used to display a specified procedure in a program text.

If '↑' follows *Edit.Show*, then the parameter is found in the selection. The selection is also searched if the text line is empty after the command name.

The viewer is automatically placed in the user track, unless overridden with the pointer (see *Edit.Open*.)

Store

Edit.Store [*name* | ↑]

In the title bar, *Edit.Store* does not take parameters. It stores its viewer in a disk file whose name is identical with the viewer name.

If executed from a main text, *Edit.Store* saves the text displayed in the marked viewer in a disk file *name*. If '↑' follows *Edit.Store*, then the name is found in the selection.

If a disk file with the given name already exists, it is renamed. The first name part is the same, the second name part is changed to 'Bak'. Further name parts are ignored. For example, if a viewer *Memo1.Text* is stored and file *Memo1.Text* already exists, the old file is renamed to *Memo1.Bak*.

Recall

Edit.Recall

Inserts the most recently deleted text at the position of the caret. The caret may be in a different viewer from the one where the text was deleted.

Note: Deletion and *Edit.Restore* can be used in combination to move text from one place to another:

(1) Delete text to be moved.

(2) Place the caret at the insertion point (may be in a different text viewer.)

(3) Execute *Edit.Recall*.

Change attributes

Edit.ChangeFont (*fontName* | ↑)
Edit.ChangeColor (*colorNumber* | ↑)
Edit.ChangeVoff (*voffNumber* | ↑)

Changes the font, color or vertical offset attributes of the selection to *fontName*, *colorNumber* or *voffNumber*, respectively. Subsequently typed text is of the global font color specified by *System.SetFont*, *System.SetColor* or *System.SetVoff*. If the command name is followed by '↑', the parameter is found in the selection.

CopyFont

Edit.CopyFont

Change the font of the selection to the font found at the place of the star-shaped pointer. Subsequently, typed text is of the global font.

Search   Edit.Search
The parameter is contained in the selection and holds a text called the pattern.

If executed from the title bar, *Edit.Search* places the caret at the place of the first occurrence of the pattern in the displayed text. If necessary, the text is scrolled such that the pattern becomes visible.

If executed from an editable text (for example, from a tool viewer), *Edit.Search* searches for a match of the pattern in the text of the marked viewer. If a caret is placed in that text, the search starts at the location of the caret. Otherwise, it starts at the beginning of the text. The search terminates at the end of the text.

Note: In both cases, repeated execution of *Edit.Search* searches for subsequent occurrences of the pattern.

Locate   Edit.Locate
The parameter contained in the selection holds a text which is scanned from left to right for the occurrence of the first integer. Assume that n denotes that integer. Execution of *Edit.Locate* places the caret in the text of the marked viewer after the nth character (note that carriage return control characters are also counted.) For example, assume that the selection in viewer *System.Log* contains 'pos 2598 err 38'. The marked viewer contains the text of an Oberon module whose compilation has caused this error message. Then the execution of *Edit.Locate* places the caret at the point of the error found by the compiler.

Finding compiler errors is a typical use of *Edit.Locate*. Therefore, it is shown in the title bar of the system log where the error messages are displayed.

Print   Edit.Print *server* (* | ({ *name* } (~ | ↑)))
Prints texts on a network server named *server*. In the first case, the text displayed in the marked viewer is printed. In the second case, all text files contained in the list of names are printed.

If the list is terminated with '↑', the search is extended to the selection for precisely one more name. This option is typically used with the empty list.

Note: System.SetUser must be executed before the printer server can be used (see Section 4.2.)

4 File administration and system commands

The user deals with files naturally through the *Open* and *Store* commands of the respective viewer class. These commands deal with the task of creating files and registering their names in the file directory.

In addition, however, a set of files needs administration facilities. When files become irrelevant, they should be deleted. Sometimes, the name of a file needs to be changed or a copy of an existing file produced for further processing. To work on files, a command providing a listing of the directory is essential.

Command module System

The command module *System* provides the facilities for file administration. It also exports commands to:

- open tool viewers and the system log;
- close, copy and enlarge viewers and tracks, recall previously closed viewers;
- display system state information;
- set user identification;
- unload modules and force garbage collection.

4.1 Commands dealing with files and the file directory

Directory

System.Directory (*template*[/d] | ↑)

Opens a viewer named 'System.Directory' which displays files controlled by *template*. If '↑' follows the command name, the template is contained in the selection. The selection is also searched if the text line is empty after the command name.

The parameter *template* is a text string which must not contain blanks. The asterisk is used as a 'wild card' – that is, a character matched by any string of non-blank characters. All file names which match the template are listed.

If the optional characters '/d' follow the template without blanks, the listing includes date of file creation and size of the file in bytes.

Examples of templates are as follows:

*	All files are listed.
*.Mod	All files with suffix 'Mod' are listed.
Test.*	All files with first name part 'Test' are listed.
.Scn.	All files with second name part 'Scn' are listed.

CopyFiles

System.CopyFiles { *name1* => *name2* } (~ | ↑)

A list of name pairs *name1* and *name2* is processed. The pairs are separated by the symbol '=>' (equal sign followed by greater than sign.) The file *name1* is duplicated and a directory entry *name2* is created. If a file *name2* already exists, it is overwritten.

If the list is terminated with '↑', the search is extended to the selection for precisely one more name pair.

RenameFiles

System.RenameFiles { *name1* => *name2* } (~ | ↑)

A list of name pairs *name1* and *name2* is processed. The pairs are separated by the symbol '=>' (equal sign followed by greater than sign.) Directory entry *name1* is renamed to *name2*. If entry *name2* already exists, it is overwritten.

If the list is terminated with '↑', the search is extended to the selection for precisely one more name pair.

DeleteFiles

System.DeleteFiles { *name* } (~ | ↑)

All file names contained in the parameter list are deleted from the directory. If the list is terminated with '↑', the search is extended to the selection for precisely one more name.

Note: If a variable of type *Files.File* providing access to one of the deleted files exists, it continues to afford read/write access to that file. *System.DeleteFiles* only deletes the directory entry, not the physical file data. Such data is only purged when the system is booting the next time (see Chapter 11.)

Caution: Don't forget to terminate the parameter list with a special symbol. Any file whose name appears after *System.DeleteFiles* will be removed from the directory without a request for confirmation or the possibility of undoing the operation.

4.2   Other commands exported by command module System

Open

System.Open (*name* | ↑)

Open a text viewer *name*. If *System.Open* is followed by '↑', the name is contained in the selection. The selection is also searched if the text line is empty after the command name.

Note: Only part of a name needs to be selected. In the following examples, the text viewer *Edit.Tool* will open in the system track in both cases.

The viewer is automatically placed in the system track, unless the star-shaped pointer is set. In this case, the viewer opens with its upper edge at the place of the pointer. This means that if the pointer is placed in the user track, the viewer will open there.

If a text with the given name has been previously stored, it is initialized from disk and shown in the newly opened viewer. If the text is a new one, the viewer is empty.

System.Open is typically used to open tool viewers.

OpenLog

System.OpenLog

Opens the system log viewer in the system track (unless overridden with the pointer.)

Close

System.Close

If executed from the title bar, *System.Close* closes the viewer which contains the bar. If executed from a main text (for example, a tool viewer), *System.Close* closes the marked viewer.

In the tool viewer, the command should be listed as 'System.Close *' to indicate that it applies to the marked viewer. Note, however, that the asterisk is not required.

A viewer which is closed is removed from the display. The viewer adjacent (on top) to the one which is closed reclaims the freed display area.

Note: The viewer's contents (for example, text) are not saved to disk. If the viewer is erroneously closed, it may be reopened with *System.Recall.*

Copy

System.Copy

Opens a copy of the viewer in which *System.Copy* is executed (from the title bar or the main text.) The copy displays the *same* document as the original viewer.

Grow

System.Grow

Enlarges the viewer in which *System.Grow* is executed (from the title bar or the main text.) An overlay track is opened and the enlarged viewer covers the area of the whole track. The enlarged viewer displays the *same* data as the original one.

In the overlay track, other viewers may open and close in the usual manner. If the last viewer in the overlay track closes, the underlying track is restored.

CloseTrack

System.CloseTrack

Closes the track which contains the star-shaped pointer. If the track is an overlay, the underlying track is recovered.

Recall

System.Recall

Reopens the viewer closed with the most recent execution of *System.Close.*

Time

System.Time [*dd mo yy hh mm ss*]

If *System.Time* has no parameter (for example, if it is followed by a special symbol), then the date and time is displayed in the system log. With parameters, date and time are reset. The symbols *dd*, *mo*, *yy*, *hh*, *mm* and *ss* are all two-digit blank delimited numbers denoting day, month, year, hour, minute and second of date and time to be set.

Watch

System.Watch

Displays the amount of currently used disk space and memory resources in the system log.

ShowModules

System.ShowModules

A map of all currently loaded modules is displayed in a viewer with name 'System.ShowModules.'

Trap

System.Trap

Displays a trap viewer.

State

System.State { *moduleName* } (~ | ↑)

The global data of the modules in the parameter list is displayed in a viewer with name 'System.State.' If the list is terminated with '↑', the search is extended to the selection for precisely one more name. This option is typically used with the empty list.

SetUser

System.SetUser *userName/password*

Sets user identification *userName* and *password*. The slash is a required separator. Blanks are not allowed between *userName* and the slash and between the slash and password. User names are restricted to eight characters while passwords may be of any length.

When *System.SetUser* is invoked, the mouse pointer is frozen. The user name, the slash and then the password must be typed blindly (that is, are not echoed on the screen.) The operation of setting user identification must be terminated with the ENTER or RETURN key.

Note: This is the only really modal command in the Oberon system which requires termination by the ENTER key.

Collect

System.Collect

Initiates an immediate garbage collection run.

Free

System.Free { *moduleName*[*] } (~ | ↑)

Unloads every module specified by the parameter list. If a module name is immediately followed by an asterisk, imported modules are also unloaded as far as possible. A module can only be unloaded if it is not imported by another module which is still loaded. Therefore, the order of the module names in the parameter list may be significant.

If the list is terminated with '↑', the search is extended to the selection for precisely one more name.

Set global attributes

System.SetFont (*fontName* | ↑)
System.SetColor (*colorNumber* | ↑)
System.SetVoff (*voffNumber* | ↑)

Sets the attributes font, color or vertical offset globally. After execution, the designated font or color will occur when text is typed. The change applies to *all* viewers where text is entered.[1] The parameter *fontName* must be a font name, *colorNumber* is an integer naming one of the hues defined in the color palette and *voffNumber* is an integer designating the vertical offset.

If '↑' follows the command name, the attribute is contained in the selection.

---

[1] Given that they observe the Oberon interface guidelines.

The standard Oberon font is called Syntax. The default size is 10 points. The following versions of 10-point Syntax are available:

Syntax10.Scn.Fnt	Normal syntax font (default.)
Syntax10i.Scn.Fnt	Italic version.
Syntax10b.Scn.Fnt	Bold face version.
Syntax10x.Scn.Fnt	Like normal syntax but fixed spacing of numbers and characters A to F.[2]

Other point sizes are available and indicated by the number after 'Syntax.'

---

[2] To facilitate the construction of tables or arrays of numbers (including the hexadecimal notation.)

5 Using the Oberon compiler

The compiler is an important component of the Oberon system. Except for parts of the inner core (and procedures in module Display), the whole Oberon system is written in the Oberon language.

This chapter is an introduction on how to work with the compiler. Familiarity with the Oberon language is a prerequisite.

5.1 Compiler commands and messages

The input to the compiler are texts. Such texts are conveniently created in text viewers using the standard system editor. The following naming convention is recommended for files storing source programs:

name.Mod

where *name* usually corresponds to the module's name.

Compile

Compiler.Compile * [/s | /d]
Compiler.Compile { *name* [/s | /d] } (~ | ↑)
Compile the source text of the marked viewer (first option) or the text files of the list of names (second option.) If the list is terminated with '↑', the search is extended to the selection for precisely one more name-suffix parameter. This option is typically used with the empty list.

The optional suffixes '/s' and '/d' follow the asterisk or the *name* without blanks.

The suffix '/s' allows the compiler to create a new symbol file. If option '/s' is not specified, a change in the interface of the module results in a compilation error.

The suffix '/d' instructs the compiler to include position references in the object code. Traps will indicate the source position which can be located using *Edit.Locate*.

59

Messages   The compiler writes completion and error messages to the system log.

name.Mod compiling *n1 n2*
name.Mod compiling new symbol file *n1 n2*
Successful compilation of program text *name* is reported. *n1* and *n2* are integers. *n1* is the size of the object code (in bytes); *n2* denotes the size of the global data area (in bytes.)

name.Mod compiling
   pos *n1* err *e1*
   pos *n2* err *e2*
Errors with error numbers *e1* and *e2* occurred at positions *n1* and *n2*, respectively.

5.2   Debugging

5.2.1   Finding compiler errors

To efficiently debug an Oberon module, the user should compile with the '/d' option and have the following viewers open:

- The system log.
- A customized system tool or private tool containing the frequently used commands.
- A text viewer in the user track displaying the module's text.
- A text viewer displaying *OberonErrors.Text*.

Error location   Compiler errors are reported in the system log. The command *Edit.Locate* provides a convenient means to find the point in the program text where the error has occurred. For this purpose, *Edit.Locate* is included in the title bar of the system log viewer.

To place the caret at the location in the program text where an error has been found:

(1) Mark the viewer which contains the module's program text.

(2) Select the line describing the error in the system log.

(3) Execute *Edit.Locate* in the menu of the system log.

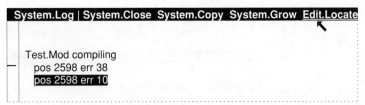

Note: Viewer Test.Mod is marked with ✳

Error description   To find the description of the error number, open a viewer displaying the text *OberonErrors.Text*. Then:

(1) Select the error number. (Be careful not to include the line break character in the selection.)

(2) Execute   *Edit.Search*   from   the   title   bar   of   viewer *OberonErrors.Text*.

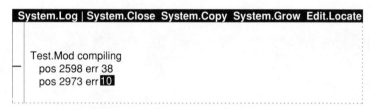

Execute Edit.Search in the title bar of OberonErrors.Text

5.2.2   Command execution and run-time errors

If a command from the module under test is invoked, the module is loaded. In this case, it must be unloaded before a new version can execute. Unloading is performed through the command *System.Free* or through an interclick with the left mouse key while executing a command with the middle mouse key.

Traps   Certain run-time errors are trapped and produce output in a text viewer called 'System.Trap'. The entire procedure activation stack is displayed. The error which produced the trap is identified with a trap code. The values of certain system registers are given. All scalar variables and strings (that is, ARRAY OF CHAR) together with their values are also listed.

For example, a floating-point division by zero produces the following trap viewer:

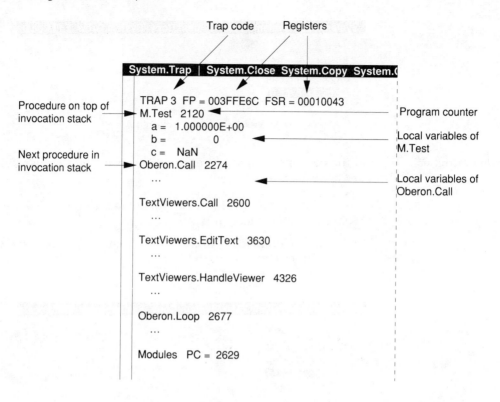

FP denotes the frame pointer, FSR the floating-point status register and NaN stands for 'not a number'.

Trap codes

The run-time errors are identified by numeric trap codes. The codes are explained at the end of *OberonErrors.Text*.

Trap from keyboard

The key combination CTRL–SHIFT–DEL produces a trap with code number 22. The keyboard-induced trap may be used to halt the execution of commands. It also allows the user to recover when he or she accidentally closes all viewers on the screen. Since the viewer named *System.Trap* is a text viewer, it is only necessary to type 'System.Open System.Tool' and resume work.

5.2.3   Writing to the system log

The system log provides a convenient output area for Oberon commands under test. The way in which commands write to the log viewer is explained in Section 18.3.

6 Using diskettes

Diskettes are primarily used to back-up files of the hard disk or to initialize RAM disks.[1] The respective command module and tool are therefore termed Backup. The commands exported by command module *Backup* serve to:

- format and initialize diskettes;
- display the directory of diskettes;
- read from diskette to hard disk and write from hard disk to diskette, delete files on diskette;
- convert formats (command module *Miscellaneous*.)

On the Oberon distribution disk (or distribution file server), the back-up tool looks as follows:

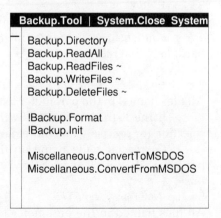

Of course, the user may change the tool or copy back-up commands into other tools (for more details see Section 2.6.3.)

---

[1] For example, in the Ceres-3 workstation, which has no built-in hard disk.

6.1   Commands dealing with diskettes

Format

Backup.Format
A two-sided diskette is formatted. *Caution:* All data the diskette may have contained is lost.

Init

Backup.Init
Initializes an already formatted diskette. *Caution:* All data the diskette may have contained is lost. *Note: Backup.Init* is much faster than *Backup.Format.*

Directory

Backup.Directory
Opens a text viewer named 'Backup.Directory' which displays the directory of the loaded diskette.

DeleteFiles

Backup.DeleteFiles { *name* } (~ | ↑)
All files named in the parameter list are deleted.
　　　　If the list is terminated with '↑', the search is extended to the selection for precisely one more name. This option is typically used with the empty list.
　　　　Caution: Don't forget to terminate the parameter list with a special symbol. Any file whose name appears after *System.DeleteFiles* will be removed from the directory without a request for confirmation or the possibility of undoing the operation.

ReadAll

Backup.ReadAll
All files contained on the diskette are copied to the hard disk.
　　　　Caution: If a file name on the diskette matches a file name on hard disk, that file is overwritten.

ReadFiles

Backup.ReadFiles { *name* } (~ | ↑)
All files named in the parameter list are copied to the hard disk.
　　　　If the list is terminated with '↑', the search is extended to the selection for precisely one more name.
　　　　Caution: If a file name on the diskette matches a file name on hard disk, that file is overwritten.

WriteFiles

Backup.WriteFiles { *name* } (~ | ↑)
All files named in the parameter list are copied from the hard disk to the diskette.
　　　　If the list is terminated with '↑', the search is extended to the selection for precisely one more name.
　　　　Caution: If a file name on the hard disk matches a file name on diskette, that file is overwritten.

6.1.1   Converting text files to MS/DOS

The diskette format used by the Oberon system is close to the format of MS/DOS. Full compatibility may be achieved through a set of commands exported by module *Miscellaneous*.

ConvertTo-
MSDOS

Miscellaneous.ConvertToMSDOS
The directory of the loaded diskette is modified to be compatible with the MS/DOS format.
Caution: File names may be changed (capitalized and truncated.)

ConvertFrom-
MSDOS

Miscellaneous.ConvertFromMSDOS
The directory of an MS/DOS diskette is modified to be readable by an Oberon system.
Note: In order to transfer a text file to an MS/DOS system, the formatting information must be removed first using Miscellaneous.Cleanup. For example the files Memo1.Text, Memo2.Text and Memo3.Text are converted to ASCII format, written to a diskette which is subsequently converted to MS/DOS format:

> Miscellaneous.Cleanup Memo1.Text Memo2.Text Memo3.Text~
> Backup.WriteFiles Memo1.Text Memo2.Text Memo3.Text~
> Miscellaneous.ConvertToMSDOS

The way in which line breaks are treated in Oberon texts and in MS/DOS text files differs. Procedures performing the necessary translations are listed in Appendix C.

7 Using networks and servers

Each system running Oberon may act as a *file server*. Special tasks installed on a dedicated machine provide *mail* and *print services* to the cluster. The servers can be accessed either by telecommunication (TC) lines (via V.24 interface) or by a local area network.

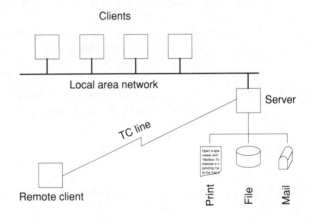

In a cluster of workstations linked by a local area network, one machine is typically dedicated as file, print and mail server. This station for the *dedicated server* has a default name which is installation specific. In the following examples, the name 'Pluto' designates the network server.

To transfer files between two workstations connected by a network, one of them must be designated a server by means of the command *Net.StartServer*. Once initiated as a server, files can be read from that station and transferred to it from any other network node. The server mode is terminated by *Net.StopServer*.

7.1 Naming conventions

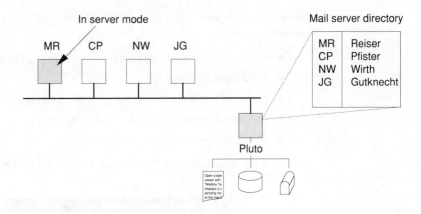

User name

If a workstation is in server mode, it is known to the network by its *user name*. The user name is set with the command:

System.SetUser userName/password

(User names are restricted to eight characters while passwords may be of any length.) To use a network and servers, it is necessary to first issue the command *System.SetUser*. Otherwise, a message 'no permission' is written to the system log.

Only stations in server mode can be recipients of files or messages sent with the command *Net.Sendfiles*. In our example, station MR is in server mode. Hence, files or messages may be sent to it with:

Net.SendFiles MR Memo1.Text Memo2.Text~
Net.SendMsg MR The files are now sent, you may switch off server mode

An attempt to send a message to station CP, for example, will result in an entry 'no recipient' in the system log.

Network name

At the mail server, participants of the mail service are registered under a *network name*. A directory at the mail server links user names and network names. The network name appears as the destination address in messages.

Typically, user names are short (for example, the user's initials) whereas network names are chosen as the full last name of participants.

7.2   Command module Net

Module *Net* exports commands for accessing the local area network, in particular, to:

- send files to a server or receive files from a server;
- send mail messages;
- get server directory and time, set password;
- process the mailbox at the mail server;
- enter and leave server mode.

On the Oberon distribution disk, the network tool looks as follows:

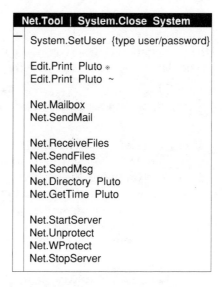

```
Net.Tool  |  System.Close  System

   System.SetUser  {type user/password}

   Edit.Print  Pluto  *
   Edit.Print  Pluto  ~

   Net.Mailbox
   Net.SendMail

   Net.ReceiveFiles
   Net.SendFiles
   Net.SendMsg
   Net.Directory  Pluto
   Net.GetTime  Pluto

   Net.StartServer
   Net.Unprotect
   Net.WProtect
   Net.StopServer
```

Of course, the user may change the tool or copy the commands into other tools (for more details see Section 2.6.)

7.2.1   Network commands

SendFiles

Net.SendFiles *server* { *name* } (~ | ↑)

Sends a list of files *name* to station *server*. The parameters *server* and *name* are names.

If the list is terminated with '↑', the search is extended to the selection for precisely one more name. This option is typically used with the empty list.

For example:

Net.SendFiles Pluto Viewers.Obj TextFrames.Obj TextViewers.Obj~

will send the files *Viewers.Obj*, *TextFrames.Obj* and *TextViewers.Obj* to the server with name *Pluto*.

ReceiveFiles   Net.ReceiveFiles *server* { *name* } (~ | ↑)
Transfer list of files *name* from *server* to the station which executes the command. The parameters *server* and *name* are names.
    If the list is terminated with '↑', the search is extended to the selection for precisely one more name.

Directory   Net.Directory *server prefix*
Fetch directory from *server* and display it in a newly opened viewer with title 'Server.Directory'. All files whose name starts with *prefix* will be listed.

Mailbox   Net.Mailbox
Open the mailbox, a special text viewer named 'Mailbox.Text', which displays a list of pending mail at the server (with default name.)

Mailbox.Text | System.Close Net.ReceiveMail Net.DeleteMail
4 21.11.89 17:34:16 Wirth 1125
3 20.11.89 14:57:20 Hiestand 1780
1 17.11.89 16:29:44 Wirth 3521

Each line starts with a message number followed by date, time, the sender's name and the document size (in bytes.)
    Note that the mailbox viewer does not display the standard text viewer commands in the title bar. Instead, *Net.ReceiveMail* and *Net.DeleteMail* are displayed, which are used to view mail and delete entries in the mailbox.

ReceiveMail   Net.ReceiveMail
The command *Net.ReceiveMail* is executed from the title bar of the mailbox. The message contained in the selection is fetched from the server and displayed in a newly opened text viewer with title 'Mailbox.Text' (see above.)

```
Mailbox.Text | System.Close  Net.ReceiveMail  Net.DeleteMail
  4 21.11.89 17:34:16 Wirth  1125
  3 20.11.89 14:57:20 Hiestand 1780
  3 20.11.89 14:57:20 Hiestand 1780
```

> *Note:* The message is conveniently selected by placing the mouse cursor to the right and double clicking with the right key. However, it is sufficient to select only the first character.

DeleteMail   Net.DeleteMail

The command *Net.DeleteMail* is executed from the title bar of the viewer 'Mailbox.Text'. The message contained in the selection is removed from the mailbox.

SendMail   Net.SendMail

The text of the marked viewer is dispatched to the mail server. To be accepted by the server, the text must observe the following syntax:

message	*toLine* { *toLine* } { *ccLine* } [*reLine*] {*textLine* CR}.
toLine	"To:" *recipient* { "," *recipient* } CR.
ccLine	"Cc:" *recipient* { "," *recipient* } CR.
reLine	"Re:" *textline* CR.
recipient	*name* ["@" *address*].
name	*letter* { *letter*	*digit*	"." }.
address	String of characters without blanks.
textline	Arbitrary text not containing CR.
CR	Carriage return.

If the *address* is present, the message is passed to a remote networks via the gateway, otherwise it is considered local. A subject may be indicated, headed by "Re:" also on one line.

```
Mail.Template | System.Close  System
  To: Wirth, Gutknecht
  Cc: Theiler
  Re: Reply to note: "Towards a final rel

  At which position is the new parameter
  procedure TextViewers.NewViewer?
```

SendMsg   Net.SendMsg *partner message*

Sends a short message to the station with name *partner* which must be in server mode (see *Net.StartServer*.) The text sent as message is the remainder of the line on which the command appears. The message is displayed in the partner's log text.

GetTime   Net.GetTime (*server* | ↑)

Synchronizes the clock of the workstation which issues the command with the clock of *server*.

If '↑' is used, the server name is contained in the selection.

SetPassword   Net.SetPassword *server "password"*

Communicates the quote enclosed *password* to *server* to be used by the mail service. This command has to be issued by the user only when he or she changes the password.

For example, a user with user id 'mr' wants to change the password from 'Heather' to 'Verena' at a mail server with name *Pluto*. He or she issues the following three commands:

```
System.SetUser mr/Heather
Net.SetPassword Pluto "Verena"
System.SetUser mr/Verena
```

First, *System.SetUser* is executed with the old password. Then *Net.Set-Password* is invoked followed with *System.SetUser* with the new password. Note how a different syntax is used to indicate the password in *System.SetUser* and in *Net.SetPassword*. The passwords in those two commands must be identical. After the change, it suffices to issue *System.SetUser* to gain network access. *Net.SetPassword* is used only to change the password at the mail server.

StartServer   Net.StartServer

The workstation which executes the command is being put in server mode; that is, a server process is initiated. Files from the workstation can be received by any other station by means of *Net.ReceiveFiles*. The workstation may be the recipient of messages sent by *Net.SendMsg*. The server is write-protected; that is, it does not accept files sent by *Net.SendFiles*.

Unprotect   Net.Unprotect

Removes write-protection of the server active at the workstation. After *Net.Unprotect* is executed, the server will accept files sent by *Net.Sendfiles*.

Caution: If received files have the same name as existing files, they will be overwritten.

WProtect   Net.WProtect

Sets the server which is active at the workstation into write-protect mode; that is, it will no longer accept files sent by *Net. SendFiles*.

StopServer   Net.StopServer

Removes the server mode of the workstation; that is, the server process is stopped.

8 Command module Miscellaneous

Command module Miscellaneous exports the following utilities.

CountLines

Miscellaneous.CountLines { *name* } (~ | ↑)
Opens a new viewer with title 'Miscellaneous.CountLines' which lists the number of non-blank lines in each text file of the parameter list. The total number of all texts is also displayed.

If the list is terminated with '↑', the search is extended to the selection for precisely one more name. This option is typically used with the empty list.

GetObjSize

Miscellaneous.GetObjSize { *name* } (~ | ↑)
Opens a new viewer with title 'Miscellaneous.GetObjSize' which lists the size of variables, constants and code (in bytes) of the files given in the parameter list. The total size is also displayed.

Note: The files must be *object files*. If the list is terminated with '↑', the search is extended to the selection for precisely one more name.

Snapshot

Miscellaneous.Snapshot *name*
Writes the pixelmap of the display from which the command was executed to the file *name*. This file may be printed (on the print server) with the command:

    Paint.Print *server name*~

Paint is the command module of the viewer class paint viewers. It is assumed that the necessary object modules are available.

Bootload

Miscellaneous.Bootload *name*
File *name* (which must be a boot file) is transferred to the special sectors of the disk reserved for booting the system. To make the new boot file active, the system must be restarted.

Cleanup   Miscellaneous.Cleanup { *name* } (~ | ↑)
Converts all text files specified in the parameter list to pure ASCII files. All formatting information of the text, such as font, color and vertical offset, is lost. Non-printable characters other than carriage returns are removed.
　　　　If the list is terminated with '↑', the search is extended to the selection for precisely one more name.

ConvertBlanks   Miscellaneous.ConvertBlanks { *name* } (~ | ↑)
In all files specified in the parameter list, pairs of leading blanks are replaced by tab characters.
　　　　If the list is terminated with '↑', the search is extended to the selection for precisely one more name.

ConvertTabs   Miscellaneous.ConvertTabs { *name* } (~ | ↑)
In all files specified in the parameter list, leading tab characters are replaced by two blanks.
　　　　If the list is terminated with '↑', the search is extended to the selection for precisely one more name.

Convert diskette   Miscellaneous.ConvertToMSDOS
formats   Miscellaneous.ConvertFromMSDOS
See Chapter 6.

Part II
Reference

9 System overview

The goals of Oberon are:

- The monolithic application with its slow loading process is disbanded. Its place is taken by a set of commands.
- The system is extensible. At any time, the user can add new commands operating on data underlying a given viewer class. Similarly, viewer classes can be added.
- The distinction between command input and text input is abolished. Commands do not write (volatile, non-editable) output to the display but produce a text which is displayed in a text viewer and hence can be edited and further processed with user-provided commands.

New architectural concepts are required to realize these goals:

- *Modules need to be memory resident* during the entire session to allow instances of abstract data types, such as texts, to exist between the execution of commands.
- *The event loop is centralized* and is part of the system architecture, rather than the application program. Oberon evolves the model of a single-process multitasking system; the indivisible unit is the procedure call.
- The fact that the event loop is centralized requires late binding of the procedures comprising the application. A special construct – *the active Oberon object* – is introduced for this purpose. Techniques from object-oriented programming are used.

A central role is played by the notion of the *Oberon object*. To show the need for such a construct, we shall discuss the consequence of moving the event loop from the application to the system. The objects *Frame* and *Viewer* are then introduced as instances of a certain record type with a procedure field. An overview of the module hierarchy completes this chapter.

9.1   Programs in the traditional sense

A program is a piece of code which can be loaded into memory and executed. We will assume that the program is written in Modula-2. Then it consists of a main module possibly with a set of imported modules.

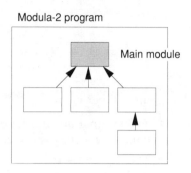

In the diagram, arrows depict the import relations that usually define a partial ordering – the module hierarchy.

The computer on which the program runs has facilities to load the set of compiled modules (object modules) into memory and to pass control to the module whose statement sequence is executed. On termination, the memory and all other resources are released. Only files provide a permanent output which may be further processed by subsequent programs.

If the program is an interactive one, its central component is a loop which executes when no other work is requested and which constantly polls for input events. In a simple case, there is only one program in memory, the keyboard is the only input device and the program polls the keyboard driver directly. This situation may be depicted as follows:

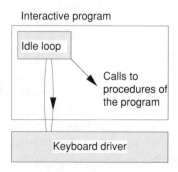

The procedure with the idle loop is also called the *command interpreter* of the interactive program.

More sophisticated systems provide multiple-screen windows and a mouse as pointing device. Each window may support an application program. Such a system has to discriminate input events, especially those from the mouse, and route them to the appropriate program. At least a limited form of multitasking is required, as indicated in the following:

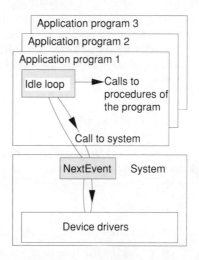

The structure of the interactive program remains the same as in the previous case. However, drivers are no longer called directly. A system routine, here termed *NextEvent*, is substituted. Whenever *NextEvent* is called, the system is in command and may decide to direct control to another program – an action called *task switch*. Enough state information is saved with the interrupted program so that it can resume execution later.

Multiprogramming systems differ in the granularity at which task switches may take place and also in the level of protection granted to the memory space of an individual program. In their most sophisticated form, the notion of an individual *virtual machine* is projected to each one of the application programs. Each one of these virtual machines is an individual process.

9.2   Oberon commands, module loading

It is an important concept of Oberon that commands communicate through instances of abstract data types of which texts are a prominent example. Since modules provide the encapsulations of abstract data types, this necessitates *modules staying in memory for the duration of the session*. Thus, the body of a main module is no longer an appropriate execution unit.[1] Its place is taken by the *statement sequence of a parameterless procedure*, which we now call a *command*.

The Oberon system provides a module loader which not only loads object modules but also allows activation of the statement sequences of procedures. *Dynamic loading* is used; that is, a module is loaded at the time a command is executed for the first time in the session. Loading of imported modules is further deferred until one of their procedures is called.

While debugging, a module must be *explicitly unloaded* before a recompiled version can be tested.

9.3   The event loop

Commands are initiated from texts which are displayed in text viewers. Like the traditional interactive application, the text viewer needs a command interpreter which:

- defines the semantics of mouse and keyboard actions;
- performs editing functions on the displayed text;
- provides the link to the module loader to start commands.

The last duty here is new – it was previously handled by the system command interpreter. A viewer's command interpreter is also called its *handler*.

Oberon introduces a novel architectural concept which differs from the standard system model: the idle loop of the interactive application becomes a central component – the *event loop*.

Viewers are represented by instances of an abstract data type *Viewer* which are record variables with a procedure field called *handle* to which a viewer's command interpreter is assigned. A viewer manager maintains a (hidden) data structure of viewers and enforces proper tiling of the screen.

In a quiescent period, control is in the event loop, which constantly polls the device driver for keyboard and mouse events. If an input event occurs, a target viewer is determined and its handler is called. On completion, the handler returns control to the calling procedure in the loop, which continues polling. Oberon has no facility to

---

[1] As is the case in Modula-2.

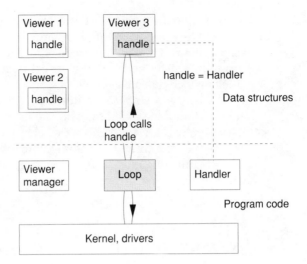

interrupt the execution of procedures. The *procedure (or command) is the indivisible unit of execution*.

The concept of a central loop has a significant advantage: since all procedures run to completion and since control follows the path defined by normal procedure calls, *no state information needs to be saved*. Oberon may thus be called a *single-process multitasking system*.

However, in the framework of the module concept of the Oberon language, the new architecture poses a problem. The event loop, which is contained in module Oberon, makes calls to handlers provided in application modules. Since applications can be added at any time, there is no way module Oberon can import such application modules and gain the required knowledge to make normal procedure calls to the handlers. (We exclude as impractical the possibility that module Oberon is modified and recompiled each time an application is added.) In the following diagram of the module hierarchy, the application modules are above the module Oberon:

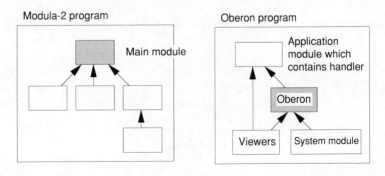

Therefore, a mechanism of *late binding* is required. The solution is provided by object-oriented design which uses the type extension facility of the Oberon language. Calls to modules higher up in the hierarchy are termed *up-calls*, in contrast to normal procedure calls which may be called *down-calls*.

Clearly, a smooth multitasking operation depends crucially on whether handlers and commands keep their processing periods short. Also, handlers are not running in protected memory regions, nor are they prevented from trespassing into other viewer frames. System integrity thus depends on the type safety of the language and on well-behaved handlers. We speak, therefore, of a *cooperating process multi-tasking system*.

9.4   System architecture for up-calls: active objects

In this section, we shall discuss the object-oriented design used in the Oberon system. The issue is late binding of procedures allowing up-calls from the main loop to viewers. The key idea is that a low level module exports the type of the handler and a public projection of all viewer types. This allows module Oberon, which contains the event loop, to make calls to the handlers within the type constraints of the Oberon language. The handler has a formal parameter *Msg* – the message. The real parameters are passed in a record variable which extends the base type of the message parameter. Type extension makes a variety of messages compatible with the formal type of *Msg*.

9.4.1   Definition of an object

An Oberon object is an instance of an abstract data type which is specified by a pointer to a descriptor record which contains state information and has a procedure field called *handle*.

The object Frame   For example, let *Frame* be the base type of such an object defining a display area:

```
TYPE
    Frame = POINTER TO FrameDesc;
    FrameDesc = RECORD
        next, dsc: Frame;
        X, Y, W, H: INTEGER;
        handle: Handler
    END;
```

The fields of *FrameDesc* describe a display frame with coordinates X and Y, width W, height H, pointers *next* and *dsc* to other frames, and a procedure *handle*.

Procedures which may be assigned to the field *handle* are termed handlers. They are of the following type:

```
TYPE Handler = PROCEDURE (F: Frame; VAR Msg: FrameMsg);
```

Thus, the handler has access to the object's state information recorded in its descriptor and to a parameter *Msg* of type *FrameMsg*.

The object Viewer

Extending the descriptor type of objects provides a powerful mechanism for adding functionality while reusing existing definitions. For example, the abstract data type *Viewer* is derived from the definition of *Frame*. It consists of an extension of the frame descriptor and a set of procedures comprising the viewer manager. These procedures implement the Oberon logical display model. The added field is *state*, which yields information about the viewer (for example, displayed, closed, suspended etc.)

```
TYPE
    Viewer = POINTER TO ViewerDesc;
    ViewerDesc = RECORD
      (FrameDesc) (* Type extension *)
      state: INTEGER
    END;
```

Viewers describe rectangular display areas together with their semantics.

Application viewer

The system, however, should allow an open-ended number of different viewer types, typically providing editing functions operating on a specific kind of document. In order to provide this functionality, the type *Viewer* is further extended and additional fields (state variables or instance variables) are added to its descriptor. For example:

```
TYPE
  MyViewer = POINTER TO MyViewerDesc;
  MyViewerDesc = RECORD
    (ViewerDesc) (* Type extension *)
      ...              (* Further state variables *)
  END;
```

Creation of an object

A variable which is an instance of type *MyViewer* is called *an active object*. It is created as follows:

```
VAR
  V: MyViewer;
  ...
  NEW(V); V.handle := MyHandler; (* Install handler *)
  ...                            (* Initialize state variables *)
```

Note: The call of NEW is always immediately followed by the installation of the handler. Failure to install a handler results in an unrecoverable system crash.

Installing a handler

We say 'the handler MyHandler is *installed* in object V', which means that procedure *MyHandler* is assigned to the field *V.handle* in object *V*.

9.4.2 Definition of a message

The type *FrameMsg* in the definition of *Handler* is a record type. The actual parameter which is passed to the handler is called a *message*. It serves to communicate information from the caller to the handler and may be visualized as the parameter list proper of the handler.

Various callers may use messages of different types all extending a common base type *FrameMsg*. No restriction is placed on the message if:

```
TYPE FrameMsg = RECORD END;
```

For example, the event loop may use messages of type *InputMsg* whereas the viewer manager defines its own type *ViewerMsg*:

```
TYPE                    TYPE
  InputMsg = RECORD       ViewerMsg = RECORD
  (FrameMsg)              (FrameMsg)
  id: INTEGER;            id: INTEGER;
  keys: SET;              X, Y: INTEGER;
  X, Y: INTEGER;          W, H: INTEGER;
  ch: CHAR                state: INTEGER
  END;                    END;
```

A message of type *InputMsg* contains information about a mouse or keyboard input event; a message of type *ViewerMsg* holds the parameters of a screen configuration change.

**Message
identifier**

To avoid proliferation of message types, the type may be used as a broader classification and use made of *message identifiers* to discriminate between message variants. An integer field called *id* is typically used as message identifier. The possible values for message identifiers are defined as a set of constants with appropriate names; for example, the type *InputMsg* may admit the identifiers:

```
CONST
    consume = 0; (∗ Character read from keyboard ∗)
    track = 1;      (∗ Mouse event ∗)
```

9.4.3 Sending a message to an object

When a handler is called, it is first necessary to fill the fields of the message. Let *V* be an object of type *Viewer*. The handler of a viewer is called from a procedure in the event loop when an input event occurs. Assume that an alphanumeric key was pressed. The calling sequence may look as follows:

```
VAR M: InputMsg;
    ...
M.id := consume;
M.ch := ...;      (∗ Character read by loop ∗)
V.handle(V, M); (∗ send message to V ∗)
```

Note: Only relevant fields of the message need to be set, in this case the *id* and the character field *ch*.

**Sending a
message**

We say 'sending a message of type *InputMsg* with *id* = *consume* to object *V*' or simply 'sending a consume message to *V*' to mean precisely:

(1) Set *M.id := consume*.

(2) Assign values to the relevant fields of message *M*.

(3) Call the handler of object *V* with the object *V* as first and the record *M* as second actual parameter; that is, *V.handle(V, M)*.

9.4.4 Structure of handlers

The definition of the procedure type *Handler* has two formal parameters. However, the true parameters for the handler are contained in the *fields* of both the message and the object's descriptor. The handler may encounter an open-ended number of message types. It discriminates between them with a *type test*. The structure of the typical handler is therefore:

```
PROCEDURE MyHandler(F: Frame; VAR M: FrameMsg);
BEGIN
  IF M IS InputMsg THEN
    WITH M:InputMsg DO
      ...   (* Process input message *)
    END
  ELSIF M IS SelectionMsg THEN
    WITH M:SelectionMsg DO
      ...   (* Process selection message *)
    END
  ELSIF ... (* Further message types *)
    ...
  END
END MyHandler;
```

The handler is at liberty to react to message types. New message types may be introduced without affecting the proper functioning of existing handlers.

9.4.5 Objects in the module hierarchy

In the preceding section, the concepts defining active Oberon objects were introduced without referring to different modules. We now place these definitions into their appropriate context. Module Display is at the bottom of the hierarchy. It exports (among other things) the base types *Frame*, *Handler* and *FrameMsg*. Module Viewers implements the abstract

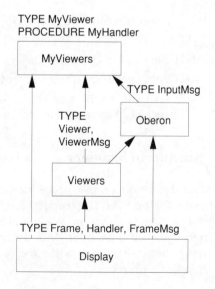

data type *Viewer*. It uses messages of type *ViewerMsg* to alert handlers about changes in the display configuration. Module Oberon contains the event loop. It imports *Viewers* in order to gain access to instances of viewers to which messages of type *InputMsg* will be sent when the loop senses a mouse or keyboard event. Module MyViewers – the one provided by an application programmer – contains the type *MyViewer* and the actual code for the handler.

It is an important design philosophy of the Oberon object concept that *message types are defined in the module which has a need to send them*.

9.5   The module hierarchy

We may now refine the module hierarchy of the Oberon system.

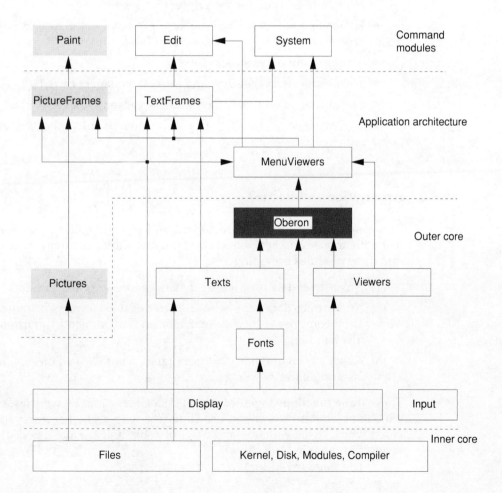

In order not to overload the figure, only major import relations are shown. The complete import lists are documented in the chapters describing each of the modules.

9.5.1   Inner and outer core

The inner core of the system provides the Oberon compiler, memory management, file management and program loading. This core is not the subject of this book, except for the module *Files*.

The modules of the outer core export procedures and abstract data types used by the application provider. It comprises:

- Drivers for the keyboard and mouse (*Input*), for the network (*V24* and *SCC*) and for the printer (*Printer.*)
- Raster operations for writing to the screen's bitmap and base types *Frame*, *Handler* and *FrameMsg* (*Display.*)
- Management of typefaces (*Fonts.*)
- The abstract data type *Text* and the text manager (*Texts.*)
- The abstract data type *Viewer* and the viewer manager (*Viewers.*)
- The event loop, facilities to call commands and other system wide resources (*Oberon.*)

9.5.2   Application architecture

Viewers normally display a document and provide editing functions using the mouse and keyboard. Their functionality is naturally divided into three modules providing:

(1) An abstract data type whose instance represents a document.
(2) An abstract data type whose instances are viewers or frames. They comprise a display manager and a command interpreter (the handler.)
(3) A set of commands, most notably *Open* which creates an instance of the viewer.

These three functions together are called a *viewer class*. Viewer classes, which implement the Oberon user interface with a title bar in reverse video which displays name and a set of commands, make use of the services of module *MenuViewers*.

The standard editor is a good example:

- The abstract data type *Texts.Text* represents the document (*Texts.*)
- The abstract data type *TextFrames.Frame* incorporates a display manager and a handler. Text frames are active objects installed in menu viewers which implement the mouse and keyboard actions of the standard editor (*TextFrames.*)
- Module *Edit* is the command module.

In order to illustrate this concept, the diagram includes another viewer class – picture viewers – comprised of abstract document *Pictures*, display manager and handler *PictureFrames* and command module *Paint*. These modules, however, are not documented in this book.

9.6   Guide to the notation used to describe the modules of the outer core

The modules of the outer core of Oberon are described in subsequent chapters with, generally, a chapter being provided for each module. The chapter starts with a summary of the abstract data types and the functions exported by the module.

A box follows with a rigorous definition in the form of a Modula-2 definition module. Thus, all imported modules are identified, the exported constants, types and variables are declared and the procedure heading of the exported procedures is listed.

Note that the Oberon programming language does not use definition modules but export marks.

Following the definition module, the concepts and the exported objects and procedures are explained in detail. To do this, we take the point of view of *being inside the module*. This means that we refer to identifiers declared in the module without module qualification. For example, module Display exports a variable *Bottom*. In Chapter 12 we refer to that variable as *Bottom* whereas the user should refer to *Display.Bottom*. In Part III we adopt the user's point of view.

10 Keyboard, mouse, network and printer

In this chapter, we describe the low-level device drivers *Input*, *V24* and *SCC* together with module *Printer* which accesses a printer server over a network.

```
DEFINITION Input;

PROCEDURE Available ( ): INTEGER;
PROCEDURE Mouse(VAR keys: SET; VAR x, y: INTEGER);
PROCEDURE Read(VAR ch: CHAR);
PROCEDURE SetMouseLimits(w, h: INTEGER);
PROCEDURE Time( ): LONGINT;

END Input.
```

```
DEFINITION V24;

IMPORT SYSTEM;

PROCEDURE Available ( ): INTEGER;
PROCEDURE Receive(VAR x: SYSTEM.BYTE);
PROCEDURE Send(x: SYSTEM.BYTE);
PROCEDURE Start(...); (* Hardware dependent parameters *)
PROCEDURE Stop;

END V24.
```

```
DEFINITION SCC;

IMPORT SYSTEM;

TYPE
  Header = RECORD
    valid: BOOLEAN;
    dadr, sadr, typ: SHORTINT;
    len, destLink, srcLink: INTEGER
  END;
```

```
PROCEDURE Available ( ): INTEGER;
PROCEDURE Receive(VAR x: SYSTEM.BYTE);
PROCEDURE ReceiveHead(VAR head: ARRAY OF SYSTEM.BYTE);
PROCEDURE SendPacket(VAR head, buf: ARRAY OF SYSTEM.BYTE);
PROCEDURE Skip(m: INTEGER);
PROCEDURE Start(filter: BOOLEAN);
PROCEDURE Stop;

END SCC.
```

```
DEFINITION Printer;

VAR
    res: INTEGER;

PROCEDURE Close;
PROCEDURE ContString(VAR s: ARRAY OF CHAR; fno: SHORTINT);
PROCEDURE Font(fno: SHORTINT; VAR name: ARRAY OF CHAR);
PROCEDURE Line(x, y, w, h: INTEGER);
PROCEDURE Open(VAR name, user: ARRAY OF CHAR;
                    password: LONGINT);
PROCEDURE Page(nofcopies: INTEGER);
PROCEDURE Picture(x, y, w, h, mode: INTEGER; adr: LONGINT);
PROCEDURE Shade(x, y, w, h, pat: INTEGER);
PROCEDURE String(x, y: INTEGER; VAR s: ARRAY OF CHAR;
                    fno: SHORTINT);

END Printer.
```

10.1 Module Input

Module Input is the device driver for the mouse and keyboard. It deals with special hardware supporting these devices. Procedures are provided which read the hardware and return typed characters and mouse events.

Note: Mouse and keyboard events are normally handled by the event loop. The programmer of commands should, therefore, refrain from reading these devices directly except in special cases, such as mouse tracking, reading a password or using a command key to interrupt a long-running command (see Part III for an example.)

Available

PROCEDURE Available ( ): INTEGER;
Returns the number of characters available from the keyboard.

Read   PROCEDURE Read(VAR ch: CHAR);
The parameter *ch* is set to the next character read from the keyboard. If no character is in the keyboard buffer, *Read* waits until a key is pressed.
Note: Procedure *Available* should be used to test whether a character is available if waiting is to be avoided.

Mouse   PROCEDURE Mouse(VAR keys: SET; VAR x, y: INTEGER);
Parameters x and y are the coordinates of the mouse at the time of the call. The status of the mouse keys are recorded in keys according to the following convention:

- 0 IN *keys* :   right key was pressed.
- 1 IN *keys* :   middle key was pressed.
- 2 IN *keys* :   left key was pressed.

SetMouseLimits PROCEDURE SetMouseLimits(w, h: INTEGER);
Defines width w and height h of the rectangle in which the mouse moves. The mouse coordinates are computed modulo w and modulo h. Therefore, when the mouse leaves the rectangle it re-enters at the opposite edge (the surface on which the mouse moves is logically a torus.)

Time   PROCEDURE Time( ): LONGINT;
Elapsed time since system startup in units of 1/300 second.

10.2   Module V24

Module V24 is the driver for an asynchronous RS232 interface. Data is sent and received in chunks of eight binary digits. The receiving end provides a *receive buffer*. The buffer has circular organization and its size is implementation dependent.

Module V24 is the device driver of the RS232 interface and in OSI (Opens Systems Interconnection) terminology handles protocols on level 2a – the *media access control*. Client modules of V24 must implement the protocols of level 2b – the *logical link control*. (Its description is beyond the scope of this book.) The receiving part is *timing critical*: the receive buffer may overflow and data may get lost as a consequence of overrun conditions.

Note: Only the more important procedures of module V24 are described below.

Available   PROCEDURE Available ( ): INTEGER;
Returns the number of bytes in the receive buffer.

Receive   PROCEDURE Receive(VAR x: SYSTEM.BYTE);
Receives one byte from the receive buffer. If no data is buffered, Receive *waits until a byte arrives*.

Send   PROCEDURE Send(x: SYSTEM.BYTE);
Sends one byte over the interface.

Start   PROCEDURE Start(...);
Starts the RS232 interface. The arguments are hardware dependent – consult documentation for specific machine. The receive buffer is cleared.

Stop   PROCEDURE Stop;
Stops the RS232 interface, so no more data is received or sent. Remaining bytes in the receive buffer are not touched.

10.3   Module SCC

Module SCC is the device driver of a synchronous *serial communication controller* which serves a network of up to 255 fully connected stations. The network accepts addressed data packets which are delivered to a destination node. On the receiving side, the packet is checked for transmission errors and invalid data is discarded.

Data is sent in *frames* which consist of a *header* and a *data block*. Sending and receiving operations are not symmetrical:

- A frame is sent in one operation by means of a call to *SendPacket*.
- Data is received in a circular buffer. The header is obtained by the procedure *ReceiveHead*; subsequent data bytes are acquired one by one using procedure *Receive*.

In OSI terminology, module SCC handles protocols on level 2a – the *media access control*. Client modules of SCC must implement the protocols of level 2b – the *logical link control*. (Its description is beyond the scope of this book.) The receiving part is *timing critical*: the receive buffer may overflow and data may get lost as a consequence of overrun conditions.

The packet header is defined by:

```
TYPE
   Header = RECORD
     valid: BOOLEAN;
     dadr, sadr, typ: SHORTINT;
     len, destLink, srcLink: INTEGER
   END;
```

where:

- *valid* is TRUE if a valid packet is in the receive buffer.
- *dadr* is the address of the destination of the packet.
- *sadr* is the source address (the address of the sending station.)
- *typ* is used by the data link control protocol.
- *len* is the length of the data block.
- *destLink* is used by the data link control protocol.
- *srcLink* is used by the data link control protocol.

Prior to sending a data frame, the user must construct a header. The fields *typ*, *destLink* and *srcLink* are used by logical link control protocols specified in client modules of SCC.

It is mandatory for SCC to specify the fields *dadr* and *len*.

Network addresses are variables of type SHORTINT and are defined by the installation. A *broadcast address* −1 is available.

The serial communication controller receives data which is stored in a (circular) receive buffer which is accessed by the procedures *Available*, *ReceiveHead*, *Receive* and *Skip*.

Available

PROCEDURE Available ( ): INTEGER;
Returns the number of bytes of available data in the receive buffer.

ReceiveHead

PROCEDURE ReceiveHead(VAR head: ARRAY OF SYSTEM.BYTE);
Returns a header from the receive buffer. The parameter *head* is of type *Header*. The field *head.valid* is TRUE if a valid header was received, FALSE otherwise.

Note: It is the responsibility of the user to ensure that when *ReceiveHead* is called, all data bytes of the preceding frame have been received. Otherwise, an erroneous header is returned with *head.valid* = TRUE.

Receive

PROCEDURE Receive(VAR x: SYSTEM.BYTE);
Receives one data byte from the receive buffer. If the buffer is empty, *Receive* waits for data to arrive.

Note: It is the responsibility of the user to make sure that *Receive* is only issued if data is in the receive buffer. When a header is properly received, its length field indicates the number of bytes to be read.

Skip

PROCEDURE Skip(m: INTEGER);
Skips over *m* data bytes in the receive buffer.

SendPacket

PROCEDURE SendPacket(VAR head, buf: ARRAY OF SYSTEM.BYTE);
Sends a packet of data comprised of header *head* and data frame *buf*.

The length of the data frame must be properly recorded in *head.len*. Also, the destination address must be set by the user.

Start
PROCEDURE Start(filter: BOOLEAN);
Starts the serial interface. If *filter* is TRUE, then interrupts are only generated if a packet with either the proper address of the receiving station or a broadcast address is received. If *filter* is set to FALSE, all packets on the network generate an interrupt; that is, are received. Their receive buffer is cleared.

Stop
PROCEDURE Stop;
Stops the serial interface. No more interrupts are generated. The receive buffer is not touched.

10.4   Module Printer

Module *Printer* provides the network interface to the printer server. A page is composed using the procedures *String*, *ContString*, *Line*, *Shade* and *Picture*. After a page is completed, it is printed with a call to *Page*, which also opens a new page to be written.

A Cartesian coordinate system is used. Its origin is in the lower left corner of the page. Points are addressed in *units of printer resolution*. For example, a 300 points per inch laser printer measures points in units of 1/300 inch. Translation from display coordinates to printer coordinates is the responsibility of the user.

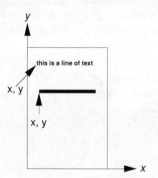

Result code
VAR res: INTEGER;
The variable *res* is an exported result code with definition:

- *res* = 0: normal completion.
- *res* = 1: no connection.
- *res* = 2: no link.
- *res* = 3: bad response.

Open   PROCEDURE Open(VAR name, user: ARRAY OF CHAR; password: LONGINT);
Opens the connection to the print server *name*. The actual parameters corresponding to *user* and *password* are normally the global variables *Oberon.User* and *Oberon.Password*. They must be set with the command *System.SetUser* prior to issuing *Open*.

Close   PROCEDURE Close;
Releases the connection to the print server.

Font   PROCEDURE Font(fno: SHORTINT; VAR name: ARRAY OF CHAR);
Assigns font identifier *fno* (specified by the user) with font *name*. The font identifier, not the font name, is subsequently used for printing characters in a given font. The reason for this indirection is to save transmission overhead.

String   PROCEDURE String(x, y: INTEGER; VAR s: ARRAY OF CHAR; fno: SHORTINT);
Prints string *s* using font described by *fno* starting at position with coordinates x and y.

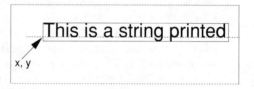

Coordinate y measures the height of the baseline of the font; x is the left edge of the character box.

ContString   PROCEDURE ContString(VAR s: ARRAY OF CHAR; fno: SHORTINT);
Continues printing string *s* from the end position of the previously printed string. *ContString* is typically used when a font change takes place.
            Note: ContString must immediately follow a call to *String* or *ContString*. It is not permissible to call procedure *Font* in between.

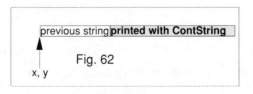
Fig. 62

Shade   PROCEDURE Shade(x, y, w, h, pat: INTEGER);
Prints a rectangle with lower left corner at coordinates x and y, width

w, height *h*, filled with a pattern determined by *pat*. If *pat* = 0, then the rectangle is white. For 1 ≤ *pat* ≤ 9, the following patterns are defined:

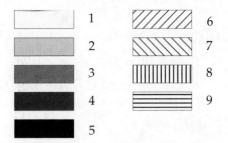

Line

PROCEDURE Line(x, y, w, h: INTEGER);
Prints a black box (line) with lower left corner at coordinates *x* and *y*, width *w* and height *h*.

Picture

PROCEDURE Picture(x, y, w, h, mode: INTEGER; adr: LONGINT);
Prints a bitmap stored in an array with base address *adr*. The bitmap is of width *w* and height *h* (in pixels.) Its lower left corner is placed at coordinates *x* and *y*. The parameter *mode* is a zoom factor. Each printed pixel is composed of a *mode* × *mode* square of printer pixels.

Note: A bitmap will print much smaller than it appears on the display if the printer is of higher resolution.

The bitmap is stored row-wise starting with the top left pixel and extending downwards. *Each row starts byte aligned*. If *w* is not a multiple of eight, then the line is padded at the right.

The base address of the array is obtained with the procedure *SYSTEM.ADR*.

Page

PROCEDURE Page(nofcopies: INTEGER);
Initiates printing of one or several copies. After *Page* has been issued, composition of a new page commences. Typically, *Page*(1) is used.

11 Module Files

The purpose of module Files is to implement the notion of a *sequence of bytes stored on disk*. It does this in terms of disk sectors presented by the disk driver.

Module Files exports:

- The abstract data type *File*. A variable of type *File* identifies the data on the disk.
- The abstract data type *Rider*. An instance of type *Rider* is associated with a file and affords read/write access. It is the rider, not the file, which has the property position (the point where read/write actions take place.)
- Procedures which interface with the *disk directory*. In particular, the procedure *Old* creates instances of type *File* from a file name contained in the directory.

The Oberon file system distinguishes clearly between three concepts:

(1) The file.
(2) The directory entry.
(3) The access method.

It differs from traditional file systems in the sense that the actions normally bundled with opening and closing files are performed explicitly.

```
DEFINITION Files;

IMPORT SYSTEM;
TYPE
   File = POINTER TO Handle;
   Handle = RECORD END;
   Rider = RECORD
      eof: BOOLEAN;
      res: LONGINT
   END;
```

```
            PROCEDURE Base(VAR r: Rider): File;
            PROCEDURE Close(f: File);
            PROCEDURE Delete(name: ARRAY OF CHAR; VAR res: INTEGER);
            PROCEDURE GetDate(f: File; VAR t, d: LONGINT);
            PROCEDURE Length(f: File): LONGINT;
            PROCEDURE New(name: ARRAY OF CHAR): File;
            PROCEDURE Old(name: ARRAY OF CHAR): File;
            PROCEDURE Pos(VAR r: Rider): LONGINT;
            PROCEDURE Purge(f: File);
            PROCEDURE Read(VAR r: Rider; VAR x: SYSTEM.BYTE);
            PROCEDURE ReadBytes(VAR r: Rider; VAR x: ARRAY OF SYSTEM.BYTE;
                          n: LONGINT);
            PROCEDURE Register(f: File);
            PROCEDURE Rename(old, new: ARRAY OF CHAR; VAR res: INTEGER);
            PROCEDURE Set(VAR r: Rider; f: File; pos: LONGINT);
            PROCEDURE Write(VAR r: Rider; x: SYSTEM.BYTE);
            PROCEDURE WriteBytes(VAR r: Rider; VAR x: ARRAY OF SYSTEM.BYTE;
                          n: LONGINT);
            END Files.
```

11.1   Files and the file directory

A file is an instance of the abstract data type *File*. Variables of type *File* identify the data on the disk comprising the file. This data is called the *physical file* which is composed of possibly non-contiguous disk sectors. The logical file provided by module Files is a simple sequence of bytes.

```
TYPE
    File = POINTER TO Handle;
    Handle = RECORD END;
```

It has the hidden properties:

- *Length* (in bytes);
- *Name*;
- *Date*.

Name and date are assigned to the file on creation. They may be obtained through the following procedures:

Length
PROCEDURE Length(f: File): LONGINT;
Returns the length of file *f* (in bytes.)

GetDate
PROCEDURE GetDate(f: File; VAR t, d: LONGINT);
Returns the date of creation *d* of file *f* (see Chapter 15 for the encoding of the date in variable *d*.)

File names   A file name is defined by the lexicographic syntax:

> *Name = NamePart* { "." *NamePart* }.
> *NamePart = letter* { *letter* | *digit* }.

The following are examples of structured names:

Viewers.Mod	For a file containing the source text of Oberon module Viewers.
Viewers.Obj	For an object file of Viewers.
Memo1.Text	For a text file containing a document.
Syntax10.Scn.Fnt	For syntax screen font.
Reiser.Mail.Memo25	For stored electronic mail of user Reiser.

File directory   To have a non-volatile record of file names and their associated physical files, a file directory is also stored on disk. The directory is a flat table, which means it is not structured into sub-directories. Structured names, defined by the above syntax, together with the facilities of the commands exported by command module *System*, provide some of the amenities of a hierarchical file system.

11.1.1   Opening files

The term 'opening a file' means initializing the resources which allow programs to access file data (that is, pointer variables providing access to physical files and the necessary buffers.)

In Oberon, *files and entries in the directory are clearly distinct entities*. Opening a file (creating an instance of the type *File*) is performed by two procedures: *Old* and *New*:

Old   PROCEDURE Old(name: ARRAY OF CHAR): File;
Creates a file from directory entry *name*. If *name* does not exist, the result is NIL.

New   PROCEDURE New(name: ARRAY OF CHAR): File;
Creates a new file whose name is determined by parameter *name*. A new physical file is initialized. The name is bound to the file at the time of creation and may be later registered in the directory.
Note: The procedure *New does not create an entry in the directory*.
Directory entries are unique. This, however, need not be the case with file names. The following diagram illustrates this fact:

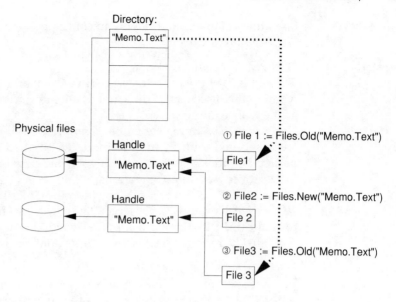

Variables *File1*, *File2* and *File3* are instances of the type *File*. Each one of them has the same name 'Memo.Text.' *File1* and *File3* point to the same handle whereas *File2* affords access to a newly initialized physical file.

11.1.2   Closing files

Normally the term 'closing a file' describes the following actions:

(1) Ensure that all buffers are written to disk.

(2) Register the file in the directory.

(3) Remove or invalidate the access handle.

In Oberon, the third task of the traditional close operation is never performed. As long as a variable of type *File* exists, it provides access to its physical file data. *During a session, disk sectors comprising physical files are never released* (unless procedure *Purge* is called.) Unused sectors (that is, sectors which do not belong to files recorded in the directory) are reclaimed when the system is booting. Oberon provides two procedures for performing tasks (1) and (2) explicitly: *Close* and *Register*.

Close

PROCEDURE Close(f: File);
Ensures that the physical file is identical with the logical state of the file. The two states may differ due to buffering. *Close* writes all buffers back to disk.

    Notes: File *f* and other files sharing *f* ↑ (that is, the handle to which *f* points) continue to provide access to the physical file and read/write operations of associated riders can continue. *Close* does *not* register the file name in the directory.

Register

PROCEDURE Register(f: File);

Closes file *f* (in the sense of procedure *Close*) and registers it under its name in the directory. If the name is already an entry in the directory, its file will be unregistered.

Note: The unregistered file is not deleted. If variables of type *File* are associated with it, they continue to point to the physical file. In particular, riders associated with such file variables continue to perform proper read/write operations.

In rare cases, there is a need to purge files (to remove their disk sectors.) An example is a server task on a machine which is never turned off. In this case, disk space of working files is never released and must be reclaimed explicitly. This is done through *Purge*.

Purge

PROCEDURE Purge(f: File);

Removes the physical file (the list of sectors) from the disk. The procedure does not invalidate file *f*, or other files sharing the same handle *f*↑. If any write operations are performed with riders associated with those files after a call to *Purge*, data is destroyed.

Note: This procedure must be invoked only if it is certain that no files and no associated riders remain active. It is used only for spool files on servers and similar applications.

11.1.3   Directory maintenance

The only way an entry in the directory can be created is through the following sequence of events:

(1) Create a file *f* (that is, an instance of type *File*) with the new name using procedure *f* := *New(name)*.

(2) Register the file *f* through *Register(f)*.

Temporary files are created with *New* and not registered. The name of temporary files may be the empty string "". Their disk space will be reclaimed at the time of the next session.

Two procedures are provided to remove entries from the directory and to change names in the directory: *Rename* and *Delete*.

Rename

PROCEDURE Rename(old, new: ARRAY OF CHAR; VAR res: INTEGER);

Renames directory entry *old* to *new*. The result code *res* reports the conditions:

- *res* = 0: file renamed.
- *res* = 1: new name already exists and is now associated with the new file.

- *res* = 2: old name is not in directory.
- *res* = 3: name is not well formed.
- *res* = 4: name is too long.

Note: This is an operation on the directory. Any variables of type *File* which are associated with the physical file retain their relationship under the old name.

Delete PROCEDURE Delete(name: ARRAY OF CHAR; VAR res: INTEGER);

Removes directory entry *name*. The result code *res* reports the conditions:

- *res* = 0: file deleted.
- *res* = 3: name is not well formed.
- *res* = 4: name is too long.

Note: The physical file is not purged. If variables of type *File* are associated with the physical file, they continue to provide valid read/write access.

The directory may change through registration of files, renaming or deletion of entries. Changing the directory does not affect existing files (that is, the variables of type *File* which provide access to the physical data.) The effect of deleting a directory entry and registering a file is shown below for the example given earlier:

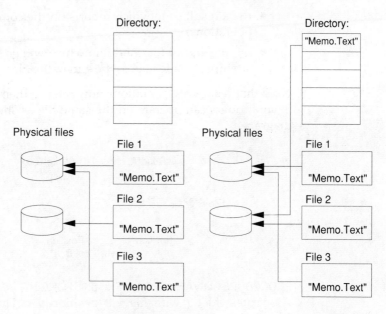

Directory entry "Memo.Text" deleted   File 2 registered

11.2   Read/write access: the rider

The abstraction provided by Oberon files is a contiguous sequence of bytes. A second abstract data type, *Rider*, provides sequential and random read/write access.

Sequential files have a *position* which designates the point in the sequence of bytes where read/write operations take place. The position is implicitly incremented after each operation.

In Oberon, this position is not a property of the file but embodied in a second abstract data type, the *Rider*. A rider (an instance of the type *Rider*) is associated with a file. It is set to a specific position in the file and then affords sequential read/write access through a set of procedures. The position is incremented upon each I/O operation.

The definition of *Rider* is:

```
TYPE
   Rider = RECORD
     eof: BOOLEAN;
     res: LONGINT
   END;
```

Its properties are:

- The file on which the rider operates (hidden.)
- The read/write position (hidden.)
- *res*: a result code which reports on the completion of read/write operations.
- *eof*: the end-of-file condition which will be set to TRUE when an attempt is made to pass the end of the file.

Note that read/write operations now refer to their rider, not to the file. Several riders can operate on the same file as shown in the following diagram:

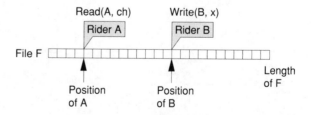

Set   PROCEDURE Set(VAR r: Rider; f: File; pos: LONGINT);
Associates rider *r* with file *f* at position *pos*. The field *r.eof* is set to FALSE.

Notes: The bytes of file *f* are numbered from 0 up to, but not including, *Length(f)*. *r.eof* is FALSE even if *pos* ≥ *Length(f)*. The user must ensure that *pos* is within the file limits.

Read

PROCEDURE Read(VAR r: Rider; VAR x: SYSTEM.BYTE);

Rider *r* reads one byte at its position and returns it in parameter *x*. The position of the rider is incremented by one. An attempt to read beyond the end of the file results in *x* = 0X and *r.eof* = TRUE.

Notes: The field *r.eof* is set at an attempt to read beyond the file, not at reading the last byte. Actual parameters of type CHAR and SHORTINT are compatible with the formal parameter *x*.

The following loop reads and processes all the bytes in a file *F*:

```
F := Files.Old("Sample.Text");
Files.Set(R, F, 0);
Files.Read(R, x);
WHILE ~R.eot DO
    ... (* Process byte x *)
    Files.Read(R, x)
END;
```

ReadBytes

PROCEDURE ReadBytes(VAR r: Rider; VAR x: ARRAY OF SYSTEM.BYTE;
                    n: LONGINT);

Rider *r* reads a block of *n* bytes at its position and returns it in parameter *x*. The position of the rider is incremented by *n*. If the request results in an attempt to read beyond the end of the file, *r.eof* = TRUE and *r.res* = number of bytes requested but not read.

Note: Actual parameters corresponding to *x* may be of any type.

Write

PROCEDURE Write(VAR r: Rider; x: SYSTEM.BYTE);

Writes byte *x* in the file associated with rider *r* at the rider's position and advances this position by one.

If *Pos(r)* = *Length(Base(r))*, then *x* is appended to the file and the length of the file is extended. Otherwise, the byte at the rider's position is replaced by the data byte *x*. Actual parameters of type CHAR and SHORTINT are compatible with the formal parameter *x*.

WriteBytes

PROCEDURE WriteBytes(VAR r: Rider; VAR x: ARRAY OF SYSTEM.BYTE;
                     n: LONGINT);

Writes block of *n* bytes contained in *x* in the file associated with rider *r* at the rider's position and advances this position by *n*.

If *Pos(r)* + *n* ≥ *Length(Base(r))*, then the length of the file is extended. If the rider is positioned at the end of the file, the data block is appended. Actual parameters corresponding to *x* may be of any type.

Examples: Write an array *A* of type *Matrix* to file *f*:

```
Files.Set(R, f, 0);
Files.WriteBytes(R, A, SIZE(Matrix));
```

Write an object *P* stored on the heap and accessed through the pointer type *Obj* to disk:

```
Files.WriteBytes(R, P↑, SIZE(Obj));
```

Note the dereferencing operator ↑. Observe that, for this to work properly, it is assumed that the writing and reading Oberon programs use the same array mapping. Compiler dependence may be avoided if the elements are written individually under the control of loop statements.

Pos

```
PROCEDURE Pos(VAR r: Rider): LONGINT;
```
Returns the position of rider *r*.

Base

```
PROCEDURE Base(VAR r: Rider): File;
```
Returns the file associated with rider *r*.

12 Module Display

The module Display provides three general functions:

(1) A set of procedures performing raster operations on pixelmaps (that is, for writing to the screen.) The data type *Pattern* provides raster data information. Variables of type *Font* are collections of patterns representing characters to be copied to the screen.

(2) A set of procedures for controlling the monochrome and color display.

(3) Export of the data types *Frame, FrameMsg* and *Handler* which are the basis for the Oberon objects *Viewers.Viewer, MenuViewers.Viewer, TextFrames.Frame* and other extensions defined by viewer classes.

For efficiency reasons, the procedures in module *Display* are written in assembler.

```
DEFINITION Display;

IMPORT SYSTEM;

CONST
    black = 0; white = 15;[1]
    replace = 0; paint = 1; invert = 2;

TYPE
    Font = POINTER TO Bytes;
    Bytes = RECORD END;

    Frame = POINTER TO FrameDesc;
    FrameDesc = RECORD
        dsc, next: Frame;
        X, Y, W, H: INTEGER;
        handle: Handler
    END;
```

[1] The value 15 applies for a 16-bit color display.

```
            FrameMsg = RECORD END;
            Handler = PROCEDURE(f: Frame; VAR msg: FrameMsg);
            Pattern = LONGINT;

        VAR
            Bottom, ColLeft, Height, Left, UBottom, Width: INTEGER;
            Unit: LONGINT;
            arrow, cross, downArrow, hook, star: Pattern;
            gray0, gray1, gray2, ticks: Pattern;

        PROCEDURE CopyBlock(sx, sy, w, h, dx, dy, mode: INTEGER);
        PROCEDURE CopyPattern(col: INTEGER; pat: Pattern;
                                    X, Y, mode: INTEGER);
        PROCEDURE DefCC(X, Y, W, H: INTEGER);
        PROCEDURE DefCP(VAR raster: ARRAY OF SYSTEM.BYTE);
        PROCEDURE DrawCX(X, Y: INTEGER);
        PROCEDURE FadeCX(X, Y: INTEGER);
        PROCEDURE GetChar(f: Font; ch: CHAR; VAR dx, x, y, w, h: INTEGER;
                                    VAR p: Pattern);
        PROCEDURE GetColor(col: INTEGER; VAR red, green, blue: INTEGER);
        PROCEDURE InitCC;
        PROCEDURE InitCP;
        PROCEDURE Map(X: INTEGER): LONGINT;
        PROCEDURE ReplConst(col, X, Y, W, H, mode: INTEGER);
        PROCEDURE ReplPattern(col: INTEGER; pat: Pattern;
                                    X, Y, W, H, mode: INTEGER);
        PROCEDURE SetColor(col, red, green, blue: INTEGER);
        PROCEDURE SetCursor(mode: SET);
        PROCEDURE SetMode(X: INTEGER; s: SET);

        END Display.
```

12.1   Bitmapped display, the display area

The Oberon display subsystem is a *pure bitmapped design*. CRT (cathode ray tube) display devices address a given number of points on their screen surface and are capable of writing dots of a given color at the location of these points. Such a picture point is called a *pixel*.

Pixel size   The size of a screen pixel in units of 1/36000 cm is recorded in the global variable:

```
        VAR Unit: LONGINT;
```

Pixelmap In a bitmapped architecture, the pixels of the device are mapped into a special memory area, the *pixelmap*. In this map, each pixel of the device has a corresponding pixel value designating its color. The display hardware reads the pixelmap and drives the CRT device. Therefore, the memory holding pixelmaps is also called *video RAM*.

Raster operations The pixelmap is accessed through a set of procedures performing raster operations which are exported by module Display. Some of these take as source a small pixelmap, suitably termed a *pattern*.

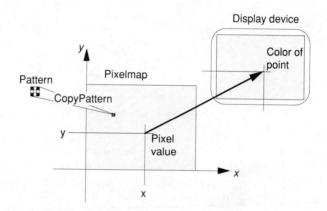

In a pure bitmapped design, everything displayed is created through raster operations on the pixelmap. Alphanumeric characters, for example, are simply patterns copied to the appropriate place in the pixelmap. The collection of such patterns is called a *font*.

The display area The *display area* is considered a plane with x and y coordinates. Three pixelmaps are defined:

(1) The primary monochrome map.

(2) The secondary monochrome map.

(3) The color map.

Their position on the Cartesian plane is shown in the following diagram:

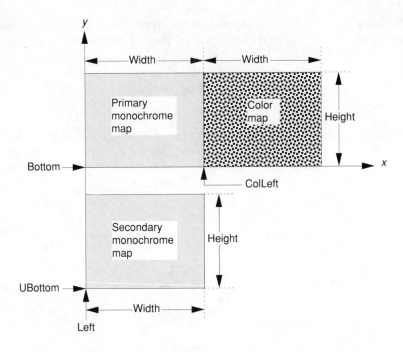

Pixel coordinates   Pixels have integer-valued coordinates X and Y which measure the position in terms of screen resolution, typically 72 to 80 points per inch.

The module Display exports variables which locate the different pixelmaps on the plane:

VAR Left, ColLeft, Bottom, UBottom, Width, Height: INTEGER;

The values are hardware dependent.[2]

Pixel values   Each pixel has a value which determines its *color*. In the case of a monochrome pixelmap, the pixel is represented by one bit and hence has values 0 (background) or 1 (inverse of background.) The background color is usually black. Reverse video mode, however, results in a white background.

In the case of a color pixelmap, each pixel is represented by an integer. The number of bits allocated to the pixel depends on the hardware.[3] The system assigns to each of the possible pixel values a particular hue mixed from the base colors.

---

[2] For the Ceres workstation with monochrome and color monitor: *Left* = 0, *ColLeft* = 1024, *Bottom* = 0, *UBottom* = −1024, *Width* = 1024, *Height* = 800.

[3] Four binary digits on Ceres.

Use of the secondary monochrome map

Only one of the monochrome maps is displayed at any given time. The user can switch between them using procedure *SetMode*. One may, for example, construct a complicated graphics using many calls to the procedures performing raster operations and, on completion, switch the display.

Organization of the video memory

The pixelmaps are stored in the video RAM, which is embedded in the general address space. Thus, access to the video RAM is no different from ordinary memory access.

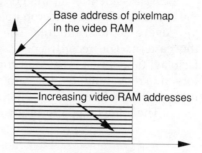

The pixel values are stored contiguously, row-wise from the top to the bottom. In a monochrome map, each pixel is represented by one bit. In the color map, the system-specific number of binary digits is allocated per pixel. The base address of the pixelmap in the video RAM is recovered using the procedure *Map*.

12.2   Raster operations

Module Display contains four procedures which perform operations on the pixelmaps:

- *ReplConst*: draws a box or a line.
- *ReplPattern*: draws a pattern in a rectangle.
- *CopyPattern*: copies a pattern to the display.
- *CopyBlock*: moves a rectangular block.

12.2.1   Patterns and fonts

The data type *Pattern* represents a program-defined source area with binary pixel values:

```
TYPE
    Pattern = LONGINT;
(* PatternDesc = RECORD
    w, h: SHORTINT;
    raster: ARRAY (w + 7) DIV 8 * h OF SYSTEM.BYTE
    END; *)
```

In *PatternDesc*, *w* is the pattern's width and *h* its height. The array *raster* carries the pixel data, line by line, ordered from bottom to top and left to right, a single bit per pixel.

    Note: Pattern is an integer type rather than a pointer type as is the case with all other Oberon objects. The reason is that it is used by a low-level assembler module. The integer holds the starting address of the pattern. The record type *PatternDesc* is not exported by module Display, therefore it is listed in comment brackets. The pattern descriptors must be built by the programmer using character constants, integers or sets (see examples in Section 19.2.)

    The following patterns are exported:

```
VAR
    arrow, star, downArrow, hook, cross: Pattern;
    gray0, gray1, gray2, ticks: Pattern;
```

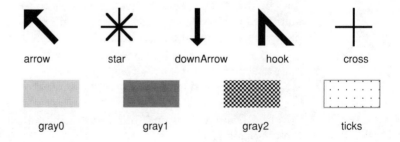

| arrow | star | downArrow | hook | cross |

| gray0 | gray1 | gray2 | ticks |

The pattern *arrow* is used for the mouse cursor, *star* for the star-shaped pointer, *downArrow* for the viewer busy signal, *hook* for the caret and cross for a special cursor (such as in a graphics editor.) The patterns *gray0* and *gray1* are two shades of gray, *gray2* is a checkerboard of 2 by 2 pixel squares and *ticks* produces a 'tick' mark in a square lattice of 16 pixels.

Type Font   A collection of patterns for screen characters which share a common typeface is called a font. The abstract data type *Font* represents such a collection.

```
TYPE
    Font = POINTER TO Bytes;
    Bytes = RECORD END;
```

The patterns of a given character are retrieved from a font by the procedure *GetChar*:

GetChar

```
PROCEDURE GetChar(f: Font; ch: CHAR; VAR dx, x, y, w, h: INTEGER;
                  VAR p: Pattern);
```

This returns the pattern *p* of character *ch* in the typeface of font *f*. The pattern is of minimal extent. The result parameters *x*, *y*, *w*, *h* and *dx* place the pattern in the character's box as shown in the following diagram:

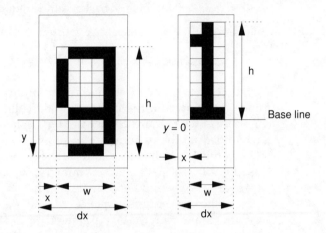

12.2.2 Procedures for raster operations

Destination

The raster operations affect a rectangular area of the pixelmap called the *destination* which is specified by its lower left corner *x*, *y* and its extent *w*, *h* measured in pixels.

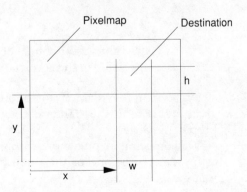

Note: The destination must be *fully contained* in the available display map, otherwise unpredictable results may occur (including address exceptions.) It is the user's responsibility to enforce this restriction. If the results are to be visible, the destination must fall in the active pixelmap of an existing device.

Color numbers

The notion of a *color number* is introduced in order to achieve a unified treatment for the monochrome and color case. In the latter, the color number is simply the hue of the pixel. In the former, the following convention holds:

- *pixel* = 0: background color.
- *pixel* > 0: inverse of background color.

The hues white and black are exported as constants:

```
CONST black = 0; white = 15;
```

On both the monochrome and the color monitor the pixel values *white* and *black* map into the corresponding colors (in the case of the color monitor, the standard color palette is assumed.) The values black and white denote the extremal color numbers; that is, $black \leq col \leq white$. The value 15 applies to a four-bit color monitor. If other hardware is used, *white* is adjusted accordingly. Note that module Display is hardware dependent and needs to be changed for different monitors.

The procedures *CopyPattern* and *ReplPattern* take as source a monochrome pattern. A parameter *col* is used to extend the binary pixel values to the range of the color numbers according to the following rules:

Modes

$dst := (\text{if } src = 0 \text{ then } 0, col \text{ otherwise})$	Replace mode
$dst := (\text{if } src = 0 \text{ then } dst, col \text{ otherwise})$	Paint mode
$dst := (\text{if } src = 0 \text{ then } dst, col - dst \text{ otherwise})$	Invert mode

where:

src is the value of the source pixel.
dst is the value of the corresponding destination pixel.

Note: In the invert mode, *col* should be set to the maximum value given by *white*. If the standard color palette is chosen, the colors are properly inverted.

For example, on a monochrome display, the effect of copying an arrow pattern in one of the three modes over the letters ABC is as follows:

replace   paint   invert

The module Display exports the following constants which are used as arguments to determine the desired mode:

CONST replace = 0; paint = 1; invert = 2;

ReplConst PROCEDURE ReplConst(col, x, y, w, h, mode: INTEGER);
Replicates color number *col* over the destination *x, y, w, h* in the specified mode. In the case of a monochrome destination, *col* = 0 represents the background color whereas *col* > 0 maps into the inverse of the background.[4]

Examples (monochrome map): Fill destination with background color:

ReplConst(Display.black, x, y, w, h, Display.replace);

Fill destination with the inverse of background color:

ReplConst(Display.white, x, y, w, h, Display.replace);

Invert destination:

ReplConst(Display.white, x, y, w, h, Display.invert);

Other combinations of the *col* and *mode* parameters do not yield new results.

ReplPattern PROCEDURE ReplPattern(col: INTEGER; pat: Pattern; x, y, w, h, mode: INTEGER);
Replicates the source pattern *pat* over the destination *x, y, w, h* in color and mode specified by the parameters *col* and *mode*, respectively. On the monochrome display, *col* is ignored.

The pattern is aligned with respect to the origin. This guarantees that overlapping destination areas are filled with a homogeneous pattern.[5]

---

[4] Current implementation restriction: In the color display, the paint mode is treated as replace mode.

[5] Current implementation restriction: The pattern width *w* is ignored. For the monochrome display, $w = 32$ and $0 \leq h < 256$. For the color display, $w = 16$ and $0 \leq h \leq 16$. If applied to the color display, 1 is subtracted from the *x* and *w* values, if they are odd. *Hint:* In order to be display independent, width should be taken as 16 and the pattern should be replicated such that, in each line, pixel values 16 .. 31 equal those of 0 .. 15.

CopyPattern   PROCEDURE CopyPattern(col: INTEGER; pat: Pattern; x, y, mode: INTEGER);
Copies the specified pattern *pat* to the screen map such that its lower left corner has coordinates *x, y*.
   The color and mode of the copied pattern are determined by the parameters *col* and *mode*. On the monochrome display, the parameter *col* is ignored.[6]

CopyBlock   PROCEDURE CopyBlock(sx, sy, w, h, dx, dy, mode: INTEGER);
Copies a rectangular screen area, the source block specified by *sx, sy, w, h* to an area of the same size with lower left corner at position *dx, dy*.[7] Source and destination areas may overlap.

12.3   Display control

The following procedures serve to control the display devices and are typically used for system initialization.

Map   PROCEDURE Map(x: INTEGER): LONGINT;
The base address of the pixelmap containing the coordinate *x*. For example, *Map(Left)* yields the base of the primary monochrome map. Similarly, *Map(ColLeft)* furnishes the base of the color map. Pixel values are stored contiguously, row-wise from the top row to the bottom row. In the monochrome map, a pixel consumes one bit; in the color map, a number of bits according to the capability of the display[8].

SetMode   PROCEDURE SetMode(X: INTEGER; s: SET);
Determines the 'mode' of operation of the device covering coordinate *X*. For the monochrome display (*Left* ≤ *X* < *Width*), the control register *s* contains the following mode elements:

- 0 IN *s* means 'display is on'.
- 1 IN *s* means 'secondary map is displayed'.
- 2 IN *s* means 'display is in reverse video mode'.

For the color display (*ColLeft* ≤ *X* < *ColLeft* + *Width*), only bit 0 is available.

---

[6] Current implementation restriction: The replace mode is not available, paint is substituted instead. The pattern must satisfy $0 < w \le 32$ and $0 \le h < 256$.
[7] Current implementation restriction: If applied to the color display, 1 is subtracted from the *x* and *w* values, if they are odd. The *mode* parameter is ignored and taken as replace.
[8] Four bits on the Ceres-2.

SetColor PROCEDURE SetColor(col, red, green, blue: INTEGER);
Defines the hue associated with color number *col*. The parameters *col*, *red*, *green* and *blue* range over the admissible pixel values.[9]
     If *col* < 0, the operation applies to the color in which the cursor is displayed.
     Each color number designates a specific hue which is mixed from the primary colors red, blue and green. In fact, the pixel value (or color number) is used to index a table of three registers which determine the weight of the primary colors. These registers can be set by means of the procedure *SetColor*.

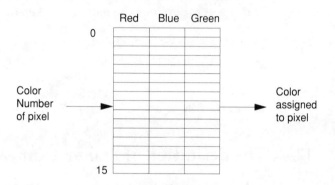

GetColor PROCEDURE GetColor(col: INTEGER; VAR red, green, blue: INTEGER);
Assigns the intensity values of the color number *col* to the variable *red*, *green* and *blue*. If *col* < 0, the intensities of the color used for the cursor are recovered.

SetCursor PROCEDURE SetCursor(mode: SET);
Determines the cursor mode of the color display. The register contains the following elements:

- 0 IN *mode* means 'display cross-hair.'
- 1 IN *mode* means 'display cursor pattern.'

InitCC PROCEDURE InitCC;
Initializes a cross-hair cursor on the color display.

InitCP PROCEDURE InitCP;
Initializes a cursor on the color display which has the shape of a default pattern.

---

[9] 0 .. 15 in the case of four-bit color displays (such as used by Ceres.)

DefCC   PROCEDURE DefCC(X, Y, W, H: INTEGER);
Defines the area on the color display in which the cross-hair is to be displayed.

DefCP   PROCEDURE DefCP(VAR raster: ARRAY OF SYSTEM.BYTE);
Allows the definition of a pattern to be used as color cursor. The array *raster* must be declared as:

          raster: ARRAY 128 OF LONGINT

and represents the pixelmap of the 64 by 64 point cursor pattern, two long integers per line. The pattern is taken top-down, left to right.

DrawCX   PROCEDURE DrawCX(X, Y: INTEGER);
Draws the color cursor with lower left corner at position X, Y.

FadeCX   PROCEDURE FadeCX(X, Y: INTEGER);
Erases the color cursor at position X, Y.

12.4   The definition of Frame, FrameMsg and Handler

A frame defines a rectangular area of the screen. The definitions of *Frame*, *FrameDesc*, *Handler* and *FrameMsg* are exported to be extended in client modules. Module Display does not perform operations with them. The type *Frame* is defined by:

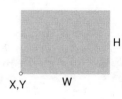

```
TYPE
  Frame = POINTER TO FrameDesc;
  FrameDesc = RECORD
    dsc, next: Frame;
    X, Y, W, H: INTEGER;
    handle: Handler
  END;
```

where:

- *next* is the link to neighbor frame.
- *dsc* is the link to subframe.
- X, Y are the absolute coordinates of the lower left corner of the frame's rectangle (in pixels.)
- W, H are the width and height of the frame (in pixels.)
- *handle* is the procedure which handles messages sent to the frame.

Each frame has a field of type *Handler* with definition:

TYPE Handler: PROCEDURE(f: Frame; VAR msg: FrameMsg);

where *FrameMsg* is a record exported by module Display with definition:

TYPE FrameMsg = RECORD END;

FrameMsg is a base type to be extended by client modules. It contains a parameter list for the handler. The handler is a procedure which reacts to messages sent to the frame (for example, to mouse and keyboard events directed at a viewer.)

13 Module Viewers

The module *Viewers* provides:

- A logical model of the display with *tracks* and *viewers*. Viewers completely tile the display. New tracks may be overlaid over existing ones. Covered tracks are restored when an overlay closes.

- The abstract data type *Track* which describes a vertical stripe of the display.

- The abstract data type *Viewer* which describes a rectangular area of the screen together with its semantics. Instances of type *Viewer* are active objects. One of their properties is a *handler* which embodies the command interpreter of the viewer and which performs all output operations to the display within its boundary.

- Procedures to manage tracks and viewers, termed *viewer manager*. The viewer manager enforces a consistent and exhaustive tiling of the display. Viewers are notified of display configuration changes by means of messages of type *ViewerMsg*.

```
DEFINITION Viewers;

  IMPORT Display;

  CONST restore = 0; modify = 1; suspend = 2;

  TYPE
    Viewer = POINTER TO ViewerDesc;
    ViewerDesc = RECORD (Display.FrameDesc)
      state: INTEGER
    END;

    ViewerMsg = RECORD (Display.FrameMsg)
      id, X, Y, W, H, state: INTEGER
    END;
```

```
    VAR curW, minH: INTEGER;

    PROCEDURE Broadcast(VAR M: Display.FrameMsg);
    PROCEDURE Change(V: Viewer; Y: INTEGER);
    PROCEDURE Close(V: Viewer);
    PROCEDURE CloseTrack(X: INTEGER);
    PROCEDURE InitTrack(W, H: INTEGER; Filler: Viewer);
    PROCEDURE Locate(X, H: INTEGER;
                        VAR fil, bot, alt, max: Display.Frame);
    PROCEDURE Next(V: Viewer): Viewer;
    PROCEDURE Open(V: Viewer; X, Y: INTEGER);
    PROCEDURE OpenTrack(X, W: INTEGER; Filler: Viewer);
    PROCEDURE Recall(VAR V: Viewer);
    PROCEDURE This(X, Y: INTEGER): Viewer;

END Viewers.
```

13.1   The logical display

Tracks

The logical display is a rectangular area which is subdivided vertically into a fixed set of adjacent tracks. A Cartesian coordinate system is defined with origin in the lower left corner.

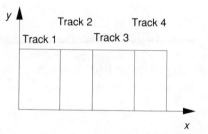

Viewers

The vertical stripe of a track is further subdivided horizontally into viewers. Viewers are stacked, one on top of another, and fill tracks from the bottom up without leaving any gaps.

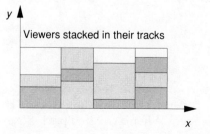

Filler viewer

It is simpler to assume that the whole logical display is *exhaustively tiled* with viewers. For this purpose, the notion of a *filler viewer* is introduced which covers the remaining area in the respective track.

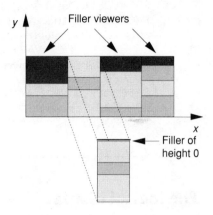

If viewers use up the whole height of their track, the filler viewer is assumed to be on top and of zero height. Thus, a track contains always at least one viewer, the filler.

Opening and closing of viewers

The tracks of the logical display form a fixed grid. Within this grid, viewers open and close under program control. Adjacent viewers either shrink or expand in such a way that the display remains exhaustively tiled. The rule is that the *change takes place at the bottom* of the viewer which expands or shrinks, as shown in the following figure:

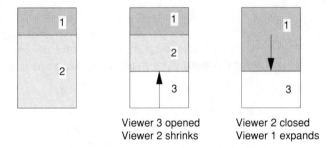

Viewer 3 opened
Viewer 2 shrinks

Viewer 2 closed
Viewer 1 expands

While the grid of tracks remains fixed, new tracks may be overlaid over existing tracks. The viewers in a covered track are hidden. When a covered track closes, the hidden track is restored.

Overlay tracks

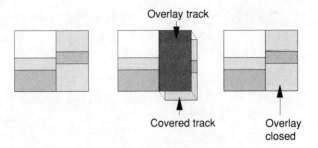

Overlay tracks may be opened to an arbitrary depth forming a stack of tracks. Only tracks on top of their stacks are visible. It is also possible to combine several tracks to form an overlay track of increased width.

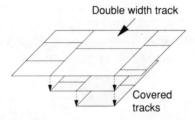

Standard layout

The logical screen model implemented by module Viewers allows an arbitrary number of tracks. The screen of an Oberon system, however, is divided into two tracks: a wide user track and a narrower system track. If a color monitor is added, it is similarly divided into two tracks. The two or four track configuration is initialized by module Oberon.

Viewer manager

Module Viewers implements the logical screen model. For this purpose, it provides:

- The abstract data type *Track* (which is completely hidden.)
- The abstract data type *Viewer*. Instances of type *Viewer* are active objects which also define the viewer's semantics.

A set of procedures – collectively termed the *viewer manager* – operates on tracks and viewers and guarantees that the logical display remains consistent.

13.2   The viewer

A viewer is an instance of the abstract data type *Viewer*:

```
TYPE
  Viewer = POINTER TO ViewerDesc;
  ViewerDesc = RECORD
    (Display.FrameDesc)
    state: INTEGER
  END;
```

The properties of a viewer are:

- Width, height and coordinates of the bottom left corner in abso-
  lute display coordinates (fields X, Y, W and H inherited from
  Display.Frame.)
- A neighbor viewer (field *next* inherited from *Display.Frame*.)
- A data structure of objects of base type *Display.Frame* (field *dsc*
  inherited from *Display.Frame*.)
- A handler which defines all mouse and keyboard commands
  and performs display output (field *handle* inherited from
  Display.Frame.)
- A state (field *state*.)

Viewer states   The viewer's state may be visualized as a priority number. This priority
defines the importance of the viewer and may be used to make
decisions regarding which viewers to display. The following conventions are defined:

- *state* > 1: the viewer is not a filler and displayed.
- *state* = 1: the viewer is a filler.
- *state* = 0: the viewer is closed.
- *state* = −1: the viewer is a suspended filler.
- *state* < −1: the viewer is not a filler and suspended.[1]

Minimal height   Requests to open or modify viewers are dependent on the *minimal
viewer height* which is exported in variable:

```
VAR minH: INTEGER;
```

---

[1] Current implementation restriction: The states are limited to the range
$-2 \leq state \leq 2$.

13.2.1 Locating viewers

The following procedures yield the viewer which satisfies certain conditions.

Locate

PROCEDURE Locate(X: INTEGER; H: INTEGER;
                  VAR fil, bot, alt, max: Display.Frame);

Within the track which contains x coordinate X, locate and return the following viewers:

- *fil*: filler viewer.
- *bot*: viewer at the bottom of the track; that is, *bot*.$Y = 0$.
- *alt*: a viewer of height *alt*.$H \geqslant H$.
- *max*: the viewer of maximum height.

This

PROCEDURE This(X, Y: INTEGER): Viewer;

Returns the viewer V whose frame contains the point with coordinates X, Y viz.

- $V.X \leqslant X < V.X + V.W$.
- $V.Y \leqslant Y < V.Y + V.H$.

Next

PROCEDURE Next(V: Viewer): Viewer;

Returns the neighbor of V. If $V.state > 1$, the neighbor is the viewer adjacent (on top) to V. If *fil*, *bot* and *top* denote the filler viewer, the bottom viewer and the top viewer, respectively, then the following relations hold:

$$Next(top) = fil, \qquad Next(fil) = bot.$$

13.3 Viewer messages

The location and size of a viewer are determined by the viewer manager. However, the contents displayed in a viewer's frame can only be produced by its handler. The viewer manager must, therefore, communicate with the handlers of affected viewers when the display configuration changes. It does this by sending a message of type *ViewerMsg*:

```
TYPE
  ViewerMsg = RECORD
  (Display.FrameMsg)
  id: INTEGER;
  X, Y, W, H: INTEGER;
  state: INTEGER
  END;
```

where:

- *id* is the message identifier: 0 (restore), 1 (modify) or 2 (suspend.)

- *X, Y* are the coordinates of the lower left corner of the changed viewer (*X* not used.)

- *W, H* are the width and height of the changed viewer (*W* not used.)

- *state* is the state of the changed viewer.

Message identifiers

The following named constants are exported serving as message identifiers with self-explanatory meaning:

```
CONST restore = 0; modify = 1; suspend = 2;
```

A variable of type *ViewerMsg* with *id = restore* is called a 'restore message.' Similarly, if *id = modify*, we speak of a 'modify message' and if *id = suspend* of a 'suspend message.'

The handler which receives a viewer message has access to:

- its viewer in the state valid *prior* to the call to the viewer manager;

- the message which indicates the state which will be valid *after* the viewer manager call is completed.

Note: While processing a viewer message, *the handler must not invoke a procedure of the viewer manager.*

Broadcast

Often, the need arises to send messages to all visible viewers. The update message mechanism of texts, for example, makes use of this facility. Such a message broadcast is performed using:

```
PROCEDURE Broadcast(VAR M: Display.FrameMsg);
```

Send message *M* to all visible viewers.

Message parameters

In an actual viewer message, only those fields which apply to a given change are set (see Table 13.1.)

Table 13.1 Fields set for a message *M: ViewerMsg.*

Event	Action	*M.id*	*M.X*	*M.Y*	*M.W*	*M.H*	*M.state*
New viewer or overlay track closed	Restore display in old boundary	*restore*	—	—	—	—	—
Display configuration changed	Change at bottom	*modify*	—	New *Y*	—	New *H*	—
Viewer will be closed	Release data structure	*suspend*	—	—	—	—	0
Overlay track opened	Release data structure	*suspend*	—	—	—	—	−*V.state*

Restore message   The viewer manager sends a restore message to all viewers which were covered by an overlay track which is closing (*CloseTrack.*) A restore message may also be sent by a command which creates an instance of a viewer.

   If the handler receives a restore message, it is expected to redraw the viewer's contents within its old boundaries, which are found in the viewer's descriptor record.

Modify message   The viewer manager sends a modify message to a viewer whose size will change as a result of another viewer which is opening, closing or moving its top edge.

   If the handler receives a modify message, it is notified that its viewer's frame will expand or reduce *at the bottom*. The handler, on receiving the message, is expected to redraw the viewer's contents within its new boundaries. The viewer's descriptor, passed to the handler, contains the frame location and extent before the change. The new *y* coordinate of the frame's lower left corner and the new height are found in the fields *M.Y* and *M.H* of the modify message *M*.

   If the viewer expands, the handler is expected to draw the new contents in the target area *V.X, M.Y, V.W, M.H.*

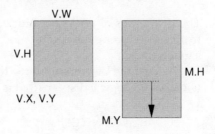

If the viewer reduces its size, the handler is still allowed to use the large area $V.X$, $V.Y$, $V.W$, $V.H$.

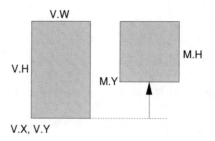

Suspend message

The viewer manager sends a suspend message to all those viewers which may be suspended due to a newly opening overlay track. It also sends a suspend message to a viewer being closed. The target state of a viewer being suspended is contained in field *state*.

If a handler receives a suspend message, it is notified that it will be removed from the screen. It may perform certain clean-up functions prior to loosing control over the display. For example, if the screen map is changed in a paint program, the bitmap must be saved before the screen is redrawn.

Note: It is not required that the handler clears the viewer's frame. The viewer claiming the space will do that.

13.4 Tracks

Tracks are instances of the abstract data type *Track*. Their properties are:

- Width, height and location of the bottom left corner (in display coordinates.)
- A filler viewer (which is always present.)
- Possibly an underlying track.

The properties of tracks are hidden and can be inferred only indirectly from procedures exported by module Oberon and from viewers within a given track.

Module Viewers exports the variable *curW* which reports the width of the logical display (that is, the sum of all track widths):

```
VAR curW: INTEGER;
```

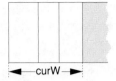

InitTrack   PROCEDURE InitTrack(W, H: INTEGER; Filler: Viewer);

Initializes a new track containing a single viewer *Filler*, provided that *Filler.state* = 0 (closed.) The new track is adjacent to the right edge of the logical display. The frame of viewer *Filler* is initialized such that it exhausts the frame of the new track and its state is set to 1 (filler.)

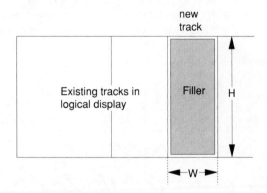

Note: The viewer manager does not send a restore message to *Filler*. All tracks should be defined with the same logical screen height.

13.5   The viewer manager

The viewer manager comprises a set of procedures to open, close and modify tracks and viewers. These procedures send viewer messages to affected viewers. They always observe the following sequence:

(1) Determine the affected viewer or viewers.

(2) Compute location and size of the modified viewer frames but do not change their frame descriptors yet.

(3) Notify the affected viewers of the change by sending a viewer message.

(4) Update the descriptors of the affected viewers to reflect the new configuration. The fields change according to:

- *X, Y, W, H*: the new frame.
- *next*: if viewer is inserted into the data structure.
- *state*: if viewer is suspended or closed.

OpenTrack   PROCEDURE OpenTrack(X, W: INTEGER; Filler: Viewer);

Creates an overlay track which spans one or several existing tracks. The new track contains a single viewer *Filler*. Suspends all viewers in the covered tracks.

Those tracks which have an *x* coordinate in the interval $[X, X + W)^2$ will be covered. The frame of the new overlay track is the union of the frames of the covered tracks. The frame of viewer *Filler* is initialized such that it exhausts the frame of the new track and its state is set to 1 (filler.)

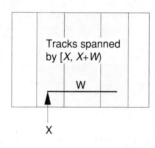
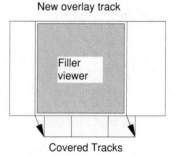

New overlay track

Tracks spanned by [*X, X+W*)

W

X

Filler viewer

Covered Tracks

All viewers *V* in the covered tracks are suspended. That means a suspend message *M* is sent with $M.state < 1$ (inverse of the state prior to suspension.) The state of the suspended viewers will be inverted subsequently.

Notes: OpenTrack has no effect unless $Filler.state = 0$ (closed.) Suspended viewers cease to receive Oberon track messages (mouse events.) However, a suspended focus viewer still receives consume and defocus messages (keyboard events.) The handler must, therefore, check whether the viewer is displayed. The viewer manager does not send a restore message to *Filler*, hence the display is left unchanged by *OpenTrack*. *OpenTrack* must not be called when a handler processes a viewer message.

---

[2] *x* is in the interval [*X, X + W*) if $X \leqslant x < X + W$.

CloseTrack

PROCEDURE CloseTrack(X: INTEGER);
If the track which contains x coordinate X is an overlay track, it is closed. All viewers in the closing track are also closed (see procedure *Close*.) The covered tracks are reinstated and the viewers in those tracks are restored. That means a restore message is sent and their state is inverted subsequently.

Notes: No action takes place if the closed track is not an overlay. *CloseTrack* must not be called when a handler processes a viewer message.

Open

PROCEDURE Open(V: Viewer; X, Y: INTEGER);
If viewer V is closed ($V.state = 0$), it will be opened in the track which contains x coordinate X. Space is claimed from viewer U which contains the point with coordinates X, Y. The height of the new viewer is controlled by Y such that the top edge of V contains the point with coordinates X, Y, except if this would result in a viewer of height less than *minH*. In this case, a viewer of height *minH* is opened.

The fate of viewer U is determined by the remaining space. If the height of this space is less than *minH*, U will be closed (see procedure *Close*.) Otherwise, a modify message is sent to U and its frame is adjusted subsequently.

Open assigns frame boundaries $V.X$, $V.Y$, $V.W$ and $V.H$ and sets $V.state := 2$ (displayed.) It inserts V into the data structure of viewers (field $V.next$.)

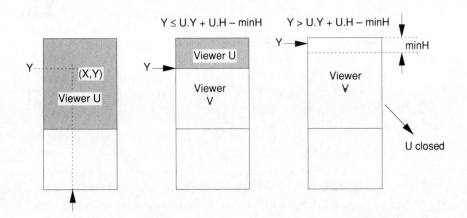

Notes: No action takes place if V is not closed prior to the call of *Open*. *Open* does not send a restore message to V. *Open* must not be called when a handler processes a viewer message.

Change

PROCEDURE Change(V: Viewer; Y: INTEGER);
Viewer V is changed with the intent of moving its top edge to the new y coordinate Y. The height of the new top edge is limited by the requirement that at least $minH$ remains for the upper neighbor U of V. Thus, the new height of V is given by:

$$h = \min(Y - V.Y, V.H + U.H - minH)$$

Viewer U is modified (that is, an appropriate modify message is sent) and its frame is adjusted subsequently. *Change* assigns the new frame boundaries $V.X$, $V.Y$, $V.W$ and $V.H$.

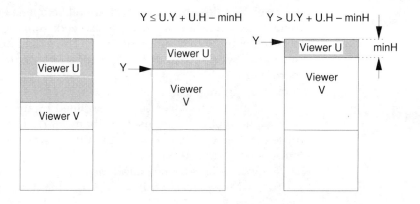

Notes: Change has an effect only if: (1) $Y - V.Y \geqslant minH$ (that is, the height of V after the intended change is at least $minH$) and (2) V is a displayed (that is, $V.state > 1$.) *Change* must not be called when a handler processes a viewer message.

Close

PROCEDURE Close(V: Viewer);
If viewer V is not a filler and displayed ($V.state > 1$), it is closed. A suspend message M with $M.state = 0$ is sent to V and its state is set to 0 (closed) subsequently.

If V is the last viewer in an overlay track (besides the filler), then that track is closed too (see procedure *CloseTrack*.)

Otherwise, the upper neighbor U of V claims its space. A modify message is sent to U and its frame is adjusted subsequently.

Note: Close must not be called when a handler processes a viewer message.

Recall

PROCEDURE Recall(VAR V: Viewer);
V is the last viewer which was previously closed by a call to *Close*. If no call to *Close* precedes the execution of *Recall*, NIL results.

13.6   The viewer data structure

Even though tracks and viewers are data abstractions, it seems useful to take a look at the data structure hidden by module Viewers. The type *Track* is an extension of the type *Viewer* with an additional field *under* which may point to overlay tracks.

Tracks and viewers are linked in a hierarchical data structure of circular lists using the fields *dsc* and *next*. Let F denote a frame (which may be of type *Track* or *Viewer*.) Then:

- $F.dsc$ points to a frame one level below F (that is, from track to viewer.)

- $F.next$ points to the next frame of the same level (that is, the adjacent track or viewer.)

The following diagram gives an example:

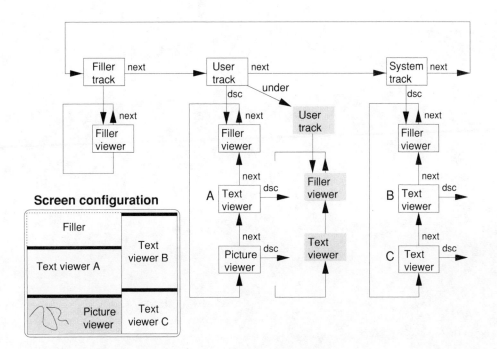

The viewer manager maintains the data structure composed of objects of type *Track* and *Viewer* which comprise the first two levels of a hierarchy. Extending the base type *Display.Frame*, the viewer too has a field *dsc*. Thus, further levels may be defined. In fact, text viewers are comprised of two frames of type *TextFrames.Frame*. Note, however, that the frames linked to viewers through *dsc* are under the control of the handler, not the viewer manager.

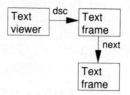

14 Module Texts

Module Texts provides the abstract data type *Text* which is a model of a *sequence of characters* with their associated properties: *font*, *color* and *vertical offset*. The text's data structure is hidden. It is accessed or changed through a set of procedures which comprise the *data manager*.

Module Texts exports:

- The abstract data type *Text*. Instances of *Text* are active Oberon objects with an installed procedure, called *notifier*, which is invoked whenever the text changes.

- The abstract data type *Buffer* to assemble and hold temporary texts.

- The abstract data type *Reader* to read the characters of a text sequentially.

- The abstract data type *Scanner* to read symbols (integers, reals, strings etc.) from texts and translate them into an internal representation.

- The abstract data type *Writer* to create texts in buffers from variables of several basic types (CHAR, INTEGER, REAL etc.)

- Procedures for changing, opening and closing texts including reading and writing to disk.

Readers, scanners and writers operate sequentially on the sequence of characters. Like riders on files, they have an implicit property, the *position*, which is incremented at each operation. In fact, they are extensions of the type *Files.Rider*.

As a preliminary, module Fonts is described which exports the abstract data type *Font*, which provides the raster data for screen fonts.

```
DEFINITION Fonts;

IMPORT Display;

TYPE
   Font = POINTER TO FontDesc;
   FontDesc = RECORD
      name: Name;
      height, minX, maxX, minY, maxY: INTEGER;
      raster: Display.Font
   END;
   Name = ARRAY 32 OF CHAR;

VAR Default: Font;

PROCEDURE This (name: ARRAY OF CHAR): Font;

END Fonts.
```

```
DEFINITION Texts;

IMPORT Display, Files, Fonts;

CONST
   Inval = 0; Name = 1; String = 2; Int = 3; Real = 4; LongReal = 5;
   Char = 6;
   replace = 0; insert = 1; delete = 2;

TYPE
   Buffer = POINTER TO BufDesc;
   BufDesc = RECORD
      len: LONGINT
   END;

   Notifier = PROCEDURE (T: Text; op: INTEGER; beg, end: LONGINT);

   Reader = RECORD (Files.Rider)
      eot: BOOLEAN;
      fnt: Fonts.Font;
      col, voff: SHORTINT
   END;

   Scanner = RECORD (Reader)
      nextCh: CHAR;
      line, class: INTEGER;
      i: LONGINT;
      x: REAL;
      y: LONGREAL;
      c: CHAR;
      len: SHORTINT;
      s: ARRAY 32 OF CHAR
   END;
```

```
      Text = POINTER TO TextDesc;
      TextDesc = RECORD
        len: LONGINT;
        notify: Notifier
      END;

      Writer = RECORD (Files.Rider)
        buf: Buffer;
        fnt: Fonts.Font;
        col, voff: SHORTINT
      END;

  PROCEDURE Append(T: Text; B: Buffer);
  PROCEDURE ChangeLooks(T: Text; beg, end: LONGINT; sel: SET;
                          fnt: Fonts.Font; col, voff: SHORTINT);
  PROCEDURE Copy(SB, DB: Buffer);
  PROCEDURE Delete(T: Text; beg, end: LONGINT);
  PROCEDURE Insert(T: Text; pos: LONGINT; B: Buffer);
  PROCEDURE Load(T: Text; f: Files.File; pos: LONGINT;
                  VAR len: LONGINT);
  PROCEDURE Open(T: Text; name: ARRAY OF CHAR);
  PROCEDURE OpenBuf(B: Buffer);
  PROCEDURE OpenReader(VAR R: Reader; T: Text; pos: LONGINT);
  PROCEDURE OpenScanner(VAR S: Scanner; T: Text; pos: LONGINT);
  PROCEDURE OpenWriter(VAR W: Writer);
  PROCEDURE Pos(VAR R: Reader): LONGINT;
  PROCEDURE Read(VAR R: Reader; VAR ch: CHAR);
  PROCEDURE Recall(VAR B: Buffer);
  PROCEDURE Save(T: Text; beg, end: LONGINT; B: Buffer);
  PROCEDURE Scan(VAR S: Scanner);
  PROCEDURE SetColor(VAR W: Writer; col: SHORTINT);
  PROCEDURE SetFont(VAR W: Writer; fnt: Fonts.Font);
  PROCEDURE SetOffset(VAR W: Writer; voff: SHORTINT);
  PROCEDURE Store(T: Text; f: Files.File; pos: LONGINT;
                  VAR len: LONGINT);
  PROCEDURE Write(VAR W: Writer; ch: CHAR);
  PROCEDURE WriteDate(VAR W: Writer; t, d: LONGINT);
  PROCEDURE WriteHex(VAR W: Writer; i: LONGINT);
  PROCEDURE WriteInt(VAR W: Writer; i, n: LONGINT);
  PROCEDURE WriteLn(VAR W: Writer);
  PROCEDURE WriteLongReal(VAR W: Writer; y: LONGREAL;
                          n: INTEGER);
  PROCEDURE WriteLongRealHex(VAR W: Writer; y: LONGREAL);
  PROCEDURE WriteReal(VAR W: Writer; x: REAL; n: INTEGER);
  PROCEDURE WriteRealFix(VAR W: Writer; x: REAL; n, k: INTEGER);
  PROCEDURE WriteRealHex(VAR W: Writer; x: REAL);
  PROCEDURE WriteString(VAR W: Writer; s: ARRAY OF CHAR);

END Texts.
```

14.1 Module Fonts

The term *font* refers to the set of characters of a certain design and size. The abstract data type *Font* has the following definition:

```
TYPE
  Font = POINTER TO FontDesc;
  FontDesc = RECORD
    name: ARRAY 32 OF CHAR;
    height: INTEGER;
    minX, maxX: INTEGER;
    minY, maxY: INTEGER;
    raster: Display.Font
  END;
```

where:

- *name* is the name of the file which contains font data.
- *raster* is the set of patterns used in procedure *Display.GetChar*.
- *height* is the minimum distance between text lines.
- *minX, maxX, minY, maxY* are the extremal values of the box which encloses the raster points of all characters of the font when their base points are aligned at (0, 0).

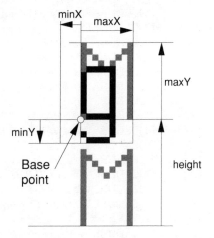

Note: The extremal values are algebraically defined; that is, *minX* ≤ 0 and *minY* ≤ 0. Module Fonts exports a variable designating the default font which is initialized from Syntax10.Scn.Fnt:

```
VAR Default: Font;
```

This   PROCEDURE This(name: ARRAY OF CHAR): Font;
Initializes the returned font from data stored in a file whose name is indicated in parameter *name*. If the file does not exist, the default font is returned.

14.2   Text and buffer

14.2.1   Text

A text is an active object which is an instance of the abstract data type *Text*, which implements the notion of a sequence of characters with their associated properties. Characters may be retrieved based on their position with respect to the start of the text.

Numbering   In line with the Oberon language conventions used for arrays, the first text element has ordinal number 0.

Stretch   A *stretch* denotes a subsequence of a text beginning with element *beg* up to but not including *end*. The shorthand notation [*beg*, *end*) is used. The length of the stretch is always *end* − *beg*. For example, in the following diagram, the stretch [2, 5) consists of the elements *c*, *d* and *E*.

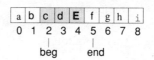

The abstract type *Text* is defined by:

```
TYPE
    Text = POINTER TO TextDesc;
    TextDesc = RECORD
        len: LONGINT;
        notify: Notifier
    END;
```

It has the properties:

- *len*: the text's length (in characters.)
- *notify*: a procedure invoked when the text is changed.

A text element has the properties:

- *fnt*: the character's font (type Fonts.Font.)
- *color*: the character's color numberer[1] (type SHORTINT.)
- *voff*: vertical offset in pixels (type SHORTINT.)

Notifier

The procedure value of *notify*, termed the text's notifier, is called whenever the text is changed. It is of type:

```
TYPE Notifier = PROCEDURE(T: Text; op: INTEGER;
                          beg, end: LONGINT);
```

where:

- *T* is the text changed prior to the call of the notifier.
- *op* is an operation code defining the nature of the change.
- *beg, end* are the stretch [*beg, end*) which were changed.

Module Texts exports the following named constants defining the operation codes in a self-explanatory manner:

```
CONST replace = 0; insert = 1; delete = 2;
```

Open

```
PROCEDURE Open(T: Text; name: ARRAY OF CHAR);
```
Loads the text stored on disk in the file whose name is contained in the parameter *name*. Initializes the text *T*. The field *T.len* is set to the text's length (in characters.)

If name = " " (empty string) or if no file with that name exists, a new text is created.

The file must be marked either as a text file or an ASCII file. A text file is preceded by a text block identifier 0F001H (−4095 decimal) two bytes in length. Files created with *Edit.Store* are so marked. If it is an ASCII file, the default font color and vertical offset values are applied.

For example, an instance of type *Text* is created as follows:

```
NEW(Txt); Txt.notify := TextFrames.NotifyDisplay;
Texts.Open(Txt, "InputFile");
```

TextFrames.NotifyDisplay is a notifier for standard texts.

---

[1] See Chapter 12.

14.2.2   Display of texts in viewers

Texts are typically displayed in a text viewer. The displayed view of the text must reflect all changes. The task of synchronizing the viewers is complicated if the same text is displayed in more than one viewer. The notifier concept provides an elegant solution. The notifier is called whenever the text is modified. Texts which are to be displayed in standard text viewers use the notifier *TextFrames.NotifyDisplay* which broadcasts messages of type *TextFrames.UpdateMsg*, indicating the nature of the change and allowing the display managers of the affected viewers to update their views of the text.

The following diagram depicts creation of a text viewer, installation of the notifier and broadcast of update messages.

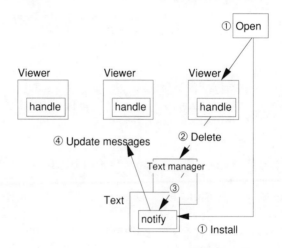

(1) The command *Open* creates the viewer, opens the displayed text and installs the notifier.

(2) Later, the handler may invoke a procedure which changes the text (for example, *Delete*.)

(3) The text manager performs the operation on the text's data structure and calls *notify*.

(4) The procedure *notify* sends update messages to all visible viewers including the one where the text was modified. These viewers may actualize their display if they show the changed text.

We wish to point to the great generality of the scheme. Texts make no assumption about message sending. It is the programmer of the viewer class who chooses the appropriate update mechanism.

14.2.3   The buffer

A buffer is another abstract data type describing a sequence of characters with their properties. It differs from a text in two respects:

(1) There is no notifier.

(2) No procedures are provided to store buffers on disk.

Buffers provide, therefore, temporary text data structures which exist no longer than the duration of a session. The absence of a notifier makes a buffer more efficient when assembling the characters comprising a text. Buffers are, therefore, used by writers for that purpose.
  The abstract data type *Buffer* has the following definition:

```
TYPE
   Buffer = POINTER TO BufferDesc;
   BufferDesc = RECORD
     len: LONGINT (* Length of the buffer *)
   END;
```

OpenBuf

PROCEDURE OpenBuf(B: Buffer);
Initializes the buffer *B*. The field *B.len* is set to 0. As in the case of text, *B* must be created first with NEW(*B*).

14.2.4   Operations on texts and buffers

ChangeLooks

PROCEDURE ChangeLooks(T: Text; beg, end: LONGINT; sel: SET;
                                    fnt: Fonts.Font; col, voff: SHORTINT);
Changes the attributes color, font or vertical offset of the stretch [*beg, end*) in text *T*. The notifier *T.notify* is called. Results are undefined if the stretch [*beg, end*) is not valid.
  Which of the attributes is changed is directed by the parameter *sel*:

- 0 IN *sel*: the font is changed to *fnt*.
- 1 IN *sel*: the color is changed to *col*.
- 2 IN *sel*: the vertical offset is changed to *voff*.

Delete

PROCEDURE Delete(T: Text; beg, end: LONGINT);
Deletes stretch [*beg, end*) in text *T*. The notifier *T.notify* is called. Results are not defined if the stretch is invalid.

Copy

PROCEDURE Copy(SB: Buffer; DB: Buffer);
Appends a copy of buffer *SB* to buffer *DB*. The source buffer is not cleared.

Recall
    PROCEDURE Recall(VAR B: Buffer);
Recalls the most recently deleted stretch of text in buffer B. There is no need to open the buffer prior to passing it as actual parameter.

Save
    PROCEDURE Save(T: Text: beg, end: LONGINT; B: Buffer);
Appends stretch $[beg, end)$ in text T to the end of buffer B.

Insert
    PROCEDURE Insert(T: Text; pos: LONGINT; B: Buffer);
Inserts the contents of buffer B into text T at position *pos*. After completion, the first character of B occupies position *pos* in T. The buffer B is cleared. The notifier $T.notify$ is called. Results are undefined if *pos* is outside of the text.

    For example, if T has textual value 'This␣is␣the␣Oberon␣guide', and B = 'new␣', where the character '␣' denotes a space, then *Texts.Insert*(T, 12, B) yields a text T with value:

"This␣is␣the␣new␣Oberon␣guide"

Append
    PROCEDURE Append(T: Text; B: Buffer);
Appends the contents of buffer B to text T. The buffer B is cleared ($B.len = 0$.) The notifier $T.notify$ is called. Append is an abbreviation for *Insert*(T, $T.len$, B).

14.3   Reading from texts, writing to buffers

Texts and buffers are sequential data structures with many similarities to files. In fact, they are implemented as extensions of the Oberon file system. As with the file's rider, the read/write operations on texts are performed through instances of abstract data types. There are three:

(1) *Reader*: to read characters from a text.

(2) *Scanner*: to read symbols (integers, reals etc.) and translate them to an internal representation.

(3) *Writer*: to assemble text data in buffers.

It is the reader, the scanner and the writer which possess the property *position*, not the object text. Several readers and scanners may operate on the same text.

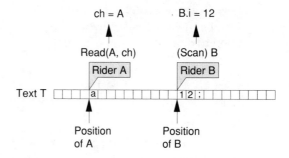

Writers only operate on an associated buffer. The written characters are always appended. When a chunk of text is assembled, the buffer is typically inserted into a text. At that moment, the notifier is called. If the text is displayed and uses message passing, all views are updated.

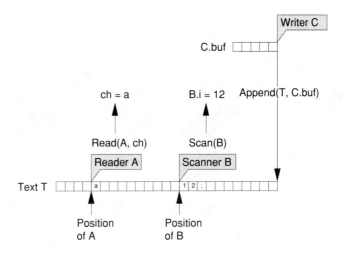

14.3.1 The reader

A reader is an instance of the abstract data type *Reader* and affords sequential read access to the elements of an associated text. It has the following definition:

```
TYPE
    Reader = RECORD
        (Files.Rider)
        eot: BOOLEAN;
        fnt: Fonts.Font;
        col, voff: SHORTINT
    END;
```

The reader's properties are:

- *an associated text* on which the reader operates (hidden.)
- *a position* in the text (hidden.)
- *eot*: an end-of-text condition.
- *fnt*: the font of the character which was last read.
- *col*: the color number of the character which was last read.
- *voff*: the vertical offset of the character which was last read.

Note: The reader also inherits properties from the rider which it extends. However, these play no role in the application of the reader.

OpenReader PROCEDURE OpenReader(VAR R: Reader; T: Text; pos: LONGINT);
Initializes reader R and sets it at position *pos* in text T. The field $R.eot$ is set to FALSE; the attribute fields remain unspecified. The first read operation after the reader is opened will return the character at position *pos* in text T.

If *pos* is outside the text ($pos \geq T.len$), the result is unspecified. The programmer cannot rely on $R.eot$ being TRUE.

Read PROCEDURE Read(VAR R: Reader; VAR ch: CHAR);
The character *ch* found at the position of the reader R is returned and that position is incremented by 1. If an attempt is made to read beyond the text's length, then $R.eot$ = TRUE and *ch* remains undefined. Otherwise, the reader's fields are set:

- $R.eof$ to FALSE.
- $R.fnt$, $R.col$ and $R.voff$ to the attributes of *ch*.

Pos PROCEDURE Pos(VAR R: Reader): LONGINT;
Returns the position of reader R in its associated text. At the end of text, the result is unspecified.

14.3.2 The scanner

A scanner is an instance of the abstract data type *Scanner*. It parses an associated text for tokens of the following kind:

- numbers (of various types);
- strings;
- names;
- special symbols.

Tokens are scanned sequentially, translated to an internal representation and returned by the scanner in one of its result fields.

A scanner has the following definition:

```
TYPE
  Scanner = RECORD
    (Reader)
    nextCh: CHAR;
    line, class: INTEGER;
    i: LONGINT;
    x: REAL;
    y: LONGREAL;
    c: CHAR;
    len: SHORTINT;
    s: ARRAY 32 OF CHAR
  END;
```

The properties of a scanner are:

- *an associated text* on which the scanner operates (hidden.)
- *a position* in the text (hidden.)
- *nextCh*: the character in the text which immediately follows a scanned symbol.
- *line*: the line number of the scanned symbol.
- *class*: a code indicating the type of the scanned symbol (see definition later.)
- *i, x, y, c*: fields of appropriate type in which results are returned.
- *len*: the length of a name or string.
- *s*: field in which names or strings are returned.

Note: The scanner also inherits properties from the underlying reader and rider. Except possibly for *eot*, thesé are not productive in the use of the scanner.

Scanner class codes

The field *class* which identifies the type of the scanned symbol admits values $0..6$. The following constants define the meaning of *class*:

```
CONST Inval = 0; Name = 1; String = 2; Int = 3; Real = 4; LongReal = 5;
  Char = 6;
```

Scanned symbols

The scanner parses the associated text for tokens. While parsing, blanks (SP or 20X) and tab characters (HT or 09X) are ignored. Carriage return characters (CR or 0DX) are also skipped but they have the effect of incrementing the line count. Tokens are defined by the lexicographic syntax:

$Name = NamePart \{ "." NamePart \}.$
$NamePart = letter \{ letter \mid digit \}.$
$String = """ \{ letter \mid digit \mid specialChar \} """ \mid$
$\qquad "'" \{ letter \mid digit \mid SpecialChar \} "'".$
$Integer = ["+" \mid "-"] digit \{ digit \} \mid$
$\qquad ["+" \mid "-"] digit \{ hexDigit \} "H".$
$Real = ["+" \mid "-"] digit \{ digit \} "." digit \{ digit \}$
$\qquad ["E" ["+" \mid "-"] digit \{ digit \}].$
$LongReal = ["+" \mid "-"] digit \{ digit \} "." digit \{ digit \}$
$\qquad ["D" ["+" \mid "-"] digit \{ digit \}].^{2}$
$Char = specialChar \mid ctlChar.^{3}$
$specialChar =$ Printable ASCII characters other than letters or
$\qquad$ number $("\sim" \mid "!" \mid "@" \mid "\#" \mid "\$" \ldots).$
$ctlChar =$ The control character of the ASCII code (that is,
$\qquad$ ordinal number $< 20X$) except HT or CR.

OpenScanner

PROCEDURE OpenScanner(VAR S: Scanner; T: Text; pos: LONGINT);
Opens scanner *S* and sets it at position *pos* in text *T*. The field *S.eot* is initialized to FALSE; the output fields remain unspecified. The scan operation after a call of *OpenScanner* will return the symbol starting at position *pos* in text *T*.

If *pos* is outside the text (*pos* $\geq$ *T.len*), the result is unspecified.

Scan

PROCEDURE Scan(VAR S: Scanner);
After each call to the procedure *Scan*, the associated text is parsed for a symbol, starting at the current position of the scanner in its associated text. Blanks and carriage return characters (CR or 0DX) are skipped. After a symbol is found, it is translated into an internal representation and assigned to the output field of the matching type. The type of symbol being scanned is identified by the field *S.class*.

The character immediately following the scanned symbol is the value of *S.nextCh*. The new position of the scanner is one more than the position of *S.nextCh*.

The scanner counts lines starting at 0 for the first one scanned. Each occurrence of a carriage return character (CR or 0DX) increments the field *S.line* by one.

---

[2] A number is also of type LONGREAL if the number of digits after the decimal point exceeds the precision of reals.

[3] Other than SP, HT or CR.

The Boolean variable *S.eot* (in base type reader) is accessible and can be tested for the end-of-text condition.

Note: Unlike the case of reader, *eot* may be TRUE when the last symbol is scanned, not at the attempt to scan beyond the text. This has to be taken into account when using *eot*.

For example, let *S* be a scanner operating on the text *Txt* with textual value 'Name␣=␣1000; ¶3.141', where '␣' denotes a space and '¶' a line break control character. In a text viewer, this text would look as follows:

```
Name = 1000;
3.141
```

After opening *S* at position 0 through a call to *Texts.OpenScanner* (*S, Txt*, 0), successive calls to *Scan(S)* yield the following:

Scan(S)	1st	2nd	3rd	4th	5th	6th
S.eot	FALSE	FALSE	FALSE	FALSE	TRUE	TRUE
S.nextCh	" "	" "	";"	"¶"	Undef	Undef
S.line	0	0	0	0	1	Undef
S.class	Name	Char	Int	Char	Real	Undef
S.i	Undef	Undef	1000	Undef	Undef	Undef
S.x	Undef	Undef	Undef	Undef	3.141	Undef
S.y	Undef	Undef	Undef	Undef	Undef	Undef
S.c	Undef	"="	Undef	";"	Undef	Undef
S.len	4	Undef	Undef	Undef	Undef	Undef
S.s	"Name"	Undef	Undef	Undef	Undef	Undef

Note: 'Undef' means that the programmer should not rely on the value. In the current implementation, once a field is set, it keeps its value until it is changed the next time.

If, in our example, the scanner is opened at the third character by means of *Texts.OpenScanner(S, Txt,* 2), the first call of *Scan(S)* yields:

```
S.class = Texts.Name
S.len = 2
S.s = "me"
```

14.3.3   The writer

A writer is an instance of the abstract data type *Writer*. The writer appends characters or symbols to the end of an associated buffer. Many of the write procedures serve to translate from the internal representation of numbers of the basic types (SHORTINT, INTEGER, LONGINT, REAL, LONGREAL) to textual symbols.

A writer has the following definition:

```
TYPE
  Writer = RECORD
    (Files.Rider)
    buf: Buffer;
    fnt: Fonts.Font;
    col, voff: SHORTINT
  END;
```

The properties of the writer are:

- *buf*: the associated buffer in which text data is assembled.
- *fnt*: the font in current use.
- *col*: the color number in current use.
- *voff*: the vertical offset in current use.

Note: While the writer also inherits the properties of the underlying rider, these are not used.

OpenWriter

PROCEDURE OpenWriter(VAR W: Writer);
Opens writer W. The associated buffer W.*buf* is also opened. The characteristics are W.*fnt* = *Fonts.Default*, W.*col* = *Display.white* and W.*voff* = 0.

Set attributes

PROCEDURE SetColor(VAR W: Writer; col: SHORTINT);
PROCEDURE SetFont(VAR W: Writer; fnt: Fonts.Font);
PROCEDURE SetOffset(VAR W: Writer; voff: SHORTINT);
Sets the character attributes of writer W. Subsequently written characters or symbols possess these attributes.

Write

PROCEDURE Write(VAR W: Writer; ch: CHAR);
Appends character *ch* to the end of the buffer W.*buf* of writer W.

WriteHex

PROCEDURE WriteHex(VAR W: Writer; i: LONGINT);
Converts integer *i* to a sequence of eight hexadecimal characters preceded by a blank. The resulting string is appended to the end of the buffer W.*buf* of writer W.

WriteInt

PROCEDURE WriteInt(VAR W: Writer; i, n: LONGINT);
Converts integer *i* to a character string representing *i* in decimal form. The resulting string is padded with blanks on the left up to a length of *n* and appended to the end of the buffer *W.buf* of writer *W*. The field size is adjusted if chosen too small.

For example, if *W.buf* has textual value "abc" and *i* = 17, then after *WriteInt*(*W*, *i*, 4), *W.buf* contains "abc⊔17" (⊔ represents a blank.)

WriteLn

PROCEDURE WriteLn(VAR W: Writer);
Appends a carriage return character (CR or 0DX) to the end of the buffer *W.buf* of writer *W*.

WriteLongReal

PROCEDURE WriteLongReal(VAR W: Writer; y: LONGREAL; n: INTEGER);
Converts long real *y* to a character string representing *y* in decimal form. The resulting string is padded with blanks on the left up to a length of *n* and appended to the end of the buffer *W.buf* of writer *W*. The field size is adjusted if chosen too small.

WriteLong-RealHex

PROCEDURE WriteLongRealHex(VAR W: Writer; y: LONGREAL);
Converts long real *y* to a sequence of 16 hexadecimal characters preceded by a blank. The resulting character string is appended to the end of the buffer *W.buf* of writer *W*.

WriteReal

PROCEDURE WriteReal(VAR W: Writer; x: REAL; n: INTEGER);
Converts real *x* to a character string representing *x* in decimal form. The resulting string is padded with blanks on the left up to a length of *n* and appended to the end of the buffer *W.buf* of writer *W*. The field size is adjusted if chosen too small.

WriteRealFix

PROCEDURE WriteRealFix(VAR W: Writer; x: REAL; n, k: INTEGER);
Appends the fixed-point decimal character representation of real variable *x*, right justified in a field of *n* places with *k* places for the decimal fraction to the end of the buffer *W.buf* of writer *W*. The field size is adjusted if chosen too small.

For example, if *W.buf* has textual value "abc" and *pi* = 3.14159.. (up to machine precision), then after *WriteRealFix*(*W*, *pi*, 6, 3), *W.buf* is "abc⊔3.141" (the symbol ⊔ represents blanks.)

WriteRealHex

PROCEDURE WriteRealHex(VAR W: Writer; x: REAL);
Converts real *x* to a sequence of eight hexadecimal characters preceded by a blank. The resulting character string is appended to the end of the buffer *W.buf* of writer *W*.

WriteString   PROCEDURE WriteString(VAR W: Writer; s: ARRAY OF CHAR);
Appends string *s* to the end of the buffer *W.buf* of writer *W*.

WriteDate   PROCEDURE WriteDate(VAR W: Writer; t, d: LONGINT);
Appends the date to the buffer *W.buf* of writer *W*. The parameters *t* (time) and *d* (date) are in the format defined by the procedure *Oberon.GetTime*. The format is 'dd.mm.yy hh:mm:ss' with dd: day, mm: month, yy: year, hh: hour, mm: minute and ss: second. All two digit numbers with leading zeros if necessary.

For example, the following writes the date to the system log:

VAR t, d: LONGINT; W: Texts.Writer;

Oberon.GetTime(t, d);
Texts.WriteDate(W, t, d);
Texts.WriteLn(W);
Texts.Append(Oberon.Log, W.buf);

System.Log
10.01.90 11:12:18

14.4 Text files

Texts are stored on disk files in the form of *text blocks*. A given file may contain several blocks of different type, of which text blocks are just one. A complex document, for example, may be composed of text blocks, one for each paragraph, graphics blocks and interspersed descriptor blocks.

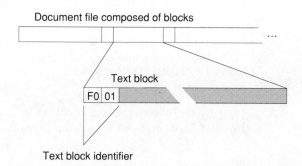

Each block is preceded by a mark composed of two bytes. The first byte is the block mark identifier (0F0X) and the second one specifies the type of block (01X for text blocks.)

Two procedures are provided to read and write text blocks: *Load* and *Store*.

Load

PROCEDURE Load(T: Text; f: Files.File; pos: LONGINT; VAR len: LONGINT);
Loads the text block stored on disk in file *f* starting at *pos*. The file position *pos* designates the start of text data after the text block identifier (0F001H.) On completion, *len* is set to the length of the block excluding the text block identifier.

It is the caller's responsibility to ensure that *pos* is a valid starting position.

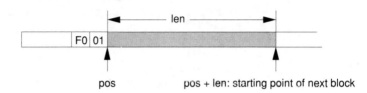

Note: *Load* knows the length of the text block from information contained in the text data. It reads only one text block (not to the end of file.)

For example, the following loads two consecutive text blocks from file *F*:

```
VAR
    F: Files.File;
    T1, T2: Texts.Text;
    pos, length: LONGINT;

pos := 2;
Texts.Load(T1, F, pos, length);
pos := pos + length + 2;
Texts.Load(T2, F, pos, length);
```

Note: In general, it is prudent to read the block identifier before the call to *Load* and test whether it is really a text block.

Store

PROCEDURE Store(T: Text; f: Files.file; pos: LONGINT; VAR len: LONGINT);
Stores the text *T* in file *f* starting at file position *pos*. The text block identifier (0F001H) is written first. On completion, *len* is set to the length of the block including the text block identifier.

It is the caller's responsibility to ensure that *pos* is a valid starting position. Also, the caller must make sure that no subsequent block is overwritten.

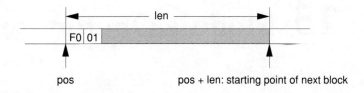

pos   pos + len: starting point of next block

Note: If an existing text block is overwritten, the user must ensure that the newly written text is not longer than the block which is overwritten. If a gap ensues, then *pos + length* is no longer the starting position of the next block. It is advisable not to overwrite existing blocks.

For example, the following appends two text blocks at the end of file *F*.

```
VAR
    F: Files.File;
    T1, T2: Texts.Text;
    pos, length: LONGINT;

pos := Files.Length(F);
Texts.Store(T1, F, pos, length);
Texts.Store(T2, F, pos + length, length);
```

15 Module Oberon

Module Oberon performs *system services* and exports:

- The *event loop* with facilities to install user-defined tasks.
- The message types *InputMsg* and *ControlMsg* which report mouse, keyboard and certain viewer control events.
- The abstract data type *Cursor* and the standard cursors *Mouse* and *Pointer* with their patterns *Arrow* and *Star*, respectively.
- The procedure *Call*, the type *ParList* and the variable *Par* which provide the link to the kernel to *start commands* from within a procedure and pass parameter information to the called command.
- The message type *SelectionMsg* and procedures which deal with the latest system-wide *selection*, the *marked viewer* and the *focus viewer*.
- Procedures for *display set-up*.
- Procedures which access the system clock, and provide user identification, password protection and a pop-up menu.
- Types and variables which define *system-wide resources*, namely *CopyMsg*, *CopyoverMsg*, *FocusViewer*, *Log* (the system log), *Par* (a parameter list), *User* (user identification), *Password*, *Mouse*, *Pointer*, *Arrow*, *Star*, *CurColor*, *CurFnt*, *CurOff* and *CurTask*.

After system start-up, the body of module Oberon gets control and:

- Initializes the monochrome display (procedure *OpenDisplay*) observing the standard Oberon model of a wide user track and a system track.
- Initializes the focus viewer (the viewer containing the point (0, 0).)
- Installs the garbage collection task in the loop.
- Initializes the cursors *Mouse* and *Pointer*.

Module *System* is then loaded whose body completes system initialization.

```
DEFINITION Oberon;

IMPORT Display, Texts, Viewers, Input, Display, Fonts, Kernel, Modules;

CONST
   consume = 0; track = 1;                    (* input message id *)
   defocus = 0; neutralize = 1; mark = 2; (* control message id *)

TYPE
   ControlMsg = RECORD(Display.FrameMsg)
     id, X, Y: INTEGER
   END;

   CopyMsg = RECORD(Display.FrameMsg)
     F: Display.Frame
   END;

   CopyOverMsg = RECORD(Display.FrameMsg)
     text: Texts.Text;
     beg, end: LONGINT
   END;

   InputMsg = RECORD(Display.FrameMsg)
     id: INTEGER;
     keys: SET;
     X, Y: INTEGER;
     ch: CHAR;
     fnt: Fonts.Font;
     col, voff: SHORTINT
   END;

   SelectionMsg = RECORD(Display.FrameMsg)
     time: LONGINT;
     text: Texts.Text;
     beg, end: LONTINT
   END;

   Cursor = RECORD
     marker: Marker;
     on: BOOLEAN;
     X, Y: INTEGER
   END;

   Marker = RECORD
     Fade, Draw: Painter
   END;
```

```
        Painter = PROCEDURE(x, y: INTEGER);
        ParList = POINTER TO ParRec;
        ParRec = RECORD
          vwr: Viewers.Viewer;
          frame: Display.Frame;
          text: Texts.Text;
          pos: LONGINT
        END;

        Task = POINTER TO TaskDesc;
        TaskDesc = RECORD
          safe: BOOLEAN;
          handle: Handler
        END;
        Handler = PROCEDURE ( );

      VAR
        Arrow, Star: Marker;
        CurColor, CurOff: SHORTINT;
        CurFnt: Fonts.Font;
        CurTask: Task;
        FocusViewer: Viewers.Viewer;
        Log: Texts.Text;
        Mouse, Pointer: Cursor;
        Par: ParList;
        Password: LONGINT;
        User: ARRAY 8 OF CHAR;

      PROCEDURE AllocateSystemViewer(DX: INTEGER; VAR X, Y: INTEGER);
      PROCEDURE AllocateUserViewer(DX: INTEGER; VAR X, Y: INTEGER);
      PROCEDURE Call(VAR name: ARRAY OF CHAR; par: ParList;
                    new: BOOLEAN; VAR res: INTEGER);
      PROCEDURE Collect(count: INTEGER);
      PROCEDURE DisplayHeight(X: INTEGER): INTEGER;
      PROCEDURE DisplayWidth(X: INTEGER): INTEGER;
      PROCEDURE DrawCursor(VAR c: Cursor; VAR m: Marker;
                          X, Y: INTEGER);
      PROCEDURE FadeCursor(VAR c: Cursor);
      PROCEDURE GetClock(VAR t, d: LONGINT);
      PROCEDURE GetSelection(VAR text: Texts.Text;
                            VAR beg, end, time: LONGINT);
      PROCEDURE Install(T: Task);
      PROCEDURE Loop;
      PROCEDURE MarkedViewer ( ): Viewers.Viewer;
      PROCEDURE OpenCursor(VAR c: Cursor);
      PROCEDURE OpenDisplay(UW, SW, H: INTEGER);
      PROCEDURE OpenTrack(X, W: INTEGER);
      PROCEDURE PassFocus(V: Viewers.Viewer);
      PROCEDURE Remove(T: Task);
```

```
PROCEDURE RemoveMarks(X, Y, W, H: INTEGER);
PROCEDURE SetClock(t, d: LONGINT);
PROCEDURE SetColor(col: SHORTINT);
PROCEDURE SetFont(fnt: Fonts.Font);
PROCEDURE SetOffset(voff: SHORTINT);
PROCEDURE SetUser(VAR user, password: ARRAY OF CHAR);
PROCEDURE ShowMenu(VAR cmd: INTEGER; X, Y: INTEGER;
                        menu: ARRAY OF CHAR);
PROCEDURE SystemTrack(X: INTEGER): INTEGER;
PROCEDURE Time ( ): LONGINT;
PROCEDURE UserTrack(X: INTEGER): INTEGER;

END Oberon.
```

15.1 Tasks and the event loop

15.1.1 The event loop

Module Oberon contains the *event loop*. A set of procedures is executed in cyclical order ad infinitum. A task is a record variable with a procedure field *handle*. The parameterless procedure assigned to *handle* is called the task's *handler*. Task records are linked in a circular list and control passes from one handler to the next one in the list. Passing of control is termed a *task switch*.

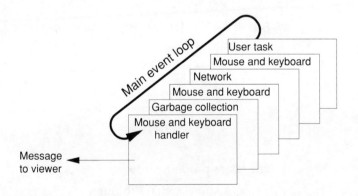

Mouse and keyboard handler

The handler for the mouse and keyboard plays a prominent role in the event loop. It is prefixed to any one of the installable tasks. This handler interfaces with module *Input* which reads hardware registers. Mouse and keyboard buffers are polled at each task switch in the loop: if events are sensed, the handler releases control by sending an input message to the appropriate viewer. The rate at which the loop cycles varies and so does the rate at which the devices are serviced.

Garbage collector   The garbage collector is the handler of a task which is installed by the statement sequence of module Oberon. It is a safe task (see Section 15.1.2) and thus remains permanently installed in the event loop.

User tasks   The user may install private tasks which participate in the multitasking provided by the event loop. Since tasks are not pre-empted by the system, it is essential that task handlers do not seize control over extended periods of time (the recommended period is less than 100 ms.) User tasks are typically unsafe and removed on the occurrence of a trap.

Tasks should be used whenever a function is executed repetitively over long periods of time but should not seize control permanently. User tasks may be viewed as background activities. Servers, simulations and network components are examples where user tasks are beneficially exploited.

Loop   The main loop is exported as procedure:

```
PROCEDURE Loop;
```

Polls mouse and keyboard prior to executing one of the installed tasks in cyclical order. Translates ASCII codes to produce a national language symbol with desired key combinations – for example, CTRL–a for ä (see Appendix B.)

15.1.2   Tasks

A task is an instance of the abstract data type *Task*:

```
TYPE
    Handler = PROCEDURE ( );
    Task = POINTER TO TaskDesc;
    TaskDesc = RECORD
        safe: BOOLEAN;
        handle: Handler
    END;
```

The task's properties are:

- A successor task (hidden.)
- *safe*: determines whether the task is removed when a trap occurs.
- *handle*: the task's handler.

Safe tasks   On occurrence of a trap, the task which caused the trap is removed from the loop if *safe* = FALSE. Normally, user tasks are not safe. An example of a safe task is the garbage collector.

Current task   Within the program text of the task handler, the task owning that handler can be accessed through the global variable:

```
VAR CurTask: Task;
```

Note: CurTask is defined only within the scope of the handler.

Install   PROCEDURE Install(T: Task);
Installs task *T* in the central loop. The handler of the task is invoked in each cycle of the event loop.
The following is an example of its use:

```
NEW (MyTask);                    (* Allocate MyTask *)
MyTask.handle := MyHandler; (* Install Handler *)
MyTask.safe := FALSE;
Oberon.Install (MyTask);         (* Install MyTask in loop *)
```

Remove   PROCEDURE Remove(T: Task);
Removes task *T* from the central loop.

Collect   PROCEDURE Collect(count: INTEGER);
Garbage collection is executed every 20 mouse events. A counter is decremented at each mouse event and garbage collection takes place when the counter is 0. The procedure *Collect* sets the counter to the value *count*.
For example, a call *Collect*(0) will force garbage collection on the next cycle of the event loop.

15.1.3   Input messages

Mouse and keyboard events are sensed prior to each task switch. Procedure *Loop* informs the affected viewer by sending a message of type:

```
TYPE
  InputMsg = RECORD
    (Display.FrameMsg)
    id: INTEGER;
    keys: SET;
    X, Y: INTEGER;
    ch: CHAR;
      fnt: Fonts.Font;
      col, voff:SHORTINT
  END;
```

where:

- *id* is the message identifier (0: consume, 1: track.)
- *keys* is the mouse keys which are pressed:
  - 0 IN *keys*: right key is pressed.
  - 1 IN *keys*: middle key is pressed.
  - 2 IN *keys*: left key is pressed.
- *X, Y* are the mouse coordinates.
- *ch* is the character typed on the keyboard.
- *fnt* is the font of *ch*.
- *col* is the color number of *ch*.
- *voff* is the vertical offset of *ch*.

Input message identifiers
The following input message identifiers are exported as named constants:

CONST consume = 0; track = 1;

For simplicity, we call a message *M of type InputMsg* with *M.id = consume* a 'consume message;' a 'track message' if *M.id = track*.

Target viewer
Each input message is sent to a single *target viewer*:

- Consume message: to the focus viewer (see Section 15.4.1.)
- Track message: to the viewer which contains the mouse cursor.

Messages of type *InputMsg* report on the mouse and keyboard events listed in Table 15.1. The table shows that, depending on the message id, only parts of the fields are actually used.

Table 15.1 Fields set for a message *M: InputMsg*

Event	Action	*M.id*	*M.X*	*M.Y*	*M.keys*	*M.ch*	*M.fnt* *M.col* *M.voff*
Character typed	Insert in text	*consume*	—	—	—	Character	Attribute
Mouse event	Viewer specific	*track*	Coordinate of mouse		Key pressed	—	—

Consume message
Hitting a key (other than SETUP, ESC or PF1 to PF4) on the keyboard generates a consume message *M* which is passed to the focus viewer. The field *M.ch* contains the ASCII equivalent of the key. The typed character has the following attributes:

- *M.fnt*: the font (default *Fonts.Default.*)
- *M.col*: the color (default value *Display.white.*)
- *M.voff*: the vertical offset (default value 0.)

The attributes can be changed using procedures *SetFont*, *SetColor* and *SetOffset*.

The typical action of a handler which receives a consume message is to insert the character into a text or a caption. *It is not guaranteed, however, that the viewer* V *receiving a consume message is displayed* (V.state > 1.) The handler (or the display manager on its behalf) must always test for visibility before writing the character to the screen.

Track message   When the mouse is moved and/or when a mouse key is pressed, a track message M is generated. This message is sent to the viewer which contains the mouse coordinates. These coordinates are reported in $M.X$ and $M.Y$. The status of the mouse keys can be deduced from the value of *M.keys*.

A handler which receives a track message draws, as a first action, the mouse cursor.

The further actions of the handler are decoding and execution of the mouse key commands (see Part III.)

15.1.4   Control messages

Certain keyboard events have system-wide significance. Rather than using a consume message, procedure *Loop* reports them to the target viewer in a message of type:

```
TYPE
  ControlMsg = RECORD
    (Display.FrameMsg)
    id: INTEGER;
    X, Y: INTEGER
  END;
```

where:

- *id* is the message identifier (0: defocus, 1: neutralize, 2: mark.)
- *X, Y* are the mouse coordinates.

Input message identifiers   The following control message identifiers are exported as named constants:

```
CONST defocus = 0; neutralize = 1; mark = 2;
```

For simplicity, we call a message *M* of type *ControlMsg* with *M.id* = *defocus* a 'defocus message;' a 'neutralize message' if *M.id* = *neutralize* and a 'mark message' if *M.id* = *mark*.

Target viewer   The target viewers of a control message are:

- Mark message: the viewer which contains the mouse cursor.
- Neutralize message: broadcast to all visible viewers.
- Defocus message: the focus viewer.

Table 15.2 summarizes the three control messages:

Table 15.2   Fields set for a message *M:ControlMsg*

Event	Action	M.id	M.X	M.Y
Focus removed	Remove caret or similar insertion marks	*defocus*	—	—
ESC key	Remove marks such as caret, selection and pointer	*neutralize*	—	—
SETUP key	Draw star-shaped pointer	*mark*	Mouse coordinates	

Defocus message   A defocus message is sent to the viewer which loses the focus as a consequence of a call to the procedure *PassFocus*. Consume messages are no longer directed at that viewer. The handler receiving a defocus message takes appropriate actions. Typically, the caret is removed if it is displayed.

Neutralize message   A neutralize message is broadcasted to all visible viewers when the ESC key is pressed. The handler which receives a neutralize message is told to remove all marks in its viewer's frame, in particular:

- the star-shaped pointer;
- the selection;
- the caret.

Mark message   A mark message *M* is sent to the viewer which contains the mouse cursor when the SETUP key is pressed. The mouse coordinates are transmitted in *M.X* and *M.Y*.

A handler which receives a mark message is told to draw the star-shaped pointer at the position of the mouse cursor.

15.2 Cursors

Cursors are patterns which move over the screen. Two such cursors are defined as global objects: the arrow of the mouse and the star-shaped pointer which designates a point on the display. Even though for the human eye the mouse cursor moves smoothly and the pointer jumps, both actually move in discrete steps. To make such a step, the cursor at the old location must be first removed, the screen content restored and then the cursor pattern drawn at the new location.

The pattern of cursors is not restricted to the arrow and the asterisk. Module Oberon provides an abstraction which allows user-defined shapes. The cursor changes its pattern properly when it moves across different viewers using differently shaped cursors.

Marker

A marker is an instance of the abstract data type *Marker*:

```
TYPE
  Painter = PROCEDURE (x, y: INTEGER);
  Marker = RECORD
    Fade, Draw: Painter;
  END;
```

where:

- *Fade* is the procedure to remove the cursor pattern at the old location.
- *Draw* is the procedure to draw the pattern at the new location.

Cursor

A cursor is an instance of the abstract data type *Cursor*:

```
TYPE
  Cursor = RECORD
    marker: Marker;
    on: BOOLEAN;
    X, Y: INTEGER
  END;
```

It has the following properties:

- *marker*: the marker of the cursor.
- *on*: TRUE if cursor is displayed, FALSE otherwise.
- *X, Y*: the position of the cursor.

Module Oberon exports two predefined cursors and two markers with self-explanatory meaning:

```
VAR
    Mouse, Pointer: Cursor;
    Arrow, Star: Marker;
```

OpenCursor

PROCEDURE OpenCursor(VAR c: Cursor);
Initializes cursor c. The cursor's fields are set such that:

- $c.on$ = FALSE.
- $c.X$ = 0.
- $c.Y$ = 0.

FadeCursor

PROCEDURE FadeCursor(VAR c: Cursor);
Removes cursor c from the screen if $c.on$ = TRUE. Sets $c.on$:= FALSE. The coordinates $c.X$ and $c.Y$ remain unchanged.

DrawCursor

PROCEDURE DrawCursor(VAR c: Cursor; VAR m: Marker; X, Y:INTEGER);
Fades cursor c at its old location recorded in $c.X$ and $c.Y$ using procedure $c.marker.Fade$. Draws new cursor pattern using $m.Draw$ and records the new location X and Y as well as the new marker m in the cursor's record. The field $c.on$ is set to TRUE. Thus, the marker in the cursor's record is used to fade the old cursor pattern and the marker passed as a parameter is used to draw the new one. This allows the cursor to change shape as it moves across viewers.

For example, the following draw the arrow-shaped mouse cursor and the star-shaped pointer, respectively:

```
Oberon.DrawCursor(Oberon.Mouse, Oberon.Arrow, X, Y);

Oberon.DrawCursor(Oberon.Pointer, Oberon.Star, X, Y);
```

RemoveMarks

PROCEDURE RemoveMarks(X, Y, W, H: INTEGER);
Fades the two cursors *Mouse* and *Pointer* if any part of their bit pattern is located in the rectangle with left lower corner coordinates X, Y, width W and height H.

RemoveMarks is conveniently used to remove the arrow and star-shaped pattern prior to writing to the display. Failure to do so can lead to 'dead' cursors and pointers (see Part III, Section 19.2.)

15.3   Command activation

Two of the important features of the Oberon system are the capabilities to:

(1) Invoke commands from ordinary texts.

(2) Create polymorphic commands.

Module Oberon provides the necessary interface to the inner core of the operating system and supplies the the command with information about the viewer and possibly the subframe from where it was called.

Parameter list

Prior to the use of the procedure *Call*, a parameter list must be built which is an instance of the following type:

```
TYPE
    ParList = POINTER TO ParRec;
    ParRec = RECORD
        vwr: Viewers.Viewer;
        frame: Display.Frame;
        text: Texts.Text;
        pos: LONGINT
    END;
```

where:

- *vwr* is the viewer which contains the text from where the command is executed.
- *frame* is the subframe which contains the text from where the command is executed.
- *text* is the text from where the command is executed.
- *pos* is the starting position of the parameter list; that is, the position of the first character in *text* after the command name.

Module Oberon exports the global variable:

```
VAR Par: ParList;
```

which is used to transfer parameter information to the command to be called.

Call

```
PROCEDURE Call(VAR name: ARRAY OF CHAR; par: ParList; new: BOOLEAN;
               VAR res: INTEGER);
```

Invokes the command whose name is the value of parameter *name*. The name must observe the Oberon convention *Mod.Proc* where *Mod* is a module name and *Proc* denotes a parameterless procedure exported by

Mod. If module *Mod* is not in memory, it is loaded first. If *new* = TRUE, then a new instance of the module is always loaded prior to passing control to *Proc*. This is important during debugging of a module when the newly compiled version should execute.

The formal parameter *par*, the parameter list, contains information about the environment from which the command is executed. An instance of a parameter list has to be created and completed prior to a call to *Call*. For example:

```
Var PL: Oberon.ParList;

NEW(PL);
PL.vwr : =     (* The viewer from which the command will be called *)
PL.frame : = (* The subframe from which the command will be called *)
PL.text : =    (* The text from which the command will be called *)
PL.pos : =     (* Position immediately after the command name in text *)
Oberon.Call("Mod.Proc", PL, FALSE, res);
```

Note: Don't forget to allocate the parameter list with a call to NEW(*PL*).

Prior to passing control to *Proc*, the parameter list *par* is assigned to the global variable *Par* which is accessible in command *Proc*. Through *Par*, the command has access to the text from which it was launched and to viewer and subframe containing that text.

Result codes   The parameter *res* is a result code which reports on the completion of the call. The following result codes are defined:

- *res* = 0: successful completion.
- *res* = 1: command does not exist.
- *res* = 2: not an object file or error in file.
- *res* = 3: module imported with bad key.
- *res* = 4: not enough space.

15.4   Focus, mark and selection

15.4.1   Focus viewer

The mouse and keyboard handler of the event loop sends consume messages to the *focus viewer* on keyboard events. The focus viewer is the value of the global variable:

```
VAR FocusViewer: Viewers.Viewer;
```

which is exported by module Oberon for use within commands. A viewer is designated the focus viewer by means of the procedure:

PassFocus   PROCEDURE PassFocus(V: Viewers.Viewer);

Viewer *V* will become the new focus viewer. A defocus message is sent to the previous focus viewer. The global variable *FocusViewer* declared in module Oberon is set to *V*.

15.4.2   Marked viewer

A viewer *V* is marked if the cursor *Pointer* is located within the viewer's frame; that is, if:

$$V.X \leqslant Pointer.X < V.X + V.W$$
$$V.Y \leqslant Pointer.Y < V.Y + V.H$$

Initial mark   *Pointer* is initialized such that *Pointer.X* = 0, *Pointer.Y* = 0 and *Pointer.on* = FALSE. Hence, after start-up, the bottom viewer located in the user track is marked.

Marking a   To mark a viewer, the cursor *Pointer* has to be set somewhere in its
viewer   frame through a call to:

Oberon.DrawCursor(Oberon.Pointer, Oberon.Star, X, Y)

Notes: It is not required that the cursor *Pointer* is *visible*. In fact, commands which take the marked viewer as a parameter often fade the star pattern. The viewer remains marked, however, until the pointer is passed to another viewer.

Since a cursor can only be at one place, the marked viewer is unique.

The cursor *Pointer* is bound to screen coordinates, and not to a particular viewer. Since a viewer is marked when *Pointer* is within its boundary, the marked viewer may change when the screen is reconfigured. For example, assume that viewer *V1* is marked. Then *V1* is closed and *V2* claims its space. Now, executing any command which takes the marked viewer as a parameter refers to *V2*.

MarkedViewer   PROCEDURE MarkedViewer ( ): Viewers.Viewer;

Returns the marked viewer. *MarkedViewer* is equivalent to *Viewers.This(Pointer.X, Pointer.Y)*.

15.4.3   Text selection

The text selection is an important parameter source for commands. System wide, the selection is not unique, like the focus or the mark. In fact, each text viewer may contain one, possibly two selections. Commands, therefore, look for the *most recent* selection for their input, which is found by the procedure:

PROCEDURE GetSelection(VAR text: Texts.Text; VAR beg, end:
                          LONGINT; VAR time: LONGINT);

The most recent text selection of any viewer is the stretch [*beg, end*) in *text*. The time of this selection is returned in the parameter *time*. If *time* < 0, then no selection exists in the system.

Having text selected is a property of the viewer. The number of viewer classes is open and their architecture is unknown to module Oberon. Therefore, the procedure *GetSelection* must rely on the cooperation of the visible viewers in the determination of the latest selection. It does this using the message-passing mechanism.

For this purpose, the type *Selection.Msg* is defined:

```
TYPE
  SelectionMsg = RECORD
    (Display.FrameMsg)
    time: LONGINT;
    text: Texts.Text;
    beg, end: LONGINT
  END;
```

where:

- *time* is the time of the selection currently contained in the message.
- *text* is the text which contains the selection.
- *beg, end* is the stretch [*beg, end*) which is selected in *text*.

The procedure *GetSelection* broadcasts a message *M* of type *SelectionMsg* to all visible viewers. *M.time* is set to −1 when *M* is sent. A handler which receives *M* will report the latest text selection, if one exists, in the fields of *M*. In particular, it carries out the following:

(1) Checks whether a selection exists. If so, it checks whether its time is more recent than *M.time*. If so, it performs steps 2 to 4.

(2) Assigns the text containing the selection to field *M.text*.

(3) Assigns the selected stretch [*beg, end*) to the fields *M.beg* and *M.end*.

(4) Assigns the time of the selection to *M.time*.

15.5   Display management

Module Oberon initializes the monochrome display and provides a set of functions which yield various display settings.

OpenDisplay

PROCEDURE OpenDisplay(UW, SW, H: INTEGER);
Opens two tracks to the right of already existing tracks with user track width UW, system track width SW and height H.[1]

OpenTrack

PROCEDURE OpenTrack(X, W: INTEGER);
Same as *Viewers.OpenTrack* except that a standard filler viewer is installed (see Chapter 13.)

DisplayWidth
DisplayHeight

PROCEDURE DisplayWidth(X: INTEGER): INTEGER;
PROCEDURE DisplayHeight(X: INTEGER): INTEGER;
Returns the width (height) of the display which contains the x coordinate X.

UserTrack
SystemTrack

PROCEDURE UserTrack(X: INTEGER): INTEGER;
PROCEDURE SystemTrack(X: INTEGER): INTEGER;
Returns the left margin of the user track (system track) of the display which contains the x coordinate X.

AllocateUser-
Viewer
AllocateSystem-
Viewer

PROCEDURE AllocateUserViewer(DX: INTEGER; VAR X, Y: INTEGER);
PROCEDURE AllocateSystemViewer(DX: INTEGER; VAR X, Y: INTEGER);
Procedures which yield a proposal for coordinates X and Y to be used to open a new viewer in the user track (system track) in the display which contains the x coordinate DX. The outcome depends on the display status of the cursor *Pointer*.

If the pointer is visible, then the values of X and Y equal the x and y coordinates of the focus of the pointer.

If the pointer is not visible, then an algorithm is used to determine X and Y in the respective track of the designated display.

Note: These procedures do *not* open viewers. They yield only a *placement suggestion* returned in parameters X and Y. An instance of the viewer is subsequently created and opened with *Viewers.Open*(V, X, Y).

---

[1] On the Ceres display, the choices are $UW = 640$, $SW = 384$ and $H = 800$.

15.6   **Miscellaneous procedures**

Set attributes   PROCEDURE SetFont(fnt: Fonts.Font);
PROCEDURE SetColor(col: SHORTINT);
PROCEDURE SetOffset(voff: SHORTINT);
Sets the attributes of typed characters globally. The attributes in effect at any given time will be transmitted in the input message. The default values are the default font, white and 0 vertical offset. The global character attributes are also the values of the global variables *CurFnt*, *CurColor* and *CurOff*.

GetClock   PROCEDURE GetClock(VAR t, d: LONGINT);
Reads the hardware clock and returns time *t* and date *d*. Time and date are encoded in 32-bit words as follows:

	7 bits	4 bits	5 bits	
High order	year	month	day	Low order

	5 bits	6 bits	6 bits
	hour	minute	second

SetClock   PROCEDURE SetClock(t, d: LONGINT);
Sets the hardware clock to time *t* and date *d*. The parameters use the same encoding as *GetClock*.

Time   PROCEDURE Time ( ): LONGINT;
Returns the time in units of 1/300 s since system start-up.

User identification   Module Oberon exports the variables:

```
VAR
    User: ARRAY 8 OF CHAR;
    Password: LONGINT;
```

These variables are set by the procedure *SetUser*.

SetUser   PROCEDURE SetUser(VAR user, password: ARRAY OF CHAR);
Assigns user identification *user* to the global variable *User*. Encrypts the password given in parameter *password* and assigns it to the global variable *Password*.

ShowMenu

PROCEDURE ShowMenu(VAR cmd: INTEGER; X, Y: INTEGER;
                                    menu: ARRAY OF CHAR);

Draws a pop-up menu at screen location *X, Y*. *ShowMenu* must be used in a loop executing while a mouse key is pressed. Dragging the mouse selects a command in the menu which, on release of the mouse key, is reported to the caller.

The menu is displayed in a rectangle which is 44 pixels wide and of height 5 * (2 + *Fonts.Default.height*) + 4. The default font height is normally 10 point, hence the menu height is 74 pixels.

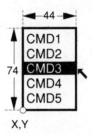

Up to five commands are allowed and their mnemonics are stored in the string *menu* according to the syntactic rule:

    command { "|" *command* }

The command selected is returned in parameter *cmd*. Assuming that the number of menu items is $m (1 \leq m \leq 5)$, then:

- $cmd < 5 - m$: no command is selected.
- $cmd = 5 - m$: the mth command is selected.
- $cmd = 5 - (m - 1)$: the $(m - 1)$ command is selected.
- $cmd = 4$: the first command is selected.
- $cmd > 4$: no command is selected.

If the string menu contains less than five commands, then the missing entries in the menu's rectangle are blank.

Note: It is the caller's responsibility to ensure that the menu rectangle does not exceed the display boundary. Otherwise, addressing exceptions may occur.

15.7   Exported system-wide resources

Module Oberon exports a set of message types to be used by client modules. It also exports global variables (most of which have been already mentioned.)

15.7.1   Copy messages

The message type *CopyMsg* is exported for use by client modules:

```
TYPE
  CopyMsg = RECORD
    (Display.FrameMsg)
    F: Display.Frame
  END;
```

Messages of type *CopyMsg* request the recipient handler to produce a copy of its object. The copy is returned in the field *F*. The type *CopyMsg* is exported by module Oberon but used by client modules, most notably module System, which broadcasts copy messages to implement the commands *System.Copy* and *System.Grow*.

A copy *Fnew* of an object *F* is a new instance of the type *F*. *Fnew* is put into exactly the same state as *F* was, when its handler was first called to put it on the display. The documents linked to *Fnew* are *identical* to those of *F*.

If *F* is a viewer (an extension of type *Viewers.Viewer*), then any subframes must be copied too and linked through *Fnew.dsc*. The copy of the viewer must be closed (*Fnew.state* = 0.)

If *F* is a frame for a menu viewer, the copy must have height zero (*F.H* = 0.)

Normally, a procedure *Open* is provided to initialize abstract data types. If available, the *Open* procedure should be used to initialize the copied objects, passing the documents of the original object as parameters (an example is given in Part III.)

15.7.2   CopyOver messages

The message type *CopyOverMsg* is exported for use by client modules:

```
TYPE
  CopyOverMsg = RECORD
  (Display.FrameMsg)
    text: Texts.Text;
    beg, end: LONGINT
  END;
```

A message *M* of type *CopyOverMsg* is sent to the focus viewer by other viewers (or commands.)

The handler which receives a copy over message *M* is requested to insert the stretch [*M.beg*, *M.end*] of *M.text* at the caret location.

The copyover message is typically used by text editors when the user interclicks the middle mouse key while selecting.

15.7.3   State variables

Module Oberon exports the following variables:

```
VAR
    CurFnt: Fonts.Fong;
    CurColor, CurOff: SHORTINT;
    CurTask: Task;
    FocusViewer: Viewers.Viewer;
    Log: Texts.Text;
    Par: ParList;
    User: ARRAY 8 OF CHAR;
    Password: LONGINT;
    Mouse, Pointer: Cursor;
    Arrow, Star: Marker;
```

where:

- *CurFnt* is the globally set font (procedure *SetFont*.)
- *CurColor* is the globally set color (procedure *SetColor*.)
- *CurOff* is the globally set vertical offset (procedure *SetOffset*.)
- *CurTask* is the current task (defined within the scope of the task handler only.)
- *FocusViewer* is the focus viewer; that is, the viewer at which keyboard events are directed.
- *Log* is the text of the system log.
- *Par* is the parameter list passed most recently to the procedure *Call*.
- *User* is the user identification used for remote server function.
- *Password* is the user's encoded password.
- *Mouse* is the mouse cursor.
- *Pointer* is the star-shaped pointer (a cursor.)
- *Arrow* is the arrow-shaped marker typically used by cursor *Mouse*.
- *Star* is the star-shaped marker typically used by cursor *Pointer*.

16 Module MenuViewers

Module MenuViewers exports the abstract data type *Viewer* which embodies the model of a viewer with two active subframes: a *menu frame* and a *main frame*. Instances of the type *Viewer* (termed menu viewers) *help to implement standard Oberon viewers.*

The handler of a menu viewer acts on the mouse command for moving the top edge of the viewer (that is, pressing the left mouse key in the upper part of the menu frame area and dragging.)

When the viewer is modified, either through dragging the menu frame or directed by a message of type *Viewers.ViewerMsg*, the position and size of the menu frame and of the main frame are newly determined. A message of type *ModifyMsg* is then sent to these active frames requesting appropriate modification of the displayed contents.

All messages which are of no concern to the handler of the menu viewer are simply passed on to the handlers of the subframes.

The standard text viewer is a menu viewer with two text frames (see Chapter 17.)

```
DEFINITION MenuViewers;

IMPORT Display, Viewers;

CONST reduce = 0; extend = 1; (* Message identifiers *)

TYPE
   ModifyMsg = RECORD(Display.FrameMsg)
     id: INTEGER;
     dY, Y, H: INTEGER
   END;

   Viewer = POINTER TO ViewerDesc;
   ViewerDesc = RECORD(Viewers.ViewerDesc)
     menuH: INTEGER
   END;
```

```
PROCEDURE Handle(V: Display.Frame; VAR M: Display.FrameMsg);
PROCEDURE New(Menu, Main: Display.Frame; menuH, X, Y: INTEGER):
    Viewer;

END MenuViewers.
```

16.1   The menu viewer

To draw a standard Oberon viewer, provide the title bar with its editable text and allow this title bar to be tracked with the mouse, turns out to be rather subtle. Since these functions are common to all viewer classes observing the Oberon interface recommendations, they are implemented once and for all in a special abstract data type *Viewer*:

```
TYPE
    Viewer = POINTER TO ViewerDesc;
    ViewerDesc = RECORD
        (Viewers.ViewerDesc)
        menuH: INTEGER
    END;
```

An instance of *Viewer* is termed a menu viewer. Its properties are:

- Width, height and coordinate of the bottom left corner (fields X, Y, W and H inherited from *Display.Frame*.)
- A neighbor viewer (field *next* inherited from *Display.Frame*.)
- Two active subframes of base type *Display.Frame* called the menu frame and the main frame (accessed through field *dsc* inherited from *Display.Frame*.)
- A handler (field *handle* inherited from *Display.Frame*.)
- A state (field *state* inherited from *Viewers.Viewer*.)
- The maximal height of the menu frame (field *menuH*.)

Functions of the handler

The handler of a menu viewer performs the following actions:

- It interprets the mouse command 'shift title bar' (that is, dragging with the left mouse key starting from the menu frame.)
- It maintains a one-pixel wide line around the viewer's perimeter.
- It sets the star-shaped pointer.
- It manages the position and size of the subframes.

Logical frame structure

The logical structure of the subframes of a menu viewer V is shown in the following diagram:

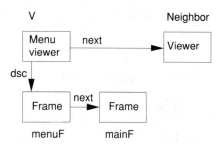

The following relations hold between a menu viewer V with menu frame *menuF* and main frame *mainF*:

$$V \text{ IS } Viewer \qquad menuF = V.dsc \qquad mainF = V.dsc.next$$

Both the menu frame and the main frame are active objects which are of base type *Display.Frame* and have a handler installed. The requirements for such a handler are discussed in Section 19.3.

Frame geometry

The menu viewer maintains a line around its perimeter which is one pixel wide. The area within this line is subdivided into the menu frame and the main frame. The maximal height of the menu frame is *menuH*. If the viewer's size does not accommodate a menu frame of full height, then the menu frame exhausts the area within the boundary line and the main frame is of height 0.

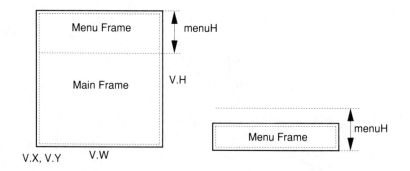

The following relations hold:

$$mainF.H + menuF.H = V.H - 2 \quad \text{and}$$
$$mainF.W = menuF.W = V.W - 2$$

Standard Oberon viewer

As the name suggests, the menu frame holds the title bar with viewer name and the local commands. For this purpose, a frame of type *TextFrames.Frame* will be installed (see Chapter 17.) The main frame is of the special type of its viewer (or frame) class. If both subframes are of type *TextFrames.Frame*, the menu viewer represents a text viewer.

New

PROCEDURE New(Menu, Main: Display.Frame; menuH, X, Y: INTEGER): Viewer; Creates an instance of a menu viewer and displays it on the screen. *Menu* and *Main* are active objects extending type *Display.Frame* which react properly to messages of type *ModifyMsg* (see Section 16.2.) Parameter *menuH* designates the height of the menu frame.

The menu viewer will open such that its top edge contains the point with coordinates X, Y provided this results in a viewer whose height is bigger than *Viewers.minH*. Otherwise, a viewer of the minimum height is opened.

For example, a standard text viewer is generated as follows (see also Chapter 17):

```
text := ...                      (* Text to be displayed *)
name := ...                      (* Name of viewer *)
cmds := "System.Close System.Copy ..." (* Commands of title bar *)
Oberon.AllocateUserViewer(X, Y);
V := MenuViewers.New(TextFrames.NewMenu(name, cmds),
                     TextFrames.NewText(text, 0),
                     TextFrames.menuH, X, Y);
```

where:

```
V: MenuViewers.Viewer; text: Texts.Text;
name, cmd: ARRAY 32 OF CHAR; X, Y: INTEGER;
```

16.2   The modify message

The handler installed in a menu viewer manages the size of its subframes. For this purpose, the message type *ModifyMsg* is defined:

```
TYPE
  ModifyMsg = RECORD
    (Display.FrameMsg)
    id: INTEGER;
    dY, Y, H: INTEGER
  END;
```

where:

- *id* is the message identifier (0 = reduce, 1 = extend.)
- *dY* is the translation.
- *Y* is the new value of the *y* coordinate of the lower left corner of the frame.
- *H* is the new height of the frame.

Note: dY, Y and *H* are related by:

$$dY = \text{ABS}(M.Y + M.H - F.Y - F.H)$$

They are chosen in such a way to make the task of the frame handler as simple as possible (see Part III, Section 19.4.)

Named constants for the message identifiers are provided:

```
CONST reduce = 0; extend = 1;
```

For simplicity, we call a message *M* of type *ModifyMsg* a 'reduce message' if *M.id = reduce*; 'extend message' if *M.id = extend*.

When we say that the handler of the menu viewer manages its subframes, we mean precisely the following:

- The handler determines the new location and size of the subframes.
- The handler sends an appropriate modify message to the subframes.
- After control is returned, the handler assigns the new frame parameters *X, Y, W* and *H* to the descriptors of the subframes.

Note: Since the subframe declaration is typically in the same module as the frame handler procedure, that frame handler is allowed to assign intermediary values to *X, Y, W* and *H*.

In the following discussion, *F* denotes the subframe prior to the change. When a modify message is sent to a subframe, its handler has access to both the frame *F* and the message *M*. The meaning of *M.dY*, *M.Y* and *M.H* is explained in the diagrams.

Extend message   The frame will expand. The handler of *F* clears the extended area and adjusts the display.

Note: The handler is expected to draw the contents of the rectangle *F.X, M.Y, F.W, M.H*.

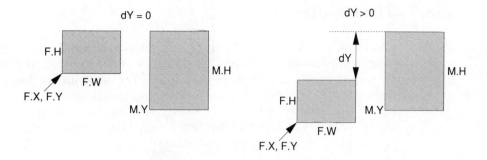

If $dY = 0$, then the area extends at the bottom. If $dY > 0$, the frame is both extended and shifted upwards by an amount dY (dY is always non-negative.)

Reduce message   The frame will shrink. The handler of F adjusts the display.

Note: The handler is still allowed to work in the large frame defined by the rectangle $F.X, F.Y, F.W, F.H$.

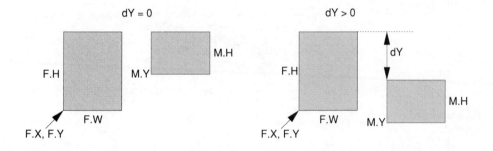

If $dY = 0$, then the area reduces at the bottom. If $dY > 0$, the frame is both reduced and shifted downwards by an amount dY (dY is always non-negative.)

Consistency   Initially, the frame is assigned zero height and the handler is called with an extend message. Then the frame is kept consistent at all times by the menu viewer. For example, when the frame is moved from one track into another one (move title bar with interclick), it is first shrunk to zero height and subsequently expanded at the new location. Similarly, if a frame is overlaid, it is reduced to zero height and when it is recovered, it is extended from there.

This consistency reduced the required procedure from four (for example, *Suspend, Restore, Extend* and *Reduce*) to just two (for example, *Extend* and *Reduce*.)

16.3 The handler

The frames under the direction of a menu viewer are active Oberon objects. This means that they have their own handler and that their type extends the base type *Display.Frame*. The semantics of the sub-frames is completely determined by the frame handlers.

The handler of the menu viewer and the handlers of the sub-frames are back-to-back and divide the work. The handler of the menu viewer receives the messages first. It acts on:

- An Oberon track message in the upper part of the menu frame.
- The Oberon mark message.
- Messages of type *Viewers.ViewerMsg*.

All other messages are simply passed on to the menu frame and to the main frame. When the menu viewer repositions its top edge or processes a viewer message, it in turn sends messages of type *ModifyMsg* to the two subframes.

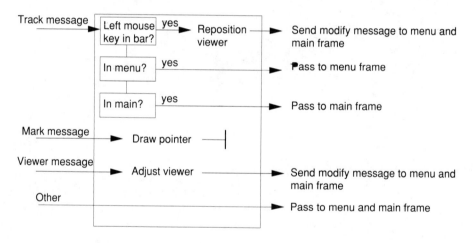

Ancestor of a subframe

The handlers installed in the subframes *V.dsc* and *V.dsc.next* of a menu viewer *V* sometimes need access to that viewer. Let *F* denote such a frame. Then the managing menu viewer *MV* of *F* is the result of the statement:

```
MV := Viewers.This(F.X, F.Y);
```

Handle

```
PROCEDURE Handle(V: Display.Frame; VAR M: Display.FrameMsg);
```
Handle is the handler installed in menu viewers. It processes the following messages: track, viewer, mark.

Track message   If the track message reports a 'shift title bar' command, the viewer will be changed at the top. 'Shift title bar' is signalled by a message M of type *Oberon.InputMsg* with:

- $M.id = Oberon.track$.
- 2 IN $M.keys$; that is, left mouse key pressed.
- $M.Y > V.Y + V.H - menuF.H - 1$; that is, the mouse is in the menu frame but not in the bottom two lines.

All other track messages are passed on to either the menu frame or the main frame, depending on which frame contains the mouse. If $(M.X, M.Y)$ is in neither frame, no action will take place.

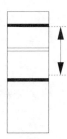

Pressing the left mouse key in the reposition-sensitive area of the menu viewer inverts the menu frame. Dragging on the left key defines the new position of the viewer's top edge. On release of the left key, the viewer is repositioned within the range shown in the diagram. If the middle key is interclicked, the viewer is repositioned without restrictions (see Part I, Section 2.4.4.)

Once the location of the repositioned viewer is established, the one-pixel wide viewer boundary is drawn or adjusted. Origin, width and height of the subframes are determined. Modify messages reporting the change are sent to both subframes. The fields X, Y, W and H of the subframes are subsequently set by *Handle*.

Viewer message   *Handle* adjusts the viewer in response to messages of type *Viewers.ViewerMsg*. The one-pixel wide viewer boundary is drawn (restore message) or adjusted (modify message.) Origin, width and height of the subframes are determined. Messages of type *ModifyMsg* reporting the change are sent to both subframes. The fields X, Y, W and H of the subframes are subsequently set by *Handle*.

If the viewer is suspended, *Handle* sends modify messages to the subframes which will result in their height being reduced to 0. Subsequently, it sets X, Y, W and H of the subframes accordingly.

If the viewer is being restored, *Handle* first assigns 0 height to both subframes and then sends appropriate extend messages. It sets the fields *X, Y, W* and *H* subsequently.

Mark message   *Handle* sets the star-shaped pointer in response to a message *M* of type *Oberon.ControlMsg* with *M.id = Oberon.mark*.

All other messages   All other messages are sent to *both* subframes.

17 Module TextFrames

Module TextFrames exports the abstract data type *Frame*. An instance of *Frame* is called a *text frame*. It is an active frame which is intended to be installed in a menu viewer. Normally, the menu frame of a menu viewer is a text frame. If both subframes are text frames, the viewer is a text viewer which represents the standard Oberon editor.

There are two sets of exported procedures:

(1) The display manager, dealing with the display of objects of type *Texts.Text*.

(2) The handler and its components dealing with different message types. The handler defines the semantics of the standard Oberon editor.

The procedures of the display manager serve to:

- Draw the text portion which falls into the frame boundary starting at an arbitrary position.

- Adjust the display to changing frame boundaries.

- Select stretches of text and display them in reverse video.

- Track and set the caret.

- Track words and lines.

- Set the position mark according to the position of the first displayed character relative to the text's length.

```
DEFINITION TextFrames;

IMPORT Input, Display, Viewers, MenuViewers, Fonts, Texts, Oberon;

CONST replace = 0; insert = 1; delete = 2;
```

```
TYPE
  Frame = POINTER TO FrameDesc;
  FrameDesc = RECORD(Display.FrameDesc)
    text: Texts.Text;
    org: LONGINT;
    col: INTEGER;
    lsp: INTEGER;
    left, right, top, bot: INTEGER;
    markH: INTEGER;
    time: LONGINT;
    mark, car, sel: INTEGER;
    carloc, selbeg, selend: Location
  END;

  Location = RECORD
    org, pos: LONGINT;
    dx, x, y: INTEGER
  END;

  UpdateMsg = RECORD(Display.FrameMsg)
    id: INTEGER;
    text: Texts.Text;
    beg, end: LONGINT
  END;

VAR
  barW, menuH: INTEGER;
  left, right, top, bot: INTEGER;
  lsp: INTEGER;

(* Display manager *)
PROCEDURE Delete(F: Frame; beg, end: LONGINT);
PROCEDURE Extend(F: Frame; newY: INTEGER);
PROCEDURE Insert(F: Frame; beg, end: LONGINT);
PROCEDURE Mark(F: Frame; mark: INTEGER);
PROCEDURE Pos(F: Frame; X, Y: INTEGER): LONGINT;
PROCEDURE Reduce(F: Frame; newY: INTEGER);
PROCEDURE RemoveCaret(F: Frame);
PROCEDURE RemoveSelection(F: Frame);
PROCEDURE Replace(F: Frame; beg, end: LONGINT);
PROCEDURE Restore(F: Frame);
PROCEDURE SetCaret(F: Frame; pos: LONGINT);
PROCEDURE SetSelection(F: Frame; beg, end: LONGINT);
PROCEDURE Show(F: Frame; pos: LONGINT);
PROCEDURE Suspend(F.Frame);
PROCEDURE TrackCaret(F: Frame; X, Y: INTEGER; VAR keysum: SET);
PROCEDURE TrackLine(F: Frame; X, Y: INTEGER; VAR org: LONGINT;
                    VAR keysum: SET);
```

```
        PROCEDURE TrackSelection(F: Frame; X, Y: INTEGER;
                            VAR keysum: SET);
        PROCEDURE TrackWord(F: Frame; X, Y: INTEGER, VAR pos: LONGINT;
                            VAR keysum: SET);

        (* Handler and its components *)
        PROCEDURE Call(F: Frame; pos: LONGINT; new: BOOLEAN);
        PROCEDURE Copy(F: Frame; VAR Fcopy: Frame);
        PROCEDURE CopyOver(F: Frame; text: Texts.Text; beg, end: LONGINT);
        PROCEDURE Defocus(F: Frame);
        PROCEDURE Edit(F: Frame; X, Y: INTEGER; keys: SET);
        PROCEDURE GetSelection(F: Frame; VAR text: Texts.Text;
                            VAR beg, end, time: LONGINT);
        PROCEDURE Handle(F: Display.Frame; VAR M: Display.FrameMsg);
        PROCEDURE Modify(F: Frame; id, dY, Y, H: INTEGER);
        PROCEDURE Neutralize(F: Frame);
        PROCEDURE Update(F: Frame; VAR M: UpdateMsg);
        PROCEDURE Write(F: Frame; ch: CHAR; fnt: Fonts.Font;
                            col, voff: SHORTINT);

        (* Texts *)
        PROCEDURE NotifyDisplay(T: Texts.Text; op: INTEGER;
                            beg, end: LONGINT);
        PROCEDURE Text(name: ARRAY OF CHAR): Texts.Text;

        (* Creation of objects *)
        PROCEDURE NewMenu(name, commands: ARRAY OF CHAR): Frame;
        PROCEDURE NewText(text: Texts.Text; pos: LONGINT): Frame;
        PROCEDURE Open(F: Frame; H: Display.Handler;
                            T: Texts.Text; org: LONGINT;
                            col, left, right, top, bot, lsp: INTEGER);
    END TextFrames.
```

17.1 The frame

A text frame is an instance of the abstract data type *Frame*. The text frame is an active frame intended to be installed either as the menu frame or the main frame in a menu viewer. *The text frame implements the standard Oberon editor*. It has the following definition:

```
    TYPE
        Frame = POINTER TO FrameDesc:
        FrameDesc = RECORD
            (Display.FrameDesc)
            text: Texts.Text;
            org: LONGINT;
            col: INTEGER;
```

```
            lsp: INTEGER;
            left, right, top, bot: INTEGER;
            markH: INTEGER;
            time: LONGINT;
            mark, car, sel: INTEGER;
            carloc, selbeg, selend: Location
         END;
```

A text frame has the following properties:

- Width, height and coordinate of the bottom left corner (fields *X*, *Y*, *W* and *H* inherited from *Display.Frame*.)
- A neighbor frame (field *next* inherited from *Display.Frame*.)
- A handler which implements the standard editor and is compatible with the requirements of *MenuViewers* (field *handle* inherited from *Display.Frame*.)
- A displayed text (fields *text* and *org*.)
- A background color (field *col*.)
- Line spacing information (field *lsp*.)
- A margin (fields *left*, *right*, *top* and *bot*.)
- A selection (fields *time*, *sel*, *selbeg* and *selend*.)
- A caret (fields *car* and *carloc*.)
- A mark (fields *mark* and *markH*.)

The text frame also inherits the field *dsc* from *Display.Frame*. This field is not normally used.

Location

The auxiliary type *Location* describes the place and properties of a given character:

```
         TYPE
            Location = RECORD
               org, pos: LONGINT;
               dx, x, y: INTEGER
            END;
```

where:

- *org* is the position in the text of the first displayed character in the line which contains the located character.
- *pos* is the position in the text of the located character.
- *dx* is the width of the located character.
- *x*, *y* are the relative positions of the located character within the frame.

Character numbering in texts starts at 0. The *relative position* of a character is given by the coordinates of the character's base point (see Chapter 14) measured in a coordinate system with origin in the lower left corner of the frame. Thus, the base point of a located character has display coordinates:

$$X = F.X + loc.x \quad \text{and} \quad Y = F.Y + loc.y$$

where F is a variable of type *Frame* and *loc* denotes a location.

Exported variables

The following variables are exported to designate standard values for various frame properties:

```
VAR
    barW: INTEGER;
    menuH: INTEGER;
    lsp: INTEGER;
    left, right, top, bot: INTEGER;
```

where:

- *barW* is the width of the standard scroll bar.
- *menuH* is the standard height of the menu frame.
- *lsp* is the standard line spacing.
- *left, right, top, bot* are the standard margins.

Frame and text

A text frame F displays the text designated in field *text*. Often, the whole text is bigger (typically longer) than the portion that fits into the boundary of frame F. The display manager provides the functions to show that portion of the text which falls into the frame, given that the first displayed character has position $F.org$.

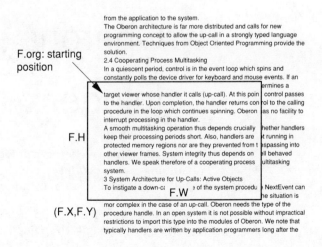

F.org: starting position

from the application to the system.
The Oberon architecture is far more distributed and calls for new programming concept to allow the up-call in a strongly typed language environment. Techniques from Object Oriented Programming provide the solution.
2.4 Cooperating Process Multitasking
In a quiescent period, control is in the event loop which spins and constantly polls the device driver for keyboard and mouse events. If an ...ermines a target viewer whose handler it calls (up-call). At this poin...control passes to the handler. Upon completion, the handler returns con...rol to the calling procedure in the loop which continues spinning. Oberon...as no facility to interrupt processing in the handler.

F.H

A smooth multitasking operation thus depends crucially...hether handlers keep their processing periods short. Also, handlers are ...t running in protected memory regions nor are they prevented from t...espassing into other viewer frames. System integrity thus depends on ...ll behaved handlers. We speak therefore of a cooperating process ...ultitasking system.
3 System Architecture for Up-Calls: Active Objects
To instigate a down-ca...e of the system procedu...e NextEvent can ...he situation is

F.W

(F.X,F.Y)

mor complex in the case of an up-call. Oberon needs the type of the procedure handle. In an open system it is not possible without impractical restrictions to import this type into the modules of Oberon. We note that typically handlers are written by application programmers long after the

Further properties of a text frame *F* are the color, the line spacing, the mark, the margin, the selection and the caret. They are depicted in the following diagram.

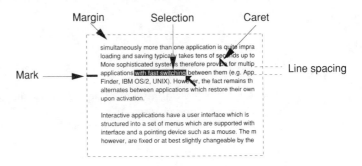

Color   The field *col* of a text frame *F* determines whether the frame has the standard background (*F.col* = *Display.black*) or an inverted background (*F.col* > 0, typically *F.col* = *Display.white*.)

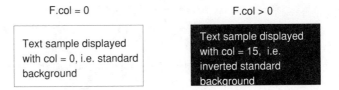

Note: In all the drawings of this book, the standard background is assumed to be white.

Spacing   The field *lsp* controls the spacing of lines:

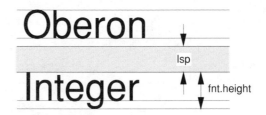

If *lsp* = 0 then the displayed (or printed) lines are separated by *fnt.height* (assuming that font *fnt* is in effect.) This is the standard value and results in the densest display or printing.

Margin   A text frame *F* has a margin around its perimeter. The size of this margin is specified by the fields *left*, *right*, *top* and *bot*.

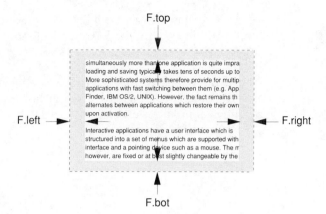

F.top

F.left →   ◄── F.right

F.bot

Restriction: The area in the margin is at the disposal of the display manager. Client modules cannot assume that pixels written into the margin will not be cleared.

Selection

A text frame may have a selection. When a selection exists, it is unique. The state of the selection is indicated by the fields *sel*, *time*, *selbeg* and *selend*:

- *sel* = 0: no selection exists.
- *sel* > 0: a selection exists.
- *time*: time of last selection.
- *selbeg*: location of begin of selection.
- *selend*: location of end of selection.

Note: selbeg and *selend* are defined only if *sel* > 0. If frame *F* has a selection, the selected stretch of text is [*beg*, *end*) with *beg* = *F.selbeg.pos* and *end* = *F.selend.pos*. The relative coordinates of the characters at positions *beg* and *end* and their respective line origins are also available (*F.selbeg.x*, *F.selbeg.y*, *F.selbeg.org* etc.)

Caret

A text frame may display a caret. The state of the caret is defined by the fields *car* and *carloc* as follows:

- *car* = 0: no caret is set.
- *car* > 0: caret is set.

Field *carloc* is defined only if *car* > 0. If frame *F* has a caret set, its position in the text of *F* is given by *F.carloc.pos*. The relative coordinates of the character to the right of the caret and its line origin are the values of *F.carloc.x*, *F.carloc.y* and *F.carloc.org*.

Note: It is the responsibility of the programmer to ensure that the caret is unique within the frame and set only if the menu viewer which supervises the frame is the focus viewer.

Mark

A text frame may display a mark in the left-hand margin. Two marks are available: position and arrow (the arrow is used when a long running command is executing.)

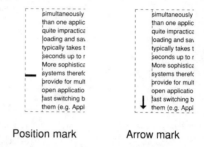

Position mark   Arrow mark

The state of the mark is given by the field *mark*:

- *mark* < 0: arrow mark is displayed.
- *mark* = 0: no mark is displayed.
- *mark* > 0: position mark is displayed.

The field *markH* defines the location of the position mark as shown in the following diagram:

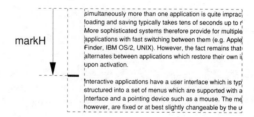

If text is drawn or changed in the frame or if the frame changes (procedures *Reduce*, *Extend*, *Show*, *Insert*, *Replace* and *Delete*), the field *markH* is adjusted such that in the actual frame *F*:

$$markH/F.H = F.org/F.text.len$$

Some procedures also reposition the position mark according to the changed display (for example, *Show*, *Insert*, *Replace* and *Delete*.) The position mark is displayed only if $F.left \geq barW$.

17.2 The display manager

Restore
PROCEDURE Restore(F: Frame);
The content of text frame F is written to the display, starting at position $F.org$ in text $F.text$. If $F.mark > 0$ (position), the position mark is restored according to $F.markH$. The frame area is cleared of its previous contents.

Suspend
PROCEDURE Suspend(F: Frame);
Suspends text frame F. The hidden data structure describing the displayed text is released.

Reduce
PROCEDURE Reduce(F: Frame; newY: INTEGER);
Reduces text frame F such that the bottom edge assumes the y coordinate $newY$. Text lines which would only be partially visible are cleared. $F.Y$ and $F.H$ are adjusted such that $F.Y = newY$ and the top edge stays fixed.
Preconditions: (1) $newY \geq F.Y$, (2) $F.mark = 0$ (that is, no marks are displayed) and (3) the frame is consistent (that is, $F.X$, $F.Y$, $F.W$, $F.H$ are not changed except in concordance with *Extend* and *Reduce* (see discussion under procedure *Extend*.)
If a position mark is displayed ($F.mark > 0$), it must be removed using *Mark*(0) prior to a call of *Reduce*. If a position mark is desired, it has to be reset with *Mark*(1) afterwards.

Extend
PROCEDURE Extend(F: Frame; newY: INTEGER);
Extends text frame F such that the bottom edge assumes the y coordinate $newY$. Clears the extended area and writes newly visible text lines. If $F.left \geq barW$, a scroll bar is drawn. The fields $F.Y$ and $F.H$ are adjusted such that $F.Y = newY$ and the top edge stays fixed.
Preconditions: (1) $newY < F.Y$, (2) $F.mark = 0$ (that is, no marks are displayed) and (3) the frame is consistent (that is, $F.X$, $F.Y$, $F.W$, $F.H$ are not changed except in concordance with *Extend* and *Reduce*.)
If a position mark is displayed ($F.mark > 0$), it must be removed using *Mark*(0) prior to a call of *Extend*. If a position mark is desired, it has to be reset with *Mark*(1) afterwards.
The following is an example of precondition (3). Assume that text frame F is to be cleared and redrawn. This is achieved as follows:

```
PROCEDURE Redraw(F);
VAR oldY: INTEGER;
BEGIN
  oldY := F.Y;
  Reduce(F, F.Y + F.H);
  Extend(F, oldY);
END Redraw;
```

The following is illegal since the frame boundaries are changed without prior invocation of *Reduce*. A frame without text results.

```
PROCEDURE Redraw(F);
VAR Y: INTEGER;
BEGIN
  Display.ReplConst
    (Display.black, F.X, F.Y, F.W, F.H, Display.replace); (* Clear frame *)
  Y := F.Y; F.Y := F.Y + F.H; F.H := 0;
  Extend(F, Y)
END Redraw;
```

Show

PROCEDURE Show(F: Frame; pos: LONGINT);

Displays the text of text frame *F* starting at position *pos*. The parameter *pos* is normally the starting position of a line (the first character after a carriage return 0DX.) If it is not, then the next line following *pos* will be the top line. If the position mark is displayed, it is adjusted.

Show has an effect only if *pos* results in a different top line. If *pos* is negative, the first character of the text is assumed. If *pos* > *F.text.len*, then the line after the last character is on top. In this case, the frame is empty.

Precondition: (1) *Show* assumes that the caret, the selection and all cursors are removed from the display. Use the procedures *RemoveCaret(F)*, *RemoveSelection(F)* and *Oberon.RemoveMarks(F.X, F.Y, F.W, F.H)* to remove marks if needed. (2) The frame is consistent (that is, *F.X, F.Y, F.W, F.H* are not changed except in concordance with *Extend* and *Reduce*.)

Mark

PROCEDURE Mark(F: Frame; mark: INTEGER);

Marks text frame *F* specified by *mark*:

- *mark* < 0: arrow mark.

- *mark* = 0: no mark.

- *mark* > 0: position mark.

Arrow mark (viewer busy) and position mark are mutually exclusive. The position mark is only drawn if *F.left* ⩾ *barW*.

Pos

PROCEDURE Pos(F: Frame; X, Y: INTEGER): LONGINT;

Returns the position of the character designated by the point with coordinates *X, Y* in text frame *F*. The point *X, Y* is measured in display coordinates. If the frame is empty, a negative value is returned.

If the point *X, Y* is:

- Within the area of the displayed text, then the position of the character whose box contains *X, Y* is returned.
- To the right of the displayed text, then the position of the last character of the text line at height *Y* is returned (usually a carriage return 0DX.)
- Below the last line of a text, then the position of the character vertically above *X, Y* is returned.
- To the right and below the last line, then the position of the last character of the text is returned.

This function is used to correlate cursor positions with text position.

SetCaret

PROCEDURE SetCaret(F: Frame; pos: LONGINT);
Sets the caret in text frame *F* at the position *pos* in the text of *F*. The field *F.car* is set to 1 and the caret location is recorded in *F.carloc*. If *pos* is less than the position of the first character displayed in *F*, then the caret is set to the left of the first character. If *pos* is bigger than the position of the last character displayed in *F*, then the caret is set to the right of the last character.
Precondition: SetCaret assumes that no caret is set.
The caret is only allowed if *V*, the ancestor viewer of *F*, is the focus viewer. The caller must request the focus first, viz.

Oberon.PassFocus(V); TextFrames.SetCaret(F, pos);

Note: If *F* showed a caret before the call to *Oberon.PassFocus*, it is removed when control returns. If it is certain that *V* is the focus viewer, *RemoveCaret* may be substituted for *Oberon.PassFocus*.

TrackCaret

PROCEDURE TrackCaret(F: Frame; X, Y: INTEGER; VAR keysum: SET);
Tracks the caret in text frame *F* from starting point *X, Y*. As long as any key is pressed, the caret follows the mouse cursor. On release of all keys, the caret is set in place. The field *F.car* is set to 1 and the final caret location is recorded in *F.carloc*.
Any mouse keys pressed during tracking are reported in parameter *keysum* which contains the sum (logical OR) of all keys:

- 0 IN *keysum*: right key pressed.
- 1 IN *keysum*: middle key pressed.
- 2 IN *keysum*: left key pressed.

Precondition: TrackCaret assumes that no caret is set (see discussion under procedure *SetCaret*.)

RemoveCaret   PROCEDURE RemoveCaret(F: Frame);
Removes the caret from text frame *F*. The field *F.car* is set to 0. *RemoveCaret* has no effect if no caret is set (*F.car* = 0.)

SetSelection   PROCEDURE SetSelection(F: Frame; beg, end: LONGINT);
Selects the stretch [*beg*, *end*) of the text frame in the text of *F*. The field *F.sel* is set to 1 and the selection is recorded in *F.selbeg* and *F.selend*. The selected stretch of text is displayed in reverse video. If the stretch [*beg*, *end*) is only partially visible in frame *F*, then only the visible portion is selected. Consequently, if the stretch is invisible, no selection is set (*F.sel* = 0.)

A text frame can contain only one selection at a time. Every call to *SetSelection* automatically clears a previous one.

TrackSelection   PROCEDURE TrackSelection(F: Frame; X, Y: INTEGER; VAR keysum: SET);
Tracks the selection in text frame *F* starting at *X*, *Y*. As long as any key is pressed, the selection follows the mouse cursor. On release of all keys, the selection is set. The field *F.sel* is set to 1 and the selection is recorded in *F.selbeg* and *F.selend*.

Any mouse keys pressed during tracking are reported in parameter *keysum* (see *TrackCaret*.)

A text frame can contain only one selection at a time. Every call to *TrackSelection* automatically clears a previous one.

RemoveSelection   PROCEDURE RemoveSelection(F: Frame);
Removes the selection from text frame *F*. If a selection exists, the reverse video is removed. The field *F.sel* is set to 0.

TrackLine   PROCEDURE TrackLine(F: Frame; X, Y: INTEGER; VAR org: LONGINT;
                VAR keysum: SET);
Tracks lines in text frame *F* from starting point *X*, *Y*. As long as any key is pressed, the line pointed at with the cursor is underlined. On release of all keys, the underlining is removed. The position of the first character of the line which was underlined last is returned in parameter *org*.

Any mouse keys pressed during tracking are reported in parameter *keysum* (see *TrackCaret*.)

This procedure is used when scrolling in a text viewer.

TrackWord   PROCEDURE TrackWord(F: Frame; X, Y: INTEGER; VAR pos: LONGINT;
                VAR keysum: SET);
Tracks words in text frame *F* from starting point *X*, *Y*. As long as any key is pressed, the word pointed at with the cursor is underlined. On release of all keys, the underlining is removed. The position of the first character of the word which was underlined last is returned in parameter *pos*.

Any mouse keys pressed during tracking are reported in parameter *keysum* (see *TrackCaret*.)

Note: A word is defined as any stretch of blank-delimited characters.

This procedure facilitates command execution from texts.

Replace
Insert
Delete

PROCEDURE Replace(F: Frame; beg, end: LONGINT);
PROCEDURE Insert(F: Frame; beg, end: LONGINT);
PROCEDURE Delete(F: Frame; beg, end: LONGINT);

The stretch [*beg, end*) is replaced, inserted or deleted in the text of *F*. The display is updated accordingly. These procedures are typically called by a handler in response to a message of type *UpdateMsg*. If the position mark is displayed, it is adjusted.

Precondition: It is assumed that the caret, the selection and all the cursors are removed from the display, use the procedures *RemoveCaret(F)*, *RemoveSelection(F)* and *Oberon.RemoveMarks(F.X, F.Y, F.W, F.H)* to remove marks if needed.

17.3 The handler and its components

Handle

PROCEDURE Handle(F: Display.Frame; VAR M: Display.FrameMsg);
Handle carries out the following:

- Tracks the mouse cursor.
- Invokes commands from the displayed text (middle mouse key.)
- Selects stretches of text (right mouse key.)
- Places the caret (left mouse key.)
- Removes marks (ESC key.)
- Inserts text from the keyboard at the caret location.
- Performs mouse editing functions such as deletion and copying of selected text (mouse interclick commands.)
- Performs scrolling (mouse events in the scroll bar.)
- Responds to messages of type *Oberon.CopyMsg*, *Oberon.SelectionMsg* and *Oberon.CopyOverMsg*.
- Adjusts the frame in response to messages of type *MenuViewers.ModifyMsg*.

Handle is the standard handler for text frames. It works in reaction to messages coming from the modules *Oberon*, *MenuViewers* and *TextFrames* itself. Typically, for each message type and each message id, a procedure is called. These procedures are exported too and described in the sequel. The program text of *Handle* is discussed in Part III.

Call

PROCEDURE Call(F: Frame; pos: LONGINT; new: BOOLEAN);

Invokes a command found in the text displayed in text frame *F*. The first name at or after *pos* is interpreted as the command name. It must observe the Oberon convention *Mod.Proc*, where *Mod* is a module name and *Proc* denotes a parameterless procedure exported by *Mod*. If module *Mod* is not in memory, it is loaded first. If *new* = TRUE, a new instance of the module is always loaded prior to passing control to *Proc*. This is useful during debugging of a module when the newly compiled version should execute.

Call builds an Oberon parameter list and invokes *Oberon.Call*. It reports error conditions in the system log.

Call is typically used in conjunction with *TrackWord*, which delivers the value of *pos*.

Defocus

PROCEDURE Defocus(F: Frame);

Removes the caret from text frame *F*. *Defocus* is called by *Handle* in response to an Oberon defocus message.

Neutralize

PROCEDURE Neutralize(F: Frame);

Removes the caret, selection and pointer from text frame *F*. *Neutralize* is called by *Handle* in response to an Oberon neutralize message.

Write

PROCEDURE Write(F: Frame; ch: CHAR: fnt: Fonts.Font; col, voff: SHORTINT);

Inserts character *ch* into text *F.text* at the position corresponding to the caret location. The inserted character is a member of font *fnt*, drawn in color *col* and with offset *voff*. If *ch* = 7FX (DEL key), the preceding character is deleted. The caret is adjusted to the right (left in the case of deletion.)

The display is subsequently updated directed by an update message originating from the notifier of *F.text*. The handler is called recursively.

Precondition: It is assumed that the caret is set.

Write is called by *Handle* in response to an Oberon consume message.

Edit

PROCEDURE Edit(F: Frame: X, Y: INTEGER; keys: SET);

Edit tracks the mouse cursor and acts on mouse key events (if any.) It executes the mouse commands defined by the standard editor, such as selecting, caret tracking, copying and deleting while tracking, scrolling and command execution. The parameters *X*, *Y*, and *keys* are the starting mouse position and key values, respectively.

Note: If the text *F.text* is changed as a result of mouse interclick commands, the handler will be called recursively with an update message originating from the notifier.

Edit is called by *Handle* in response to an Oberon track message.

GetSelection   PROCEDURE GetSelection(F: Frame; VAR text: Texts.Text;
                                    VAR beg, end, time: LONGINT);

If text frame *F* contains a selection which is more recent than indicated in *time*, the new value of *text* is the text which contains that selection and [*beg, end*) is the selected stretch. The parameters remain unchanged if no selection exists which is more recent than *time*.

GetSelection is called by *Handle* in response to an Oberon selection message.

Copy   PROCEDURE Copy(F: Frame; VAR Fcopy: Frame);

Returns a copy of text frame *F* in *Fcopy*. *Copy* is called by *Handle* in response to an Oberon copy message.

CopyOver   PROCEDURE CopyOver(F: Frame; text: Texts.Text; beg, end: LONGINT);

Copies the stretch [*beg, end*) of text *text* to the caret location *F.carloc.pos* of text *F.text*. If the caret is not set, no action occurs.

In the case that *CopyOver* changes *F.text*, the handler will be called recursively with an update message.

CopyOver is called by *Handle* in response to an Oberon copyover message.

Modify   PROCEDURE Modify(F: Frame; id, dY, Y: INTEGER);

Modifies the size of text frame *F* and adjusts the display accordingly. Parameter *id* indicates the type of the change (extend or reduce), *dY* denotes a coordinate transformation and *Y* is the new value of the *y* coordinate of the lower left corner of *F*.

Modify is called by *Handle* in response to a MenuViewers modify message.

Update   PROCEDURE Update(F: Frame; VAR M: UpdateMsg);

Removes all marks and updates the display of text frame *F* as directed by the message *M* of type *UpdateMsg*.

Update is called by *Handle* in response to an update message (see Section 17.4.)

17.4   Facilities dealing with texts

When a text changes, its notifier is invoked. Texts displayed in text frames use the notifier *NotifyDisplay* which is exported by module TextFrames:

NotifyDisplay   PROCEDURE NotifyDisplay(T: Texts.Text; op: INTEGER; beg, end: LONGINT);

In order to update all views when a change of the underlying text *T* occurs, *NotifyDisplay* broadcasts a message of type *UpdateMsg* to all visible viewers. Parameters *beg* and *end* report the changed stretch [*beg*, *end*) in *T*. The type of change is indicated in *op* which takes values:

- *op* = 0: stretch is replaced.
- *op* = 1: stretch is inserted.
- *op* = 2: stretch is deleted.

UpdateMsg   The update message sent by *NotifyDisplay* has type:

```
TYPE
  UpdateMsg = RECORD
    (Display.FrameMsg)
    id: INTEGER;
    text: Texts.Text;
    beg, end: LONGINT
  END;
```

where:

id is the message identifier.
text is the changed text.
beg, *end* is the stretch [*beg*, *end*) which is changed.

Update message identifiers   Update message identifiers are exported as named constants with obvious meaning:

```
CONST replace = 0; insert = 1; delete = 2;
```

Table 17.1 summarizes events and actions relating to update messages.

Table 17.1   Events and actions for the message *M: UpdateMsg*, process stretch [*M.beg*, *M.end*)

Event	Action	*M.id*
Stretch replaced in *M.text*	Update display if stretch is visible (call of *Replace*)	*replace*
Stretch inserted in *M.text*	Update display if stretch is visible (call of *Insert*)	*insert*
Stretch deleted in *M.text*	Update display if stretch is visible (call of *Delete*)	*delete*

Text   PROCEDURE Text(name: ARRAY OF CHAR): Texts.Text;
Creates a new text from file *name*. The notifier *NotifyDisplay* is installed. If *name* = " " or if file *name* does not exist, then an empty text is created.

17.5   Opening and creating frames

Open

PROCEDURE Open(F: Frame; H: Display.Handler; T: Texts.Text; org: LONGINT;
col, left, right, top, bot, lsp: INTEGER);

Opens text frame F and installs handler H. The text T is linked with F and positioned such that the character with position *org* is displayed at the top left corner of the frame (for details see procedure *Show*.) The fields *col*, *left*, *right*, *top*, *bot*, and *lsp* of text frame F are initialized with the values passed to the parameters with the corresponding names.

If *left* $\geq$ *barW*, then a scroll bar will be provided. Mark, caret and selection are off (that is, $F.mark = 0$, $F.car = 0$ and $F.sel = 0$.)

Note: Open does not write text to the display.

NewMenu

PROCEDURE NewMenu(name, commands: ARRAY OF CHAR): Frame;

Generates a text frame to be installed as the menu frame in a menu viewer. The background color is *Display.white* (the inverse of the normal background.) No scroll bar is provided. The standard font is used. The frame displays one text line composed of the viewer name contained in *name* and the set of commands passed in *commands*. The name is separated from the commands with the symbol '|'.

NewText

PROCEDURE NewText(text: Texts.Text; pos: LONGINT): Frame;

Generates a text frame to be installed as the main frame in a menu viewer. The text frame is associated with *text*; *pos* designates the first displayed character in the upper left corner (see procedure *Show*.) The frame has standard properties and the background color is the standard background (*Display.black*.) A scroll bar is provided.

Part III
Programming guide

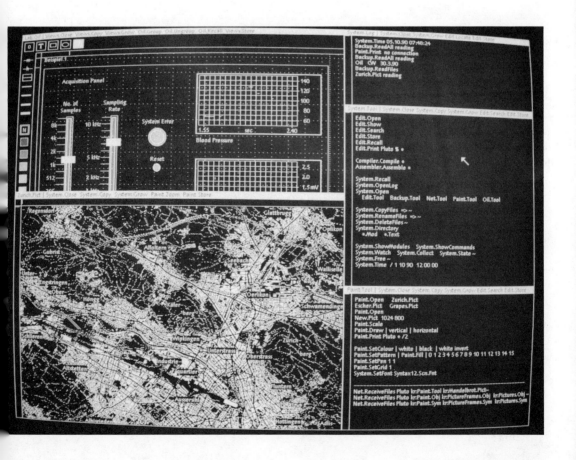

18 Programming commands

In the Oberon system, the notion of a main program is absent. The executable code unit is the *command*. The term command suggests an action in the framework of an interactive system such as *Edit.Open*, *System.Close* or *Edit.Store*.

The good old program, however, still exists. There are numerically intensive computations such as system simulations which have a natural affinity to personal workstations with their graphical capability. In Oberon terminology, such programs are commands too.

Thus, whoever writes a program for an Oberon system is writing a command. As indicated, the intent may be twofold:

(1) To write a program which performs a computation.

(2) To write a command which operates on an instance of an abstract data type such as a text or a graphic.

The second kind of activity aims at *extending the functionality* provided by an existing interactive application – termed a viewer class. That commands operating on instances of data types belonging to viewer classes can be easily written and added to the system is not self-evident – in fact, it is impossible in most systems. The factors that make it possible in Oberon are:

- The event loop is a central component.
- The absence of hidden states when control is in the event loop.
- The unified way in which commands are executed from texts.

In this chapter, we explain how to write commands. The topics discussed are how to deal with texts, how to decode parameter information, how to work with text viewers, how to use files and, finally, how to structure a long running command such that it may be installed as a task in the event loop.

18.1   General programming rules

18.1.1   Read-only nature of object descriptors

The majority of the Oberon constructs are instances of abstract data types. They are represented by variables of record type exported by their respective modules. In general, the fields of these records should be *treated as strictly read-only*. The respective modules provide procedures to initialize the objects and to change properties.

For example, a *writer* is an instance of the abstract data type:

```
TYPE
  Writer = RECORD
    (Files.Rider)
    buf: Buffer;
    fnt: Fonts.Font;
    col, voff: SHORTINT
  END;
```

The fields *fnt*, *col* and *voff* describe the attributes of the writer. They may be read at any time to find the characteristics of the next symbol written. However, the programmer *must not change the attributes with direct assignments to those fields*. For this purpose, the procedures *Texts.SetColor*, *Texts.SetFont* and *Texts.SetVoff* are provided.

There are a few *exceptions* to the read-only nature of the fields of an Oberon object, most notably the installation of handlers and notifiers. Consider a viewer, *V* say, which is initialized as follows:

```
NEW(V);                   (* Create the descriptor *)
V.handle : = HandlerProc; (* Install handler *)
V.state : = 0;            (* Set V to state closed, precondition for opening *)
Viewers.Open(V, X, Y);    (* Initialize the other public fields of V *)
...                       (* Initialize private fields, if any *)
```

Similarly, notifiers are installed in texts.

Another exception is the fields *next* and *dsc* of frames under the supervision of a handler; that is, the subframes of a viewer class. These fields, too, are set through assignment statements.

18.1.2   Responsibility for parameter correctness

The general philosophy in Oberon is that it is *the caller's responsibility to ensure correctness of the actual parameters*.

With few exceptions, parameter errors lead to undefined but not disastrous results. For example, if a reader is set beyond the end of its text, the next read operation yields an unspecified character of that text.

If correctness is not implicitly guaranteed, tests must be performed by the client of modules of the outer core. For example, if it is not guaranteed that the position of a reader is inside the text, a test is needed:

```
pos := ...              (* Position in text where reading should start *)
IF pos > T.len THEN (* Exception handling *)
ELSE ...                (* Normal read operation *)
END;
```

Special care must be used with the procedures performing raster operations (*Display.ReplConst*, *Display.ReplPattern*, *Display.CopyPattern*, *Display.CopyBlock*) and the procedure *Oberon.ShowMenu*. Attempts to draw outside the pixelmaps may result in addressing exceptions.

18.1.3   Use of exported constants, variables and functions instead of user-defined constants

Many modules export constants, variables or functions which reveal parameters of the module. The programmer is urged to use these and not substitute their numerical values.

For example, the display maps are of height *Display.Height*. The programmer should not substitute the numerical value 800 which applies to the Ceres workstation. In so doing, the user compromises his or her software in the case of a migration to new hardware with a different display size.

Similarly, module Oberon exports the procedure *Oberon.DisplayHeight*( ), which yields the height of the logical display which should not be confused with *Display.Height*, although in most cases the two coincide.

18.1.4   Strings

Often, the programmer of commands deals with strings. Oberon allows strings of varying length to be passed as open array parameters to procedures. The *special symbol 0X terminates the string*.

18.2   Modules and commands

A command is a parameterless procedure written in the language Oberon. The command can be executed from a text displayed in a text viewer. It is referred to by its name which follows the Oberon convention:

> *Mod.Proc*

where *Mod* is the module name and *Proc* designates a procedure exported by *Mod*.

Executing a command results in at least one procedure call. Since the procedure is the indivisible unit of operation in Oberon, no other activity may proceed in parallel with the command. In particular, the event loop is halted and mouse and keyboard are not polled. This means that the mouse cursor is frozen and input from the keyboard is blocked. Therefore, as long as the system should be responsive to the interactive user, *command execution must be short*.

This poses a dilemma for long running computations. Such computations should be made interruptible or, better yet, they should be installed as a task in the event loop.

However, even while a command executes, the Oberon system will react to the CTRL–SHIFT–DEL key combination. It will terminate the command in execution and display a trap viewer.

18.2.1   Dynamic loading

Modules typically export an abstract data type. Since, in Oberon, commands communicate using instances of abstract data types, such as texts, their modules must stay in memory during the entire session. However, it is wasteful if not downright impossible to load *all* modules when the system is booting. Only those modules whose data types or commands are in actual use need to be memory resident. Therefore, Oberon uses *dynamic loading*.

A module is loaded only when one of its exported procedures is called for the first time in a session. Loading of imported modules is further delayed until they are used. On loading, the statement sequence of the module executes. Then, the module stays memory resident.

While debugging a command, the programmer must be aware that a newly compiled module does *not* execute, unless the old module is purged with the command *System.Free* or with an interclick with the left mouse key while the execute key is pressed. If faced for the first time with a dynamic loading system, this may cause the novice some musing.

18.2.2   Statement sequence

A typical use of the statement sequence of the body of a module is the initialization of array or list data structures which cannot be declared as constants. Patterns used for cursors furnish a representative example.

18.3   Working with texts

In this section, we discuss common techniques for dealing with texts. The programmer deals frequently with texts since they have many uses in editors and compilers, and commands use them to display (non-volatile) output.

The reader should have a good understanding of the mechanism used by texts to update their display. We recapitulate that texts are active objects. When a standard text is changed, it broadcasts an update message to all visible viewers which indicates the change. If a viewer displays that text, it will update the display in response to the message. Therefore, the programmer does not have to worry about the display of the text – in fact, he or she does not even have to know the viewers in which the text is displayed. In a sense, Oberon displays texts automatically.

Some frequently occurring constructs are as follows:

System log text	Oberon.Log
Create an empty text	text := TextFrames.Text("");
Create a new text and initialize it from disk file *name*	text := TextFrames.Text(name);
Write to system log	Texts.OpenWriter(W);[1] ... Texts.Write(W, ch); ... Texts.Append(Oberon.Log, W.buf);
Insert buffer *buf* at position *pos* in *text*	Texts.Insert(text, pos, buf);
Append buffer *buf* to *text*	Texts.Append(text, buf);
Read sequential characters	Texts.OpenReader(R, text, pos); ... Texts.Read(R, ch); ...

---

[1] Typically in the body of the module.

Scan sequential symbols	Texts.OpenScanner(S, text, pos); ... Texts.Scan(S); IF S.class = Texts.Int THEN[2] n := S.i (* Process integer *) END; ...
Save stretch [*beg, end*) of *text* in buffer *buf*	NEW(buf); Texts.OpenBuf(buf); Texts.Save(text, beg, end, buf);

18.3.1   Creating a text

Sometimes, the text on which a command works is given, for example the text of the main frame of a text viewer. Often, however, a new instance of a text (a variable of type *Texts.Text*) needs to be created. Recall that *TextFrames.Text* serves this purpose. Its source text is a good way to learn how a text is generated:

```
PROCEDURE Text*(name: ARRAY OF CHAR): Texts.Text;
VAR text: Texts.Text;
BEGIN
    (* Create an instance and install notifier *)
    NEW(text);
    text.notify := TextFrames.NotifyDisplay;
    Texts.Open(text, name); (* Initialize text from file name *)
    RETURN text
END Text;
```

In most cases, *TextFrames.Text* can be used to generate a text. If it is necessary to create an instance of *Texts.Text* explicitly, it is important *not to forget to install the notifier*. Otherwise, addressing exceptions will result.

18.3.2   Reading from a text

A reader is used to access the characters in a text in sequential order. The reader is associated with the text and can be set to an arbitrary initial position. Each call returns a character, one after another.

The following program excerpt is typical for the use of a reader. It processes all the characters in a text, starting at a given position *pos*:

---

[2] Other class codes are *Texts.Char, Texts.Inval, Texts.LongReal, Texts.Name, Texts.Real* and *Texts.String* (see Chapter 14.)

```
PROCEDURE ProcessText(text: Texts.Text; pos: LONGINT);
VAR R: Texts.Reader; ch: CHAR;
BEGIN
    IF pos < text.len THEN (* The position is within the text *)
        Texts.OpenReader(R, text, pos);
        Texts.Read(R, ch);     (* Read character at position pos *)
        WHILE ~R.eot DO
            ...                        (* Process character ch *)
            Texts.Read(R, ch)  (* Read next character *)
        END;
    END
END ProcessText;
```

If it is not guaranteed that the starting position is within the text, a test must be performed as in our example.

Let us look at a complete example of a procedure which is patterned after the preceding program skeleton. The procedure *GetItalics* searches a text from the initial position *pos* for the first occurrence of an italics font. It returns this position, if it exists, otherwise −1 results.

```
PROCEDURE GetItalics(text: Texts.Text; pos: LONGINT): LONGINT;
VAR R: Texts.Reader; ch: CHAR; Syntax10i: Fonts.Font;
BEGIN
    IF pos < text.len THEN
        Syntax10i := Fonts.This("Syntax10i.Scn.Fnt"); (* The italics font *)
        Texts.OpenReader(R, text, pos);
        Texts.Read(R, ch);                              (* Read first character *)
        WHILE ~R.eot DO
            IF R.fnt = Syntax10i THEN RETURN Texts.Pos(R) − 1 END;
            Texts.Read(R, ch)                           (* Read next character *)
        END
    END;
    RETURN − 1
END GetItalics;
```

Observe that we made use of the field *R.fnt* which reports the font of the last character read.

18.3.3   Scanning a text

The reader provides sequential access to the characters comprising a text. Using a reader, texts can be analyzed and processed as shown in the previous example.

A frequently recurring task, however, is parsing a text for numbers, names, strings and special characters and translating the textual representation of these symbols to internal values. The *scanner* is provided to facilitate these jobs.

Scanners are frequently used to parse parameter lists. Examples of such use will be given in Section 18.4. Another typical use is to read numerical parameters from input files.

The basic principle in using a scanner is simple. A symbol is scanned, its type tested and then the appropriate output field of the scanner is further processed:

```
pos := (* Determine starting position *)
Texts.OpenScanner(S, text, pos);  (* Set scanner to starting position *)
Texts.Scan(S);                    (* Scan a symbol *)
IF S.class = Texts.Name THEN      (* Test whether it is a name *)
   name := S.s;
   ...   (* Process name *)
ELSIF S.class = Texts.Int THEN    (* Test whether it is an integer *)
   i := S.i;
   ...   (* Process integer *)
END;
```

where:

```
text: Texts.Text;
pos: LONGINT;
S: Texts.Scanner;
name: ARRAY 32 OF CHAR;
i: INTEGER;
```

Again, if it is not guaranteed that *pos* is within the text, a test must be performed.

If the whole text is to be processed by the scanner, special precautions are required at the end. In the case of a reader *R*, the predicate ~*R.eot* provides a natural stopping condition for the WHILE loop reading all characters of a text. The scanner inherits field *eot* from the reader. However, the end-of-text condition *S.eot* may already yield TRUE while the last valid symbol is returned, not only after an attempt to scan beyond the end of the text. In this case, a WHILE loop using the predicate ~*S.eot* misses the last symbol. Therefore, it is always preferable to terminate a sequence of scan operations with a definite symbol.

18.3.4   Writing a text

The conversion of the internal representation of basic types, such as integers, reals and characters, to textual representation is a frequent operation. The writer performs this conversion using an associated variable of type *Texts.Buffer*. Each call to a write procedure appends the buffer. When a suitable chunk of text is composed, the writer's buffer can be inserted into a text by means of the procedures *Texts.Insert* and *Texts.Append*. At this point, the text's notifier is activated. If it is a standard notifier, it alerts all visible viewers of the change, which will be reflected on the display.

Thus, writing a text to the screen requires:

(1) Installing the text in a viewer and opening that viewer.

(2) Changing the text using a procedure of the text manager.

The manner in which the first is performed will be explained later. In our next example, we will write to the system log. The text *Oberon.Log* already exists and is installed in the log viewer. If the log viewer is visible, then changing the log text will automatically display the change in the system log and all its clones (produced with *System.Copy*, for example.)

Module LogOut   Module *LogOut* exports procedures which write variables to the system log in symbolic form. It is a useful utility for debugging commands.

```
MODULE LogOut;

IMPORT Texts, Oberon;

VAR W: Texts.Writer;

PROCEDURE PutInt*(txt: ARRAY OF CHAR; i: LONGINT);
BEGIN
   Texts.WriteString(W, txt);  (* Append string txt to W.buf *)
   Texts.WriteInt(W, i, 1);      (* Convert i to text and append to W.buf *)
   Texts.WriteLn(W);            (* Append a carriage return character to W.buf *)
   Texts.Append(Oberon.Log, W.buf) (* Display W.buf in log *)
END PutInt;

PROCEDURE PutString*(txt: ARRAY OF CHAR);
BEGIN
   Texts.WriteString(W, txt);  (* Append string txt to W.buf *)
   Texts.WriteLn(W);            (* Append a carriage return character to W.buf *)
   Texts.Append(Oberon.Log, W.buf) (* Display W.buf in log *)
END PutInt;

(* Other procedures for reals etc. *)

BEGIN
   Texts.OpenWriter(W)
END LogOut.
```

After a call:

```
LogOut.PutInt("i =", i)
```

a line "i = 36" (assuming that i = 36) appears at the end of the system log text in the log viewer.

Only one writer per module

The writer is based on the file system. Opening a writer opens a work file – a relatively complex operation. In most cases, one writer per module is enough. It is, therefore, good practice to open the writer once per session in the module's body, as shown in the foregoing example. *Local writers should be avoided.*

Output of a matrix

Our next example deals with the output of a matrix of real numbers. The procedure *MatrixOut* produces a buffer which is returned as result. The buffer can later be inserted into a text by means of *Texts.Insert* or *Texts.Append*. Since these procedures invoke the notifier, the result will be displayed at that point in time.

```
PROCEDURE MatrixOut(VAR A: ARRAY OF ARRAY OF REAL): Texts.Buffer;
VAR
  i, j: INTEGER;
  Syntax10x: Fonts.Font;
BEGIN
  Syntax10x := Fonts.This("Syntax10x.Scn.Fnt");
  Texts.SetFont(W, Syntax10x);
  i := 0;
  WHILE i < LEN(A, 0) DO
    j := 0;
    WHILE j < LEN(A, 1) DO
      Texts.WriteRealFix(W, A[i, j], 15, 5); (* 15 places, 5 decimal places *)
      INC(j)
    END;
    Texts.WriteLn(W);                         (* Write carriage return *)
    INC(i)
  END;
  RETURN W.buf
END MatrixOut;
```

W is a variable of type *Texts.Writer* which is globally defined and opened in the module's body. The formal parameter *A* is a VAR parameter to avoid copying of an array. Compared to the use of a value parameter, this is more efficient and saves memory, too.

18.4   Accessing parameters

In the sense of the programming language Oberon, commands are procedures without formal parameters. This does not mean, of course, that commands have no need for an input mechanism. The command *Edit.Open*, for example, must be told which text file to load from disk. Commands which perform computations are typically parameterized by a number of variables which must be initialized prior to each run.

There are three major sources of parameter information:

(1) The text which contains the command name.

(2) The selection.

(3) The marked viewer.

Module Oberon provides the global variable *Oberon.Par* through which commands gain access to the text and the frames from where they were executed. The following diagram recalls the fields of *Oberon.Par*.

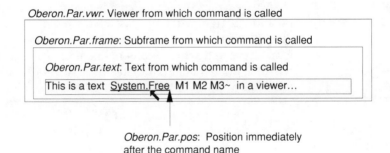

Examining the environment from which a command is invoked allows the design of polymorphic commands. Take *Edit.Store* for example. If executed from the title bar, it stores that viewer. However, if activated from a tool, it operates on the marked viewer and stores it under a name found in the called text.

The following lists ways to locate parameter information and provides tests which are useful in polymorphic commands:

System parameter list	Oberon.Par
Viewer from which command is issued	Oberon.Par.vwr
Frame from which command is issued	Oberon.Par.frame
Text from which command is issued	Oberon.Par.text
Start of parameter list	Oberon.Par.pos

The most recent selection in the system	Oberon.GetSelection(text, beg, end, time)
The marked viewer	Oberon.MarkedViewer( )
Open scanner for parameter list	Text.OpenScanner (S, Oberon.Par.text, Oberon.Par.pos)
Was command issued from a menu frame of any viewer?	IF Oberon.Par.frame = Oberon.Par.vwr.dsc THEN ...

18.4.1   Parameters in the source text

Frequently, the command information follows the command name. The scanner is a powerful tool for decoding the parameters.

List of names   Many standard Oberon commands expect a parameter list composed of blank delimited names, terminated by the character "~". Typically, the names designate files to be processed.

Our first example is the following skeleton of a procedure *ProcessNames* which expects such a list of names. A scanner is opened and positioned right after the last character of the command name. The global variable *Oberon.Par* contains the necessary information. Then a loop is entered which scans name after name in the list. Any symbol which is not a name terminates the list. As in the Oberon implementation, the '~' is not enforced.

```
PROCEDURE ProcessNames*;
VAR S: Texts.Scanner;
BEGIN
    Texts.OpenScanner(S, Oberon.Par.text, Oberon.Par.pos);
    Texts.Scan(S);
    WHILE S.class = Texts.Name DO
        name := S.s;
        ... (* Process object with name S.s *)
        Texts.Scan(S)
    END;
END ProcessNames;
```

Numerical parameters   Our next example is of a different nature. Consider a command *MM1* exported by module Sim which simulates a certain queuing system. This system is parameterized by a real number *Rho*. It is good practice in this case to include hints such as "Rho =" in the parameter text. Our goal is to start a simulation run by clicking with the middle mouse key at the word 'MM1' in a text which may show:

```
Sim.MM1 Rho = 0.9
```

Again, the scanner is used to decode the parameter of the command *MM1*:

```
PROCEDURE MM1*;
VAR
  Rho: REAL;
  S: Texts.Scanner;
  error: BOOLEAN;
  ... (* Other variables *)
BEGIN
  Texts.OpenScanner(S, Oberon.Par.text, Oberon.Par.pos);
  Texts.Scan(S);
  IF ~((S.class = Texts.Name) & (S.s = "Rho")) THEN
      LogOut.PutString("Parameter error"); RETURN
  END;
  Texts.Scan(S);
  IF ~((S.class = Texts.Char) & (S.c = "=")) THEN
      LogOut.PutString("Parameter error"); RETURN
  END;
  Texts.Scan(S);
  IF S.class # Texts.Real THEN
      LogOut.PutString("Parameter error"); RETURN
  END;
  Rho := S.x;
  ... (* Perform simulation *)
END MM1;
```

MM1 tests whether the parameter text is well formed; that is, consists of the name *Rho* followed by the equal sign followed by a real number. In this procedure, the simulation is only performed if the parameter is read properly. Otherwise, a message 'Parameter error' is written to the system log. We recommend such tests, otherwise unpredictable errors may occur.

The two examples show how the scanner is used to decode parameter lists. More complex syntactical structures can be built in a similar manner.

18.4.2   Parameters in the selection

The selection provides a parameter source across viewer boundaries. This is in contrast to the local parameter information contained in the same text adjacent to the command name. The selection is unique only within a text frame. This means that each text viewer may contain two selections at a time, one in the menu frame and one in the main frame.

Commands, therefore, refer to the *most recent selection* in the system which is located by means of a call to *Oberon.GetSelection*.

The selection is used as a parameter in two ways:

(1) The selected text is the object of the command and is changed or otherwise processed. Take *Edit.CopyFont* for example. This command changes the font of the stretch contained in the selection.

(2) The selection contains a name (or list of names) designating objects to be processed. In this case, the selected stretch may be viewed as an extension of the text following the command name.

Edit.Open is an example of a command that operates in this way. It first looks for a parameter on the same text line as the command name. If none is there or if the symbol '↑'[3] terminates the command name, it considers the selection to be an extension and searches it for a name. If none is found, a default applies.

The following sketch of a procedure *ProcessSelection* exhibits the technique to access the selection:

```
PROCEDURE ProcessSelection*;
VAR
   T: Texts.Text;         (* The text of the selection *)
   beg, end: LONGINT; (* The stretch in T which is selected *)
   time: LONGINT;        (* The time of the most recent selection *)
BEGIN
   Oberon.GetSelection(T, beg, end, time);
   IF time > 0 THEN     (* The selection exists *)
      ...                        (* Process selection *)
   END
END ProcessSelection;
```

Note: The test whether *time* > 0 is mandatory since it is not guaranteed that a selection exists.

We are now ready to modify the example *ProcessNames* to comply with the Oberon convention that when the list of names is terminated by the symbol '↑', the selection is scanned for one more name.

```
PROCEDURE ProcessNames*;
VAR
   S: Texts.Scanner;
   text: Texts.Text;
   beg, end, time: LONGINT;
```

---

[3] The code for the upward pointing arrow is 5EX, the ASCII equivalent of '^'.

```
BEGIN
    Texts.OpenScanner(S, Oberon.Par.text, Oberon.Par.pos);
    Texts.Scan(S);
    WHILE S.class = Texts.Name DO
        ...                     (* Process object with name S.s *)
        Texts.Scan(S)
    END;
    IF (S.class = Texts.Char) & (S.c = " ↑ ") THEN
        Oberon.GetSelection(text, beg, end, time);
        IF time > 0 THEN    (* The selection exists *)
            Texts.OpenScanner(S, text, beg);
            Texts.Scan(S);
            IF S.class = Texts.Name THEN
                ...                 (* Process object with name S.s *)
            END
        END
    END
END ProcessNames;
```

18.4.3   The marked viewer as parameter

One of the uses of the star-shaped pointer, technically the cursor *Oberon.Pointer*, is to designate viewers as objects of commands. The marked viewer is available from *Oberon.MarkedViewer( )*.

For example, the following command *Close* closes the marked viewer. Unlike *System.Close*, it tests whether the command has an asterisk as parameter; that is, it enforces the syntax 'Close *'.

```
PROCEDURE Close*;
VAR V: Viewers.Viewer; S: Texts.Scanner;
BEGIN
    Texts.OpenScanner(S, Oberon.Par.text, Oberon.Par.pos);
    Texts.Scan(S);
    IF (S.class = Texts.Char) & (S.c = "*") THEN
        V := Oberon.MarkedViewer( );
        Viewers.Close(V)
    END
END;
```

We recall that the procedure *Oberon.MarkedViewer( )* does not require the pointer to be visible. The programmer may, however, insist on a visible star-shaped pointer with the test:

```
IF Oberon.Pointer.on THEN ...
```

18.5   Working with text viewers

Text viewers play a prominent role in Oberon as:

- The place from where commands are executed.
- The place where programs and simple office texts are edited.
- The means for commands to display textual output.

A programmer attempting to extend Oberon is, therefore, often faced with the task of working with text viewers. To enter this endeavor, a good understanding of the text viewer structure is required. Recall that a text viewer is a menu viewer with two installed text frames.

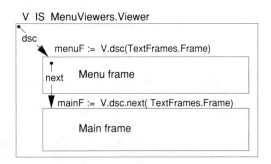

The following summarizes frequently used objects, tests and operations:

Position of star-shaped pointer	X := Oberon.Pointer.X; Y := Oberon.Pointer.Y;
The marked viewer	Oberon.MarkedViewer( )
Position of the mouse	X := Oberon.Mouse.X; Y := Oberon.Mouse.Y;
Viewer which contains mouse	Viewers.This(Oberon.Mouse.X, Oberon.Mouse.Y)
Focus viewer	Oberon.FocusViewer

Is viewer *V* a standard text viewer?	IF (V IS MenuViewers.Viewer) &
	    (V.dsc IS TextFrames.Frame) &
	    (V.dsc.next IS TextFrames.Frame THEN ...

Has viewer *V* a text frame as menu frame?	IF V.dsc IS TextFrames.Frame THEN ...
Has viewer *V* a text frame as main frame?	IF (V.dsc # NIL) & (V.dsc.next IS TextFrames.Frame) THEN
The menu frame of a text viewer *V*	V.dsc(TextFrames.Frame)
The menu text of a text viewer	V.dsc(TextFrames.Frame).text

The main frame of a text viewer	V.dsc.next(TextFrames.Frame)
The main text of a text viewer	V.dsc.next(TextFrames.Frame).text
The most recent selection	Oberon.GetSelection(text, beg, end, time)
Is the command executed from the menu frame?	V := Oberon.Par.vwr; IF (Oberon.Par.frame IS TextFrames.Frame) & (V.dsc = Oberon.Par.frame) THEN
Placement of the viewer in the user track of the display which contains the mouse	Oberon.AllocateUserViewer(Oberon.Mouse.X, X, Y);
Placement of the viewer in the system track of the display which contains the mouse	Oberon.AllocateSystemViewer(Oberon.Mouse.X, X, Y);

Open a new text viewer: *X* and *Y* are determined by *AllocateUserViewer* or *AllocateSystemViewer*	text := TextFrames.Text(name);
	V := MenuViewers.New(
	   TextFrames.NewMenu(name, commands),
	   TextFrames.NewText(text, 0),
	   TextFrames.menuH, X, Y);

18.5.1   Processing the text of the main frame

Obviously, the text displayed in the main frame of a text viewer *V* is frequently the operand of commands. It is the value of *V.dsc.next(TextFrames.Frame).text*. In many cases, however, it is not guaranteed that the viewer is a text viewer. It is, therefore, required that prior to an attempt to access the text a type test be performed:

```
IF (V.dsc # NIL) & (V.dsc.next IS TextFrames.Frame) THEN
    ... (* Process text *)
END;
```

Let us elaborate a more ambitious example. The command *CopyFont* copies the font of the character underneath the star-shaped pointer to the selection. Besides accessing the text of a viewer, this example illustrates various techniques:

- How to deal with the pointer and the marked viewer.
- The use of the selection as operand of the command.
- The use of texts and readers.
- The use of several functions from the display manager of module TextFrames.

We first access the selection. If it exists, the text of the marked viewer is located (*Viewers.This.*) The position of the pointer is correlated with the text position (*TextFrames.Pos*) and that character read. Once

read, its font attribute is deduced and applied to the selection
(*Text.ChangeLooks.*)

```
PROCEDURE CopyFont*;
VAR
  F: TextFrames.Frame;
  T: Texts.Text;
  R: Texts.Reader;
  V: Viewers.Viewer;
  beg, end, time: LONGINT; (* Time and stretch of selection *)
  X, Y: INTEGER; (* A position designated by the pointer *)
  pos: LONGINT; (* The character equivalent of X, Y *)
  ch: CHAR;
BEGIN
  Oberon.GetSelection(T, beg, end, time); (* Most recent selection *)
  IF (time > 0) (* Selection exists *)
  & Oberon.Pointer.on (* Pointer is visible *) THEN
    X := Oberon.Pointer.X; Y := Oberon.Pointer.Y;
    V := Viewers.This(X, Y); (* The viewer which contains the pointer *)
    IF (V.dsc # NIL) & (V.dsc.next IS TextFrames.Frame) THEN
      (* Second frame is a text frame *)
      F := V.dsc.next(TextFrames.Frame); (* The main frame *)
      IF (X >= F.X) & (X < F.X + F.W) & (Y >= F.Y) & (Y < F.Y + F.H) THEN
        (* The pointer is in the main frame *)
        pos := TextFrames.Pos(F, X, Y); (* Convert X, Y to text position *)
        IF pos >= 0 THEN
          (* Position is valid *)
          Texts.OpenReader(R, F.text, pos);
          Texts.Read(R, ch); (* Read character at pos to access its font *)
          Texts.ChangeLooks(T, beg, end, {0}, R.fnt, 0, 0)
          (* the font of the stretch [beg, end) is changed and
             the display is updated *)
        END
      END
    END
  END
END CopyFont;
```

Due to the active nature of the text, we do not have to know the
viewers which show the changed text *T*. When *T* is changed, it broadcasts an update message to all visible viewers which refresh the
display.

Writing to a
viewer

Once the text of a viewer is accessed, its characteristics may be changed
(as in the foregoing example) or output may be added to the text with
Texts.Append or *Texts.Insert* and displayed in the viewer. This works
exactly as in the example of the module *LogOut*.

18.5.2   Commands which open viewers

In the previous example, the command operated on the text of a viewer which is already displayed. Another situation arises when a command produces textual output which is ready for display. We encountered a first example in module *LogOut* and its procedures which write to the system log. The system log, however, is reserved for short status reports of commands. If the command has more voluminous output, it needs to open a text viewer. *Commands communicate through texts* and refrain from writing to the screen directly.

The following steps are typical to open a text viewer:

(1) Create the menu frame using *TextFrames.NewMenu*.

(2) Create the text of the main frame (often *TextFrames.Text* is helpful.)

(3) Create the main frame using *TextFrames.NewText*.

(4) Determine a point *X*, *Y* on the top edge of the viewer to be opened, using *Oberon.AllocateUserViewer* if the viewer should open in the user track, otherwise *Oberon.AllocateSystemViewer*.

(5) Open the viewer with *MenuViewers.New* such that its top edge contains *X*, *Y*.

Placement proposition

To open a viewer means to reduce the space of an existing one (possibly the filler viewer.) Where to place a new viewer may depend on various considerations. In most cases, the procedures *Oberon.AllocateUserViewer* and *Oberon.AllocateSystemViewer* are used to make a placement suggestion in the user track and the system track, respectively. *Oberon.AllocateUserViewer* is typically called as follows:

```
Oberon.AllocateUserViewer(Oberon.Mouse.X, X, Y);
```

The first actual parameter determines that the new viewer will open in the display which contains the mouse cursor. Thus, if a second display is present (color), the user can control whether the new viewer will appear in the user track of the monochrome or color display. If:

```
Oberon.AllocateUserViewer(Display.Left, X, Y);
```

is used, then the viewer will always open on the monochrome display. The VAR parameters *X* and *Y* return the placement proposition which is in turn used in the call of *MenuViewers.New*.

Let us recall *MatrixOut* which produced a buffer containing the textual representation of a matrix of real numbers. We will use *Matrix-Out* in our next example which represents a command *InvertMatrix*. As its name implies, a matrix of real numbers is inverted. Once the inverse is computed, *MatrixOut* is used to format the output and a new text viewer is opened to display the results.

```
PROCEDURE InvertMatrix*;
CONST origin = 0;
VAR
   menuF, mainF: TextFrames.Frame;
   matrixText: Texts.Text; (* Text of the main frame *)
   V: MenuViewers.Viewer;
BEGIN
   Invert(A, B); (* A procedure which inverts A and stores result in B *)
   matrixText := TextFrames.Text(""); (* Create empty text *)
   Texts.Append(matrixText, MatrixOut(B)); (* Create display text *)
   menuF := TextFrames.NewMenu("Matrix.Output",
      "System.Close  System.Copy  System.Grow  Edit.Store");
   mainF := TextFrames.NewText(matrixText, origin);
   Oberon.AllocateUserViewer(Oberon.Mouse.X, X, Y); (* Placement *)
   V := MenuViewers.New(menuF, mainF, TextFrames.menuH, X, Y)
END InvertMatrix;
```

Variables *A* and *B* are externally defined and are of type ARRAY N, N OF REAL. A writer *W* used by the procedure *MatrixOut* is also externally defined and opened in the module's body.

At first sight, it might be surprising that the viewer *V*, created by *InvertMatrix*, is a local variable. What happens is that *MenuViewers.New* creates the viewer's descriptor and calls the viewer manager to insert it in its data structure of visible viewers. The fact that the viewer is in this structure protects it from falling prey to the garbage collector.

18.5.3   The Open command, custom menu

The standard title bar of Oberon text viewers (also termed the *menu*) contains the viewer name and the commands *System.Close*, *System.Copy*, *System.Grow*, *Edit.Search* and *Edit.Store*. This choice is well tried in practice. However, a user may wish to change this convention for several reasons; for example:

- Other commands are used frequently (for example, *Edit.Recall*.)
- The viewer performs a special task whose commands should appear in the title bar.

The command *Net.Mailbox* opens such a specialized text viewer (see Chapter 7.) Its title bar shows the commands *Net.ReceiveMail* and *Net.DeleteMail* which both operate on the text displayed in the mailbox viewer. Note, however, that it is still a standard text viewer and not an instance of a new viewer class.

   To open text viewers with a different set of commands in the title bar, the user needs to provide his or her own *Open* command. We shall portray a command *Open* which replaces the menu command *Edit.Search* with *Edit.Recall*. A scanner first scans the text after the command. If a name is found it is opened. On the other hand, if the scanned symbol equals " ↑ ", the selection is scanned for the name. If none is found, a default applies. Once the name is determined, a text viewer is opened.

```
PROCEDURE Open*;
CONST origin = 0;
VAR
   S: Texts.Scanner;
   menuF, mainF: TextFrames.Frame;
   mainT: Texts.Text;
   X, Y: INTEGER;
   beg, end, time: LONGINT;
   V: MenuViewers.Viewer;
BEGIN
   Texts.OpenScanner(S, Oberon.Par.text, Oberon.Par.pos);
   Texts.Scan(S); (* Scan symbol immediately after command name *)
   IF S.class # Texts.Name THEN
      S.s := "Temp.Text";           (* Default name *)
      IF (S.class = Texts.Char) & (S.c = " ↑ ") THEN
         (* The scanned symbol is " ↑ " *)
         Oberon.GetSelection(text, beg, end, time);
         IF time > 0 THEN           (* Selection exists *)
            Texts.OpenScanner(S, text, beg);
            Texts.Scan(S)          (* Scan for name in selection *)
         END
      END
   END;
   mainT := TextFrames.Text(S.s); (* Open text S.s from disk *)
   mainF := TextFrames.NewText(mainT, origin);
   menuF := TextFrames.NewMenu(S.s,
      "System.Close System.Copy System.Grow Edit.Recall Edit.Store");
   Oberon.AllocateUserViewer(Oberon.Mouse.X, X, Y);
   V := MenuViewers.New(menuF, mainF, TextFrames.menuH, X, Y)
END Open;
```

18.5.4 Menu commands

The menu frame of a text viewer is an ordinary text frame. Any command can be issued from the menu in the same way as it is executed from the main frame. However, it turns out that commands issued from the menu frame (the title bar) are most useful if they implicitly refer to the viewer which contains the menu frame. Therefore, commands intended to be used in the menu should be polymorphic; that is, they should differentiate between whether they were activated from a menu frame or from a main frame. *Edit.Store* is an example. Issued from the menu, it operates on the viewer containing that particular menu. Issued from a main frame, it requests a name parameter and stores the marked viewer under that name.

A menu frame is defined to be a text frame linked to viewer *V* by *V.dsc*. Whether a command was issued from the menu can be learned from the fields of *Oberon.Par*:

```
IF (Oberon.Par.frame IS TextFrames.Frame) &
   (Oberon.Par.frame = Oberon.Par.vwr.dsc) THEN ...
```

As an example, consider the following excerpt of a command *ProcessText* which operates on texts. If the command is issued from an editable text (for example, a tool text), it admits a parameter list. All texts in the list will be processed. If, on the other hand, *ProcessText* is issued from the menu, it will work on the text contained in the main frame of the viewer which contains the menu.

```
PROCEDURE ProcessText*;
VAR
    text: Texts.text; (* Text to be processed *)
    V: Viewers.Viewer; S: Texts.Scanner;
BEGIN
    V := Oberon.Par.vwr;
    IF (Oberon.Par.frame IS TextFrames.Frame) &
       (Oberon.Par.frame = V.dsc)THEN
       (* Command is issued from the menu *)
       IF (V.dsc # NIL) & (V.dsc.next IS TextFrames.Frame) THEN
          (* The second frame of viewer is a text frame *)
          text := Oberon.Par.vwr.dsc.next(TextFrames.Frame).text;
          ... (* Process text *)
       END
    ELSE   (* Command issued from an editable text frame *)
       Texts.OpenScanner(S, Oberon.Par.text, Oberon.Par.pos);
       Scan(S);
       WHILE S.class = Texts.Name DO
          text := TextFrames.Text(S.s); (* Open text from file with name S.s*)
          ... (* Process text *)
          Scan(S)
       END
    END
END ProcessText;
```

18.6 Working with text frames

Text frames embody the standard Oberon editor. Module TextFrames exports a set of procedures called display manager. If the programmer of commands wishes to deal with the selection, the caret or with scrolling operations, the services of the display manager are needed. Using these facilities, the commands of module Edit (for example, *Edit.Search, Edit.CopyFont, Edit.Recall*) may be augmented.

The following summarizes frequently used tests and operations:

Has viewer *V* a main frame?	IF (V.dsc # NIL) & (V.dsc.next IS TextFrames.Frame) THEN
The focus viewer	Oberon.FocusViewer
Text of text frame *F*	F.text
Position of first displayed character	F.org
A caret is set in text frame *F*	IF F.car # 0 THEN ...
Position of the caret, if one is set	IF F.car # 0 THEN pos : = F.carloc.pos END;
A selection exists in text frame *F*	IF F.sel # 0 THEN ...
Start of the selection, if one exists	IF F.sel # 0 THEN pos : = F.selbeg.pos END;
End of the selection, if one exists	IF F.sel # 0 THEN pos : = F.selend.pos END;
Set the caret at *pos* in text frame *F* installed in menu viewer *V*	Oberon.PassFocus(V); TextFrames.SetCaret(F, pos);
Select stretch [*beg, end*) in text frame *F*	TextFrames.SetSelection(F, beg, end);
Scroll text such that line with origin at *org* will be displayed on top of the viewer	TextFrames.RemoveSelection(F); TextFrames.RemoveCaret(F); Oberon.RemoveMarks(F.X, F.Y, F.W, F.H); TextFrames.Show(F, org);

The following points should be kept in mind when using procedures of the display manager operating on a text frame *F*:

- A caret is only allowed if the viewer which manages *F* is the focus viewer.
- If a caret is displayed (*F.car* > 0), it must be removed prior to using *TextFrames.SetCaret*.
- Prior to using *TextFrames.Show*, the caret, the selection, the mouse cursor and the pointer must be removed.

The caret is removed either by a call of *TextFrames.Remove-Caret(F)* or as a consequence of *Oberon.PassFocus(V)*. Thus, if the focus has to be requested, a call to *TextFrames.RemoveCaret* is superfluous.

As a first example, we examine the command *Edit.Recall* which inserts the most recently deleted stretch of text at the caret location.

```
PROCEDURE Recall*;
VAR
  F: TextFrames.Frame;
  buf: Texts.Buffer;
  V: Viewers.Viewer;
  pos: LONGINT;
BEGIN
  V := Oberon.FocusViewer;
  IF (V.dsc # NIL) & (V.dsc.next IS TextFrames.Frame) THEN
    (* Focus viewer has a main frame which is a text frame *)
    F := V.dsc.next(TextFrames.Frame); (* The main frame *)
    IF F.car > 0 THEN                    (* A caret is set *)
      Texts.Recall(buf); (* The most recently deleted text *)
      pos := F.carloc.pos + buf.len;       (* Caret position after insert *)
      Texts.Insert(F.text, F.text.carloc.pos, buf);
      TextFrames.SetCaret(F, pos)
    END
  END
END Recall;
```

Note that since *V* is the focus viewer, there is no need to request the focus through a call to *Oberon.PassFocus*. The call of *Texts.Insert* invokes the handler which updates the display. In doing so, it clears the caret, the precondition for *TextFrames.SetCaret*.

A further example is a command *SearchItalics*. The text of the main frame of the marked viewer is searched for the occurrence of a character in the italics font *Syntax10i.Scn.Fnt*. The search is started at the caret position or at the beginning of the text if no caret is set. If a character is located, the text is scrolled such that it is displayed near the top line and the caret is positioned.

Command *SearchItalics* uses procedure *GetItalics* developed in a previous example. An ancillary problem arises. If *TextFrames.Show(F, pos)* is called with a position which is not the origin of a line, the line *after pos* will be the first one displayed. Therefore, we invoke *TextFrames.Pos(F, pos − 200)* which positions the text near the top.

```
PROCEDURE SearchItalics*;
VAR
  V: Viewers.Viewer;
  pos, carPos: LONGINT;
  F: TextFrames.Frame;
```

```
BEGIN
  V := Oberon.MarkedViewer( );
  IF (V.dsc # NIL) & (V.dsc.next IS TextFrames.Frame) THEN
    (* Marked viewer has a main frame which is a text frame *)
    F := V.dsc.next(TextFrames.Frame); (* The main frame *)
    IF F.car # 0 THEN (* A caret is displayed *)
      carPos := F.carloc.pos
    ELSE
      carPos := 0
    END;
    pos := GetItalics(F.text, carPos);
    IF pos < 0 THEN RETURN (* No italics font found *)
    ELSE
      Oberon.PassFocus(V);   (* Request focus, clear caret if one is set *)
      TextFrames.RemoveSelection(F);
      Oberon.RemoveMarks(F.X, F.Y, F.W, F.H);
      TextFrames.Show(F, pos − 200); (* Scroll viewer *)
      TextFrames.SetCaret(F, pos)       (* Set the caret *)
    END
  END
END SearchItalics;
```

18.7   Working with files

The Oberon file system differs from the standard model. The user has to be especially aware that the name of a file (that is, an instance of the abstract data type *Files.File*) and the directory entry are distinct. Also, the procedure *Close* differs from its ordinary meaning. Let us recapitulate the major characteristics which have to be kept in mind when working with Oberon files:

- Files and directory entries are distinct entities.

- Files are created with a name. In the case of a new file, the name must be explicitly registered in the directory (if the file is not a temporary one.)

- The access mechanism is separated from the file and embodied in the abstract data type *Files.Rider*. Several riders may operate on the same file.

- Physical data is never purged during a session. As long as a variable of type *File* exists, it affords access to its data.

- Unused disk sectors (not belonging to a file registered in the directory) are reclaimed when the system is booting.

The following lists some useful constructs:

Open a new file *name*	F := Files.New (name);
Open an existing file *name*	F := Files.Old (name);
Write buffers to disk sectors	Files.Close (F);
Write buffers to disk and register file *F* in directory	Files.Register (F);
Sequential read access through rider *R*	Files.Set (R, F, 0); Files.Read (R, ch); Files.Read (R, ch); ...
Sequential write access through rider *R*	Files.Set (R, F, 0); Files.Write (R, ch); Files.Write (R, ch); ...
Random access at position *pos*	Files.Set (R, F, pos); Files.Read (R, ch); ... Files.Write(R, ch);
Read/write a record *A* of type *T*	Files.ReadBytes (R, A, SIZE(T)); Files.WriteBytes (R, A, SIZE(T));
Read/write a record of type *T* accessed with a pointer *P*	Files.ReadBytes (R, P↑, SIZE(T)); Files.WriteBytes (R, P↑, SIZE(T));

8.7.1   Opening and closing of files

Opening a file means creating an instance of type *Files.File*. If the file already exists, *Files.Old* creates such an instance. Otherwise, *Files.New* is used.

The first example covers the simplest case: the file exists, is opened, processed and then closed. In this case, *Files.Close* is used since the directory entry is already in existence.

```
PROCEDURE ProcessFile(name: ARRAY OF CHAR);
VAR file: Files.File;
BEGIN
    file := Files.Old (name); (* Create file variable from directory entry name *)
    IF file = NIL THEN        (* No entry name exists in the directory *)
        ...                   (* Exception handling *)
    ELSE
        ...                   (* Process file *)
        Files.Close (file)    (* Write buffers to disk *)
END;
```

Note, however, that unlike the close operation in other systems, *the file F is still valid after Files.Close is called* and read/write operations can be performed. The file is valid as long as its variable exists.

Sometimes, a command will attempt to open an old file and, if none exists, create a new one. The corresponding program text looks as follows:

```
PROCEDURE ProcessFile(name: ARRAY OF CHAR);
VAR file: Files.File;
BEGIN
   file := Files.Old(name);      (* Create file from directory *)
   IF file = NIL THEN            (* No entry in directory *)
      file := Files.New(name)    (* Create new file *)
   END;
   ...                           (* Process file *)
   Files.Register(file);         (* Write buffers to disk and register file *)
END;
```

Here, it is not certain that the file name is already in the directory. Therefore, *Files.Close* must be replaced by *Files.Register* which also closes the file and, in addition, writes an entry into the directory. Thus, in the event the file already existed, it will be closed. On the other hand, the newly created file will be closed and registered.

Initialize data structure

It is quite typical for files to be used to initialize a data structure, often an instance of an abstract data type such as a text, graphic, bitmap, spreadsheet etc. The following is an example of how an open procedure for such a data structure X of hypothetical type *DataStructure* may read:

```
PROCEDURE Open(X: DataStructure; name: ARRAY OF CHAR);
VAR file: Files.File;
BEGIN
   file := Files.Old(name); (* Create a file from the directory *)
   IF file = NIL THEN
      (* No such file exists *)
      ...                       (* Create a new instance of the data structure X *)
   ELSE
      ...                       (* Read data from disk and build X *)
   END
END Open;
```

Note that the data structure needs to be mapped on to the file. It typically consists of a header followed by descriptors and data blocks. An example is given in Section 18.7.3.

Save with back-up

Recall that commands such as *Edit.Store*, which save a data structure to disk, rename the old file if it is overwritten. This allows the user to undo an erroneous change. A program excerpt which retains a back-up of the old copy while saving the data structure is as follows:

```
PROCEDURE Save(X: DataStructure; name: ARRAY OF CHAR);
VAR
  file: Files File;
  backupName: ARRAY 32 OF CHAR;
  res: INTEGER;
BEGIN
  file := Files.New(name);        (* Create an output file *)
  ...                             (* Write data structure to file *)
  Backup(name, backupName); (* Create a backup name *)
  Files.Rename(name, backupName, res);
  Files.Register(file)            (* Register the newly created output file *)
END;
```

The data structure is written to a new file, even if it was initialized from an old file *name*. The directory entry *name* is first changed to a back-up name derived from *name* and then the new file is registered. If a file *name* existed prior to the call to *Save*, it is still available under the back-up name.

The procedure *Files.Rename* returns a result variable *res* which may be decoded as follows:

```
CASE res OF
    0:          (* Normal termination *)
  | 1: ...      (* New name existed already *)
  | 2: ...      (* Old name is not in directory *)
  | 3: ...      (* Name is not well formed *)
  | 4: ...      (* Name is too long *)
END;
```

Back-up name   A suggestion for the procedure *Backup* which derives a back-up name from the original file name is:

```
PROCEDURE Backup(VAR name; bak: ARRAY OF CHAR);
VAR i, j: INTEGER;
BEGIN
  i := 0; j := 0;
  LOOP
    WHILE (name[i] # 0X) & (name[i] # ".") DO INC(i) END;
    IF name[i] = 0X THEN EXIT END;
    INC(i);
    WHILE j # i DO bak[j] := name[j]; INC(j) END
  END;
  bak[j] := "B"; bak[j + 1] := "a"; bak[j + 2] := "k"; bak[j + 3] := 0X
END Backup;
```

The procedure *Backup* substitutes "Bak" for the file suffix; for example, *Backup*("Test.Mod", *backup*) yields *backup* = "Test.Bak". The character 0X is used to terminate a string.

18.7.2   Read/write operations of files

Read/write operations are performed with a rider. Several riders may operate on the same file. A single byte is read or written by means of a call to *Files.Read* and *Files.Write*. Whole blocks are processed by *Files.ReadBytes* and *Files.WriteBytes*.

Sequential access   File data is accessed sequentially by means of a sequence of *Read* or *Write* calls to the rider *R*, viz.

```
VAR
    R: Files.Rider;
    F: Files.File;
    ch: CHAR;

Files.Set (R, F, 0);  (* Position rider R at the beginning of the file F *)
Files.Read (R, ch); (* Read first byte *)
Files.Read (R, ch); (* Read second byte *)
    . . .
```

Random access   Random access is achieved with a pair of procedure calls *Set* followed by *Read* or *Write*:

```
VAR
    R: Files.Rider;
    F: Files.File;
    ch: CHAR;

Files.Set (R, F, 0);   (* Position rider R at the beginning of the file F *)
Files.Read(R, ch);     (* Read first byte *)

pos := 10;
Files.Set(R, F, pos); (* Position rider *)
Files.Read(R, ch);    (* Read eleventh byte *)

pos := Files.Length (F);
Files.Set(R, F, pos); (* Position rider *)
Files.Write(R, ch);   (* Append a byte to the end of the file F *)
    . . .
```

Note: Numbering of bytes in the file starts with 0.

Record types   In the following example, we update a file which contains records of type *Person*. All records are read sequentially, processed and rewritten to the same position in the file. Whole records are read and written using the procedures *Files.ReadBytes* and *Files.WriteBytes*.

```
TYPE Person = RECORD
    Name: ARRAY 32 OF CHAR;
    ... (* Other fields *)
END;

PROCEDURE UpdateFile(F: Files.File);
CONST beginning = 0;
VAR
    Customer: Person;
    readR, writeR: Files.Rider;
BEGIN
    F := Files.Old(name);
    IF F = NIL THEN LogOut.PutString("file does not exist"); RETURN END;

    Files.Set(readR, F, beginning);
    Files.Set(writeR, F, beginning);
    Files.ReadBytes(readR, Customer, SIZE(Person));
    WHILE ~readR.eof DO
        ... (* Process Customer record *)
        Files.WriteBytes(writeR, Customer, SIZE(Person));
        Files.ReadBytes(readR, Customer, SIZE(Person))
    END;
    Files.Register(file)
END UpdateFile;
```

This example shows how two riders operating on the same file can be used. The rider, *readR*, reads records sequentially. The rider, *writeR*, trails *readR* and updates the record in place.

Observe the use of the function *SIZE* to determine the number of bytes in a record. The use of *SIZE* is preferable to using numeric constants.

If a record is read or written as an aggregate (that is, with *ReadBytes(readR, Customer, SIZE(Person))*), it can only be read subsequently if the compiler mapping the aggregate is the same as the one used when writing. Field-wise reading (or writing) is less implementation dependent.

```
Files.WriteBytes(writeR, Customer.Name, LEN(Customer.Name));
Files.WriteBytes(writeR, ... (* Other fields *)
```

Records accessed through pointers

Often, records are stored on the heap and accessed through pointers. In this case, it is *important to dereference the pointer* in the read and write procedures. The dereferencing operator is the upward pointing arrow '↑'.[4]

```
TYPE
   Person = POINTER TO PersonDesc;
   PersonDesc = RECORD
      Name: ARRAY 32 OF CHAR;
      ... (* Other fields *)
   END;
VAR Customer: Person;
   ...
   Files.Read(readR, Customer↑, SIZE (PersonDesc));
   Files.Write(writeR, Customer↑, SIZE (PersonDesc));
```

Array types

The following procedure *ReadMatrix* initializes a two-dimensional array of reals from a file. It is assumed that the number of rows and columns are recorded at the beginning of the file.

```
PROCEDURE ReadMatrix(VAR A: ARRAY OF ARRAY OF REAL;
                     file: Files.File);
VAR
   R: Files.Rider;
   M, N: INTEGER;                      (* Row and column number *)
   i, j: INTEGER;
BEGIN
   Files.Set(R, file, 0);              (* Set rider R at file origin *)
   Files.ReadBytes(R, M, SIZE (INTEGER)); (* Initialize M *)
   Files.ReadBytes(R, N, SIZE (INTEGER)); (* Initialize N *)
   i := 0;
   WHILE i < M DO
      j := 0;
      WHILE j < N DO
         Files.ReadBytes(R, A[i, j], SIZE(REAL));
         INC (j)
      END;
      INC (i)
   END
END ReadMatrix;
```

---

[4] The code for the upward pointing arrow is 5EX, the ASCII equivalent of '^'.

Procedure *ReadMatrix* reads the array element-wise. Using *Files.ReadBytes*, the array can be initialized with a single procedure call. Assume that *A* is of type *Matrix* which specifies a two-dimensional array of reals. Then:

```
Files.ReadBytes(R, M, SIZE (INTEGER)); (* Initialize M *)
Files.ReadBytes(R, N, SIZE (INTEGER));  (* Initialize N *)
Files.ReadBytes(R, A, SIZE (Matrix));
```

This technique may, however, waste disk space if the actual array bounds *M* and *N* are not of a size close to the maximum value specified in the declaration of type *Matrix*. Also, files written in the abbreviated manner can only be read if the implementations use the same array mapping. In this respect, element-wise reading and writing is less implementation dependent.

18.7.3　A note on complex file organizations

Complex data structures require a corresponding file organization. Such organizations can be built using the primitive functions exported by module *Files*.

Using an electronic mail system, many small text files arise. It is wasteful and tedious to maintain such a collection of file names. The need arises to store mail in a repository.

Our next example is a complete module MailFile which provides such a repository. The file organization is shown in the following diagram.

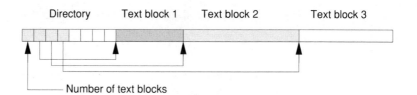

Text files are stored as contiguous data blocks. Prior to text data is a directory which is an array of integers. The first word in the directory indicates the number of texts in the file. It is followed by contiguous records of the starting positions of corresponding text blocks.

Module *Texts* provides the procedures *Texts.Load* and *Texts.Store* which transfer text blocks to and from disk. To append a text block to a file, the rider is positioned at the file before the block is written. Note the offset of 2 required in *Texts.Load* (see Chapter 14.)

```
MODULE MailFile;

IMPORT Texts, Files;

CONST max = 200;

TYPE Directory = ARRAY max OF LONGINT;

PROCEDURE Store(text: Texts.Text; file: Files.File; VAR res: INTEGER);
VAR
   dir: Directory;
   R: Files.Rider;
   pos, len: LONGINT;
BEGIN
   res := 0; (* Result code for normal termination *)
   Files.Set(R, file, 0); (* Set rider at beginning of file *)
   Files.ReadBytes(R, dir, SIZE(Directory)); (* Read directory *)
   INC (dir[0]); (* Increment the number of files *)
   IF dir[0] >= max THEN
      res := 1; (* Result code for directory overflow *)
      RETURN
   END;
   pos := Files.Length(file);
   Texts.Store(text, file, pos, len); (* Append a text block to file *)
   dir[dir[0]] := pos; (* Record directory entry *)
   Files.Set(R, file, 0); (* Reset rider at beginning of file *)
   Files.WriteBytes(R, dir, SIZE(Directory)) (* Write modified directory *)
END Store;


PROCEDURE Fetch (i: INTEGER; file: Files.File; text: Texts.Text;
                      VAR res: INTEGER);
VAR
   dir: Directory;
   R: Files.Rider;
   pos, len: LONGINT;
BEGIN
   res := 0; (* Result code for normal termination *)
   Files.Set(R, file, 0); (* Set rider at beginning of file *)
   Files.ReadBytes(R, dir, SIZE(Directory)); (* Read directory *)
   IF i > dir[0] THEN
      res := 1; (* Result code for out of range position parameter i *)
      RETURN
   END;
   pos := dir[i] + 2; (* Starting position of text block *)
   Texts.Load(text, file, pos, len) (* Initialize text *)
END Store;

... (* Further procedures, in particular commands *)

END MailFile.
```

Our example only illustrates the procedures to add a text block to the file and to fetch a text block given its index number. For a complete application, commands have to be added to open a new repository file, to access the text coming from the mail system and to provide a variety of search functions.

18.7.4   Operating on groups of files

Commands which operate on groups of files can be a significant help in maintaining files. For example, one might want to back up all files which were changed in a given working day.

We recall that the command *System.Directory* opens a text viewer with name 'System.Directory.' The text displayed in this viewer contains a list of files which match a template. Date, time and size may be optionally obtained. The text of this viewer can be accessed as any displayed text (see Section 18.3) and processed by means of a scanner. For example, the file list may be sorted according to name, time or size.

Sometimes, opening a viewer is not adequate. In this case the procedure *FileDir.Enumerate* of module FileDir is needed. FileDir is part of the inner core and thus the following discussion should be considered an advanced topic.

Enumerate

PROCEDURE Enumerate(prefix: ARRAY OF CHAR; Handle: EntryHandler);

All directory entries whose name start with *prefix* are processed. For each matching entry, the procedure *Handle* is invoked. *Handle* is of type:

TYPE EntryHandler = PROCEDURE(name: FileDir.FileName;
                    sector: DiskAdr; VAR cont: BOOLEAN);

Within the scope of the handler, the formal parameter *name* corresponds to the name of the directory entry, *sector* is the address of the first disk sector of the file and *cont* controls the enumeration operation. As long as *cont* = TRUE at the point of return, the enumeration proceeds. If *cont* = FALSE, the enumeration is terminated.

Important note: The handler **must not change the directory** while *Enumerate* runs. Otherwise, the disk may become inconsistent and data may be lost permanently.

The following example prints a list of file names in the system log.

```
MODULE FileList;
IMPORT FileDir,

PROCEDURE * Handle(name: FileDir.FileName; adr: FileDir.DiskAdr;
                   cont: BOOLEAN);
BEGIN
  LogOut.PutString(name);
  cont := TRUE
END Handle;

PROCEDURE Show*;
BEGIN
  FileDir.Enumerate("", Handle)
END Show;

... (* Further procedures *)
END FileList.
```

18.8 Long running commands, background tasks

While control is in a command, the Oberon system ceases to admit input from the mouse and keyboard. This interferes notably with the responsiveness of the system, if the processing time of commands exceeds a certain threshold, which is around a tenth of a second. The reader is most likely familiar with the interrupts produced by disk access and compilations.

Besides commands which run for a few tenths of a second to a few seconds, there is a class of very long running commands, such as numerically intensive computation and system simulation. Fortunately, it is often quite easy to design such programs so that they can be interrupted and restarted. With such a design, it will be possible to:

- Make the very long running command interruptible in a controlled way.

- Run the very long running command in the background, thus preserving an interactive system for the user who can simultaneously perform other activities.

Other applications of background tasks are:

- An animated display; for example, a running clock.

- Servers which need to react to network traffic.

18.8.1   Setting the arrow mark

Any command running longer that about a tenth of a second should show a busy viewer mark. According to Oberon conventions, this mark is a downward pointing arrow in the lower left corner of the viewer. This alerts the user to be patient. The pattern for the arrow is exported by module Display in the global variable *Display.downArrow* and can be drawn using *Display.CopyPattern*.

If the frame enclosing the lower left corner is a text frame, then the procedure *TextFrames.Mark* can be used to display the arrow mark as shown in the following example of a command *Process.Text*, which performs some lengthy computation with the text of a text viewer.

```
PROCEDURE ProcessText*;
CONST arrow = −1; position = 1;
VAR mainF: TextFrames.Frame;
BEGIN
  V := Oberon.Par.vwr;
  IF (V.dsc NL) & (V.dsc.next IS TextFrames.Frame) THEN
    mainF := V.dsc.next(TextFrames.Frame);
    TextFrames.Mark(mainF, arrow);    (* Show busy arrow *)
    ... (* Decode parameter list and process text files *)
    TextFrames.Mark(mainF, position)  (* Restore position mark *)
  END
END ProcessText;
```

18.8.2   Very long running commands in the foreground

Some computations may monopolize the system for arbitrarily long periods of time and shut down interaction with the user. Unless special precautions are taken, the only communication left is CTRL–SHIFT–DEL, to halt their execution. A more controlled interruption is clearly desirable.

Key is a design which provides interrupt/restart points. In system simulations, for example, such restart points are naturally available. Numerical programs too can often be made interruptible without undue difficulty.

In our next example, we show how to make a simulation interruptible from the keyboard. Since the Oberon loop is halted, the keyboard must be read directly using *Input.Read*. Note that this is the only exception to the rule, that the keyboard is exclusively handled through the event loop. When the simulation runs, pressing the "s" key will interrupt it and return control to the user.

The command *Setup* will read parameters and set up a run which is started with *Simulation*. The run may be interrupted by pressing the "s" key. Subsequent activation of *Simulation* continues the run.

```
MODULE Sim;

IMPORT Oberon, Texts, LogOut, Input, ...;

VAR
    interval: LONGINT;      (* Number of steps performed
                               between checkpoints *)
    stepCnt: LONGINT;
    maxCnt: LONGINT;        (* Maximum number of simulation steps *)
    ch: CHAR;               (* Read from keyboard: "r" = resume, "s" = stop *)
    ...                     (* Declarations of other variables *)

PROCEDURE Simulate*;
BEGIN
  REPEAT
    ch := "r";              (* Set control character to "run" *)
    IF Input.Available() > 0 THEN Input.Read(ch) END;
      IF ch = "s" THEN (* Stop key was pressed *)
        LogOut.PutInt("simulation interrupted, stepCnt =", stepCnt);
      RETURN
      END;
      REPEAT
        ...                 (* Perform one simulation step *)
        INC(stepCnt)
      UNTIL stepCnt MOD interval = 0
    UNTIL stepCnt = maxCnt
END Simulate;

PROCEDURE Setup*;
VAR S: Texts.Scanner;
BEGIN
  stepCnt := 0;
  Texts.OpenScanner(S, Oberon.Par.text, Oberon.Par.pos);
  Texts.Scan(S); interval := S.i;
  Texts.Scan(S); maxCnt := S.i
  ...                       (* Read further parameters *)
END Setup;
END Sim.
```

Note that prior to the call of *Input.Read* it is necessary to test whether there are characters in the keyboard buffer (*Input.Available.*) Otherwise, *Input.Read* will wait for a character to be typed, hence no simulation would take place.

18.8.3   Very long running commands in the background

In the preceding section, we have seen how to make a very long running command interruptible in a controlled way. However, as long as the command keeps control, no other activity can go on in the system (except for interrupt-driven handlers.) If the long running job can be partitioned into short slices, then it can be installed in a task running in the event loop. Commands to be installed in tasks must satisfy the following:

- Have short execution time (less than a tenth of a second.)
- Be Oberon procedures without parameters.

While commands should be short in general, this is a *must* for commands to be installed in the background. Otherwise, a truly jerky behavior of the mouse cursor results.

The following program piece shows how to create an instance of a task, install handler *SimulationProc* and insert the task into the event loop:

```
VAR
    SimulationTask: Oberon.Task;
    ...
NEW(SimulationTask);
SimulationTask.handle : = SimulationProc;
Simulation.Task.safe : = FALSE;
Oberon.Install(SimulationTask);
```

After *Oberon.Install*, the procedure variable handle of task *Simulation-Task* is called at every cycle of the event loop. The task is removed from the loop using:

```
Oberon.Remove(SimulationTask);
```

Let us sketch the simulation example with more detail.

```
running: BOOLEAN;
MODULE Sim;

IMPORT Oberon, Texts, LogOut ... ;

VAR
    steps: INTEGER;   (* Number of steps performed in one call
                            of Simulation*)
    running:
    BOOLEAN;        (* TRUE if the simulation task is in the event loop *)
    SimulationTask: Oberon.Task;
    ... (* Declarations of other parameters and variables *)

PROCEDURE Simulate*;
(* Procedure to be run as task in the background *)
```

```
VAR i: INTEGER;
  ... (* Declarations of other parameters and variables *)
BEGIN
  i := 0;
  WHILE i < steps DO
    ... (* Perform one simulation step *)
    INC(i)
  END
END Simulate;

PROCEDURE: Start*;
(* Command that starts the simulation *)
VAR
  S: Texts.Scanner;
  ... (* Declarations of other parameters and variables *)
BEGIN
  IF running THEN
    LogOut.PutString("simulation already running");
    RETURN
  ELSE
    Texts.OpenScanner(S, Oberon.Par.text, Oberon.Par.pos);
    Texts.Scan(S); steps := S.i;
    ... (* Read further parameters *)
    Oberon.Install(SimulationTask); (* Install task in event loop *)
    running := TRUE (* Task is running *)
    LogOut.PutString("simulation started")
  END
END Start;

PROCEDURE Stop*;
(* Command to stop simulation in background *)
BEGIN
  IF running THEN
    Oberon.Remove(SimulationTask);
    running := FALSE;
    ... (* Open a viewer and display results *)
  ELSE
    LogOut.PutString("simulation not running");
    RETURN
  END
END Stop;

BEGIN
  NEW(SimulationTask); (* Create a task *)
  SimulationTask.handle := Simulate; (* Install handler *)
  SimulationTask.safe := FALSE; (* A normal task, removed upon failure *)
  running := FALSE
END Sim.
```

Our example exhibits several typical features of an application running in the background:

- The variable *steps* to control the amount of computing done in each cycle of the event loop.
- A procedure *Start* to start the background activity by installing a task in the loop.
- A procedure *Stop* to halt the background activity and display results.
- A Boolean variable *running* to prevent installation of multiple tasks with the same handler.

18.8.4   Garbage collection

The garbage collector is a task in the event loop. It is activated after every 20 mouse clicks. Therefore, if no mouse activity takes place, garbage collection is suppressed. If a long running command creates variables on the heap (calls to NEW), then there is a danger that storage overflow may happen. User tasks in the background which do produce rubbish must, therefore, force garbage collection from time to time through a call to *Oberon.Collect*. The simulation command, for example, should be modified according to:

```
PROCEDURE Simulation*;
VAR i: INTEGER;
BEGIN
  INC(count);
  i := 0;
  WHILE i < steps DO
    ... (* Perform one simulation step *)
    INC(i)
  END;
  IF MOD(count, collectInterval) = 0 THEN Oberon.Collect(0) END
END Simulation;
```

The variable *count* is an externally defined counter that records invocations of *Simulation* while *collectInterval* measures the maximal interval between garbage collections.

18.9   Rules for well-behaved commands

Let us conclude this chapter with a set of guidelines for the programmer of commands.

- Commands do *not leave the system in a hidden state*.

- Commands are uninterruptible atomic actions. They do not perform a dialog with the user. This means that with few exceptions[5] commands *do not deal with the mouse and keyboard driver directly* (module Input.) The job of dealing with these input devices is performed by the handler of a viewer reacting to Oberon messages (see Chapter 19.)

- Output written by commands is a (non-volatile) text which is displayed in a viewer. Commands do not write text to the screen directly using functions from module Display.

- *Commands have a visible consequence*. They open or close a viewer, for example. If their action is not visible a priori, they write a completion or error message to the system log.

- If commands are not instantaneous, they *write an arrow mark* to signal 'viewer is busy.'

- Long running commands should be designed to *run in slices* and installed in the background. They explicitly activate the garbage collector.

- Commands *test the parameters* for validity and report errors in the system log.

- Commands, especially when taking the marked viewer as a parameter, *check the type of the accessed frames*. If they operate on text viewers, for example, they always make sure that a menu frame and a main frame exist, which are of type *TextFrames.Frame*.

- When taking the selection as a parameter, it is the *most recent selection*.

- An asterisk following the command name means that the command operates on the marked viewer.

- An upward pointing arrow '↑' following the command name means that the parameters are found in the selection.

- If commands draw to the pixelmaps directly (using the procedures for raster operations of module Display), they *strictly respect the boundary of the viewer* and its subframes. They also refrain from output operation to the display if the viewer state is suspended or closed.

- Commands executing in the background must have very short execution times.

---

[5] Providing a controlled break point and tracking the mouse on a key, for example.

19 Programming viewers and frames

In Oberon, an interactive application is called a *viewer class*. A particular viewer on the display is an instance of such a class. Adding viewer classes is the most powerful way of extending the Oberon system.

While adding a single command is usually simple, creating a viewer class is often a major task comprised of programming:

(1) An abstract data type whose instances are *documents*, such as texts, graphics, bitmaps or spreadsheets. The procedures operating on the abstract data type are called the *data manager*.

(2) A handler which interprets the mouse and keyboard and which produces (all) screen output. Usually, screen output is delivered by a set of procedures known as the *display manager*. The handler also interacts with the data manager of the displayed document.

(3) A set of commands which create an instance of the viewer class (usually called *Open*) and perform other operations relating to the display or to the document.

Each one of the three parts is typically encapsulated into a module. A viewer class is, thus, a *module triplet*; for example:

Function	Standard editor	Bitmap editor	Graphics editor
Commands	Edit	Paint	Draw
Handler	TextFrames	PictureFrames	GraphicFrames
Data manager	Texts	Pictures	Graphics

Evidently, creating a viewer class touches on all aspects of programming – data structures, algorithms and special fields such as editor design. Clearly, a comprehensive coverage is beyond the scope of this book. In this chapter, we shall *concentrate on the handler and on programming the display*.

The relation of the document to the viewer is depicted in the following diagram which shows the three major sources of messages: module Oberon, module Viewers and the data managers.

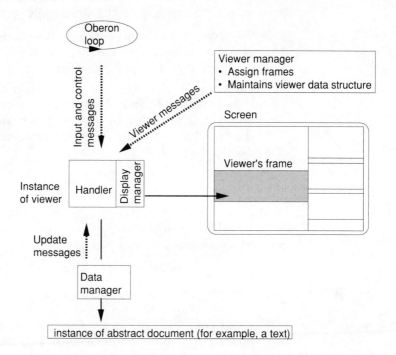

The provider of a viewer class can choose between two levels of abstraction and:

(1) *program a viewer*;

(2) *program a frame* which will be installed in a menu viewer.

The first approach is completely general within the framework of the tiled display model provided by module Viewers. No restriction is imposed on the viewer's appearance and how the mouse and keyboard are interpreted.

The second approach prescribes that the viewer has standard layout with a wire frame and a title bar. The viewer also reacts to the left mouse key within the title bar and repositions its top edge. Within the frame (to be precise the main frame), interpretation of the mouse and keyboard are still completely under the control of the user.

Thus, in most cases, the programmer of a viewer class will follow the second approach. It relieves him or her from the conceptually simple but tedious chore of computing the boundaries of two frames within the viewer and of handling title bar tracking.

19.1   The design of a viewer class

The design of a typical viewer class (which observes standard Oberon conventions) is comprised of the following elements:

- Specifying a data representation of the underlying logical model of the document (for example, text, graphic etc.) and defining the operations to be performed on the document.
- Designing a *frame* which is installed in a menu viewer. The frame is linked to an instance of the document. It has a *handler* and a data structure of objects which are visible within the frame. Objects in that data structure may be termed *display descriptors*.
- The use of *update messages* to synchronize document state and display state.

We shall sketch essential features of such a design. For this purpose, we sketch a highly simplified graphics editor. A complete example of a viewer class is furnished in Appendix A.

19.1.1   The document and data manager

Document

A graphic is composed of elements such as lines, rectangles, circles, text captions etc. The logical model is a Cartesian plane. We have to find an appropriate data structure for such a plane. We call this data structure the *document*.

A simple data representation of such a graphic is a list of descriptors of graphical objects. The following figure shows a graphic composed of a rectangle, a circle and two line segments. Both the plane and the data representation are shown.

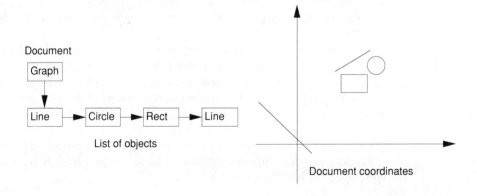

The type declarations for such a graphic may look as follows:

```
TYPE
   Graph = POINTER TO GraphDesc;
   GraphDesc = RECORD
      ...              (* Graph specific data *)
      list: Object (* Link to object list *)
   END;
```

```
TYPE                                    TYPE
   Object = POINTER TO ObjectDesc;         Rect = POINTER TO RectDesc;
   ObjectDesc = RECORD                     RectDesc = RECORD
      ... (* Data common to all objects *)    (ObjectDesc)
      next: Object                            X, Y, W, H: INTEGER;
   END;                                    END;
```

Thus, a graphic is an instance of the data type *Graph*. A variety of graphics objects may be defined as extensions of the base type *Object*. We have outlined the definition of a rectangle.

Data manager

We have to provide operations on the graphical object. The following are typical functions:

- Initialize a graphic (typically called *Open* or *New*.)
- Create an object and add it to the data structure.
- Delete or modify an object.
- Provide access to all objects; for example, with an abstract data type *Reader* similar to the readers for texts.

The set of these procedures is the *document manager*. When the document manager makes changes to the data structure, it broadcasts an *update message* to all visible viewers. The essence of the definition of such a message is:

```
TYPE
   UpdateMsg = RECORD
      (Display.FrameMsg)
      id: INTEGER;
      graph: Graph;   (* The graph which is updated *)
      object: Object; (* The object which is updated *)
      ...                 (* Other information related to the update *)
   END;
```

The message identifies the document and the object which is changed. The type of change is determined by the message identifier for which we declare constants with names which are suggestive of the update action; for example:

```
CONST delete = 0;
```

It is good practice to make *Graph* an abstract data type which is encapsulated in a module with an appropriate name, Graphics, say.

19.1.2   The frame and display manager

Frame

The next step in our design is to create a viewer. Since we plan to adhere to Oberon user interface guidelines, we will program a frame to be installed in a menu viewer. This involves the design of an appropriate frame data structure and programming the handler. First, we turn our attention to the issue of the data structure.

The frame is an extension of the type *Display.Frame* and inherits all its properties, most notably the frame's rectangle *X, Y, W* and *H* and the field *handle*. Our frame displays a single document which is an instance of the type *Graph*. The frame deals with those objects of the graph which are visible in its rectangle. For this purpose, the frame needs additional properties; for example:

- The graph being handled by the frame.
- A data structure of *display descriptors*.
- A data structure of special objects, such as a *selection*.
- The *frame position* in the document space.

The following diagram shows a graphics frame and its relation to the displayed document. Since the graph is a simple list of graphics objects, it is straightforward to attach a similar list of display descriptors to the frame. Each one of these descriptors points to the graphics object which it represents. Note that the relation is not the other way around, since the concept of an abstract document precludes 'knowledge' of the viewers in which the document is rendered. The frame itself points to the graph displayed in its boundary. It also has a second list of objects which have a special status: they are 'selected' and serve as operand of subsequent operations (such as *move* or *delete*.)

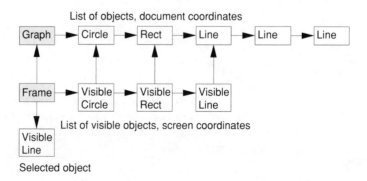

The display descriptors are instances of types which we call *VisibleLine*, *VisibleRect* etc. and which may have the following declarations:

```
TYPE                                    TYPE
  VisibleObject = POINTER TO VDesc;       VisibleRect = POINTER TO VRectDesc;
  VDesc = RECORD                          VRectDesc = RECORD
    object: Graphics.Object;                (VDesc)
    next: VisibleObject                     X, Y, W, H: INTEGER
  END;                                    END;
```

Coordinate systems

Documents are, at least potentially, larger than the available frame size. Therefore, the frame's location in the document space is an additional property of the frame. Also, Oberon raster operations use (absolute) screen coordinates. Therefore, document coordinates and display coordinates have to be transformed into each other. The following diagram depicts screen and viewer superimposed on the graphics plane.

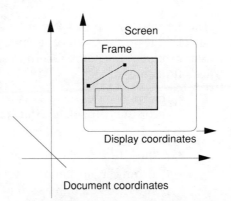

We are now ready for the declaration of the type *Frame*:

```
TYPE Frame = POINTER TO FrameDesc;
  FrameDesc = RECORD
    (Display.Frame)
    graph: Graphics.Graph; (* The rendered graph *)
    XUL, YUL: INTEGER;    (* upper left frame corner, in document
                                            coordinates *)
    DisplayList: VisibleObject;
    SelectionList: VisibleObject;
    ...                            (* Other frame data *)
  END;
```

Note that if the upper left corner is chosen to fix the frame position in the document plane, frame repositioning will become particularly easy, since the upper left corner stays fixed in such moves.

Display manager The handler uses a set of procedures to update the display which, as we mentioned, is termed the display manager. Typical functions are:

- Display those objects which fall in the frame's rectangle.
- Display those objects which will become visible when the frame extends (typically called *Extend*.)
- Remove objects which will become invisible (or partially visible) when the frame reduces its size (typically called *Reduce*.)
- Locate the display descriptor for a given document object.
- Deal with the selection.
- Deal with update messages from changed graphics documents.

19.1.3   The handler

The handler is the heart of the viewer class. Recall that everything visible (including the mouse cursor) is drawn by the handler which also produces the entire Oberon user interface. Specifically, the handler's functions are:

- Interpret mouse and keyboard input and act on the document accordingly (using the data manger.)
- Draw and write to the display.
- Adjust the size of the frame.
- Perform certain standard system functions (for example, set the pointer, copy a frame, report the selection, copy a stretch of text to the caret etc.)

Each handler has to implement the Oberon interface conventions, including command activation with the mouse. How this is done will be described in detail in subsequent sections. However, central to the design of an Oberon viewer class is the update mechanism using messages – a topic to which we now turn. The essence of this is that handlers do *not* deal with the update of the document and the display *in parallel*. Assume that in our example the graphic is changed in one of the viewers. Then:

- The handler of the viewer in which the user edited the graphic invokes one of the functions of the data manager to change the document.

- The data manager updates its data structure and broadcasts an update message.

- All handlers which receive the update message check whether they display the object and, if so, update the screen. The handler which instigates the change is called *recursively*.

This mechanism leads to the fact that both the module defining the document and the frame module declare procedures have the same name. Text viewers are a typical example. The document module, Texts, exports *Texts.Insert*. Similarly, the display manager in Text-Frames knows a procedure *TextFrames.Insert* which is called in response to an update message communicating an insert event. A similar correspondence is found in our viewer class.

Structure of the handler

We know that the handler does its work exclusively in reaction to messages sent to it by various parts of the system. It is in essence a large IF ... ELSIF ... ELSIF ... END statement. Type tests are used to discriminate between message types. Further tests on message identifiers determine the actions to be taken. Type guards (often using WITH statements) are required to access the fields of the viewer's descriptor and the actual message passed as a parameter.

The update mechanism is highlighted in the following excerpt of a frame handler which exhibits the following:

- The decoding of a mouse command to delete a specified object designated by the variable *Rect*.

- The processing of the resulting update message *M*.

```
PROCEDURE Handler*(F: Display.Frame; VAR: M: Display.FrameMsg);
BEGIN
WITH F: Frame DO
   IF M IS Oberon.InputMsg THEN
      WITH M: Oberon.InputMsg DO
         IF M.id = Oberon.track THEN
            (* A mouse event occurred *)
            Oberon.DrawCursor(Oberon.Mouse, Oberon.Arrow, M.X, M.Y);
            IF ...                    (* Decode delete command *) THEN
               Graphics.Delete(Rect)  (* Use the data manger *)
            END
         ELSIF ...                    (* Other input message id's *)
      END
END
```

```
ELSIF M IS Graphics.UpdateMsg THEN
    WITH M: Graphics.UpdateMsg DO
        IF M.graph = F.graph THEN
            (* The graph is displayed in this frame *)
            IF M.id = Graphics.delete THEN
                Delete(M.object);        (* Invoke the display manager *)
            ELSIF ...                    (* Other update messages *)
            END
        END
    END
ELSIF ...                                (* All other message types *)
END
END
END Handler;
```

Recursive calls to handlers

It is important that the programmer grasps the recursive nature of the update mechanism, otherwise he or she might have a few surprises. Assume for example that in response to an update message the procedure *LogOut.PutInt* is called to display the message identifier in the system log. Once the newly compiled handler is installed in an instance of the viewer class under test, the system stops and does not react to any control (other than the reset button.) We leave it as an exercise for the reader to find out why.

19.1.4   Sample event trail

A good understanding of the update mechanism is essential. We, therefore, discuss a sample event trail. The example chosen is text deletion with the standard Oberon editor. Recall that this entails the following:

(1) Move with the mouse cursor to the beginning of the stretch to be deleted.

(2) Press the left mouse key and track the selection.

(3) Before release of the left key, interclick the right mouse key. On release of all keys, the selected stretch is deleted. Both the document and the display are synchronized.

We shall follow these three phases, which are depicted in the following diagrams.

Recall from Part II that a text viewer, *V* say, is of type *Menu-Viewers.Viewer* with a main frame of type *TextFrames.Frame*. Both *V* and the main frame have a handler which work in tandem. In our example, the handler of *V* simply passes the messages to the handler of the main frame. In order not to overload the diagrams, we have combined the two handlers under *V.handle*.

Phase 1

The mouse moves to the starting point of the selection. The event loop polls the mouse (call to *Input.Mouse*) and sends a track message (TM) to the handler of viewer *V* indicating that the mouse position has changed. The handler draws the mouse cursor and relinquishes control back to the loop, since no mouse keys have been pressed. The events happen in quick succession; the mouse cursor moves smoothly over the viewer frame.

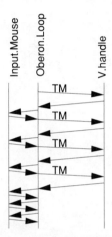

Phase 2

This phase commences with a right mouse key down event which is also reported in a track message (TM-MR.) The handler determines that the mouse is in the main frame and invokes *Text-Frames.TrackSelection* which seizes control and polls the mouse directly. Between calls to *Input.Mouse*, the selection is made visible (reverse video.) This loop continues until all mouse keys are released. At this point, control returns to the handler.

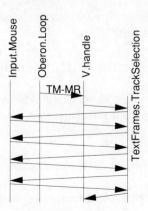

Phase 3   The handler recognizes that the left mouse key has been interclicked during tracking. It calls *Texts.Delete* to remove the stretch which corresponds to the selection. The text manager invokes the text's notifier which in turn sends an update message (UM) to all visible viewers, hence also to *V*, whose handler is activated recursively. The handler now draws on the services of *TextFrames.Delete* to adjust the display to the change in the underlying text data.

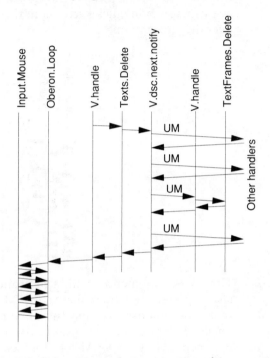

At this point, the delete action is completed. All pending procedures relinquish control which returns to the event loop. Mouse and keyboard are quiescent, hence the loop polls the mouse and keyboard at a fast rate.

19.2   Working with the display

In general, a substantial portion of the program text of a viewer class is devoted to the display manager. In this section, we discuss basic techniques for programming a monochrome display.

19.2.1   Common raster operations

Some useful constructs are summarized as follows:

Constants	CONST fgnd = Display.white; bkgnd = Display.black;
Clear a rectangular area	Oberon.RemoveMarks(X, Y, W, H); Display.ReplConst(bkgnd, X, Y, W, H, Display.replace);
Draw a filled rectangle	Display.ReplConst(fgnd, X, Y, W, H, Display.replace);
Draw a horizontal line of length L	Display.ReplConst(fgnd, X, Y, L, 1, Display.replace);
Draw a vertical line of height H	Display.ReplConst(fgnd, X, Y, 1, H, Display.replace);
Draw a dot at X, Y	Display.ReplConst(fgnd, X, Y, 1, 1, Display.replace);
Draw a pattern and remove it afterwards	Display.CopyPattern(fgnd, pat, X, Y, Display.invert); ... Display.CopyPattern(fgnd, pat, X, Y, Display.invert);
Mark a rectangular selection and remove it afterwards	Display.ReplConst(fgnd, X, Y, W, H, Display.invert); ... Display.ReplConst(fgnd, X, Y, W, H, Display.invert);
Write a character *ch* in a font *fnt*. The previous character is at X, Y	Display.GetChar(fnt.raster, ch, dx, x, y, w, h, pat); Display.CopyPattern(fgnd, pat, X + x, Y + y, Display.invert);

Foreground/ background color   The named constant *bkgnd* denotes the background color and *fgnd* the foreground color. If the monitor operates in normal mode, then the foreground color is white and the background color is black; thus:

$$fgnd = Display.white \quad \text{and} \quad bkgnd = Display.black$$

If the monitor is set to reverse video mode, the opposite is the case.

Note: The drawings in this book assume reverse video mode; that is, the characters are drawn in black on a white background.

On the monochrome monitor, any value *col* > 0 will print in the foreground color. Our particular choice, *fgnd* = *Display.white*, yields proper black background and a white foreground on a color monitor, provided the standard color palette is in use.

Raster operations   The basis for programming the display are the following procedures:

- *Display.ReplConst*: to draw a dot, a line and a rectangle.
- *Display.ReplPattern*: to fill a rectangle with a pattern.
- *Display.CopyPattern*: to copy a pattern (such as a character) to a given position.
- *Display.CopyBlock*: to copy a rectangle on the display to a new location.
- *Fonts.This*(*name*): to initialize a font.
- *Display.GetChar*: to obtain the pattern of a given character from a font.

Rules

When using procedures from the module Display, always ensure that:

- the parameters W and H in the definition of the destination are *positive integers*;
- no raster operations are performed outside the defined pixelmaps;
- cursors and marks (such as selection and caret) are cleared before writing in replace or paint mode (see discussion later.)

19.2.2 Drawing and removing mark patterns

Drawing marks

Animated marks such as the mouse cursor, the pointer or the caret play a fundamental role in the design of graphical user interfaces. To implement such moving marks, a method is needed to draw and remove the mark pattern. The invert mode provides a simple solution:

(1) Draw the pattern (here an arrow) at the position $X1, Y1$:

Display.CopyPattern(fgnd, Display.arrow, X1, Y1, Display.invert)

X1, Y1

(2) Remove (fade) the pattern at the same position $X1, Y1$ and recover the original display:

Display.CopyPattern(fgnd, Display.arrow, X1, Y1, Display.invert)

X1, Y1

(3) Draw the pattern at a new location $X2, Y2$:

Display.CopyPattern(fgnd, Display.arrow, X2, Y2, Display.invert)

X2,Y2

Removing marks It is clear that this method only works if the display within the rectangle of the pattern does not change between steps 1 and 2. Assume that the mouse cursor is visible in a frame *F*. Now, the area of *F* is cleared with a call to *Display.ReplConst(bkgnd, F.X, F.Y, F.W, F.H, Display.replace.*) Then, at the instance of the next track message, a ghost image of the cursor is created which will stay on the display.

It is, therefore, compulsory that all marks be cleared prior to changing the display in replace or paint mode. This is achieved with the following procedures:

- *Oberon.RemoveMarks(X, Y, W, H)*: remove mouse cursor and pointer in the rectangular area *X, Y, W, H*.
- *TextFrames.RemoveCaret(F)*: remove the caret from text frame *F*
- *TextFrames.RemoveSelection(F)*: remove the selection from text frame *F*.

Note: Writing in invert mode does not require removal of marks such as the mouse cursor, star-shaped marker, selection and caret.

19.2.3   Programming patterns

Patterns have to be built using the binary representation of standard data types. The first byte is interpreted as a SHORTINT denoting the pattern's width, the second byte is taken likewise as the pattern's height. The bits that follow are the pattern's bitmap rendered row-wise, left to right from the bottom up.

Bitmapping The mapping from low- to high-order bits to corresponding left to right positions in the pattern is hardware dependent. In the following two examples, we assume that the low-order byte is first in the address space and similarly the low-order bit is first within a byte. Thus, 1X puts a foreground pixel in the leftmost position of a row of eight pixels and 80X puts a foreground pixel in the rightmost position, respectively.[1] Hardware using the reverse mapping is also common.

---

[1] This is the mapping used on Ceres on which the examples were developed.

As an illustrative example, let us generate the pattern of a cross-shaped pattern which may be used for a cursor, for example:

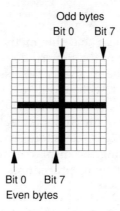

Pattern as an array of bytes

We will build the pattern from an array of bytes:

```
PROCEDURE InitCross(VAR Xpattern: Display.Pattern);
VAR
  X: ARRAY 32 OF SYSTEM.BYTE;
  j: INTEGER;
BEGIN
  X[0] := 16;                    (* Width of pattern *)
  X[1] := 15;                    (* Height of pattern *)
  i := 2;
  WHILE i < 32 DO
    IF ODD[i] THEN X[i] := 1X;   (* Vertical beam pixels *)
    ELSE X[i] := 0X;
    END;
    INC(i)
  END;
  X[16] := 0FEX; X[17] := 0FFX; (* Horizontal cross beam *)
  Xpattern := SYSTEM.ADR(X)
END InitCross;
```

We are now ready to present the program text of a module which exports a marker using the cross-pattern. The marker is an abstraction of a pattern used by cursors. It consists of a record with two procedure fields, *Draw* and *Fade*. The procedure assigned to *Draw* produces the cursor pattern at a given location; the one held in *Fade* removes it and restores the original display content.

Cross-beam marker

Using the technique based on the invert mode, we obtain the following:

```
MODULE Marks;

IMPORT Oberon, Display;

VAR
   Xpattern: Display.Pattern; (* Cross pattern for marker *)
   Cross*: Oberon.Marker;   (* The exported marker *)
   left, top: INTEGER;

PROCEDURE InitCross(VAR Xpattern: Display.Pattern);
BEGIN
   ...                         (* See above *)
END InitCross;

PROCEDURE DrawFade*(X, Y: INTEGER);
BEGIN
   IF X < left THEN X := left END; IF X > right THEN X := right END;
   IF Y < bot THEN Y := bot; IF Y > top THEN Y := top END;
   Display.CopyPattern(Display.white, Xpattern, X − 8, Y − 7, Display.invert)
END DrawFade;

BEGIN
   left := Display.Left + 8; right := Display.Left + Display.Width − 8;
   bot := Display.Bottom + 8; top := Display.Bottom + Display.Height − 8;
   InitCross(Xpattern);
   Cross.Fade := DrawFade; Cross.Draw := DrawFade
END Marks.
```

Note the tests in procedure *DrawFade*. They insure that the pattern is fully contained in the primary monochrome map. Their omission would lead to addressing exceptions if the cursor moves to the boundaries. A cross-shaped mouse cursor can be drawn with:

Oberon.DrawCursor(Oberon.Mouse, Marks.Cross, X, Y)

Pattern as an array of SET   There is a different way to specify a pattern using an array of SET. Again, the method is hardware and to some extent compiler dependent. Typically, a variable of type SET is a 32-bit word. This time, we define a checkerboard pattern useful as background shading.

```
TYPE
  Pattern = RECORD
    filler: INTEGER; (* To obtain proper alignment of w and h fields *)
    w: SHORTINT;  (* Pattern width *)
    h: SHORTINT;  (* Pattern height *)
    X: ARRAY 2 OF SET
  END;
VAR
  P: Pattern;
  Checkerboard: Display.Pattern;
  ...
  P.w := 16;        (* See recommendation in Chapter 12 *)
  P.h := 2;
  X[0] := {0, 2, 4, 6, 8, 10, 12, 14, 16, 18, 20, 22, 24, 26, 28, 30};
  X[1] := {1, 3, 5, 7, 9, 11, 13, 15, 17, 19, 21, 23, 25, 27, 29, 31};
  Checkerboard := SYSTEM.ADR(P + 2);
```

Specifying a pattern as an ARRAY OF SET has the advantage that individual bits can be easily set using their position.

Dashed lines   If a line is drawn using:

```
Display.ReplPattern(fgnd, Checkerboard, X, Y, W, 1, Display.replace)
```

a finely dashed horizontal line is drawn. Other dashing can be easily generated.

19.2.4   Basic techniques

In this section, we will show how to mark a selected object in reverse video, how to draw a viewer frame and how to write text.

Marking a selection   The method used to render a selection in reverse video is similar to the ones discussed for drawing and fading a marker.

Suppose that the object to be selected is contained in the rectangle X, Y, W and H. Then, a selection is set, as well as removed, by means of a call to:

```
Display.ReplConst(fgnd, X, Y, W, H, Display.invert)
```

Drawing a viewer frame   The following procedure is an example of how *Display.ReplConst* is used to draw lines and rectangles. A viewer frame is produced.

```
PROCEDURE DrawViewerFrame(X, Y, W, H: INTEGER);
CONST
    bkgnd = Display.black;
    fgnd = Display.white;
    barH = 14;
    replace = Display.replace;
BEGIN
    Oberon.RemoveMarks(X, Y, W, H); (* Clear mouse and pointer *)
    Display.ReplConst(bkgnd, X, Y, W, H, replace);          (* Clear area *)
    Display.ReplConst(fgnd, X, Y, 1, H, replace);           (* Left *)
    Display.ReplConst(fgnd, X + W, Y, 1, H, replace);       (* Right *)
    Display.ReplConst(fgnd, X + 1, Y, W − 2, 1, replace); (* Bottom *)
    Display.ReplConst(fgnd, X + 1, Y + H − barH, W − 2, barH, replace)
END DrawViewerFrame;
```

Observe that cursors must first be removed prior to writing in replace mode. The first statement fills the viewer area with the background color.

Horizontal lines are rectangles of height 1 drawn by the procedure *Display.ReplConst* as shown by the bottom edge. Vertical lines are analogously rectangles of width 1.

Writing text

Display managers often write text characters. The method is always the same:

- Open the appropriate font *fnt* using *fnt := Fonts.This(name)*.

- Obtain the pattern of character *ch* with *Display.GetChar(fnt, ch, dx, x, y, w, h, pattern)*.

- Display the pattern by means of *Display.CopyPattern(fgnd, pattern, X + x, Y + y, Display.invert)* where *X* and *Y* are the writing coordinates.

- Determine the new *x* coordinate $X := \text{INC}(X, dx)$.

Details are visible in the following example of a procedure *WriteStretch* which writes a stretch [*beg, end*) of text *txt* to the screen, using font *fnt*, starting at position *X*, *Y* with left margin at *Xleft*, right margin *Xright* and line spacing *lsp*. It is assumed that the text is displayed line-wise with carriage return control characters (0DX) forcing line breaks.

```
PROCEDURE WriteStretch(txt: Texts.Text; beg, end: LONGINT;
                       fnt: Fonts.Font; X, Y: INTEGER;
                       Xleft, Xright, lsp: INTEGER);
CONST
  fgnd = Display.white; CR = 0DX;
VAR
  ch: CHAR;                (* Character to be written *)
  pat: Display.Pattern;    (* Pattern of character to be written *)
  dx, x, y, w, h: INTEGER; (* Font metric data *)
  R: Texts.Reader;
  i: LONGINT;
BEGIN
  (* Precondition: writing area is cleared *)
  Texts.OpenReader(R, txt, beg);
  Texts.Read(R, ch);       (* Read first character *)
  i := beg;
  WHILE i < end DO
    REPEAT
      Display.GetChar(fnt.raster, ch, dx, x, y, w, h, pat);
      IF (X + dx) < Xright THEN
        Display.CopyPattern(fgnd, pat, X + x, Y + y, Display.invert)
      END;
      INC(X, dx);          (* Determine new X for next character *)
      Texts.Read(R, ch);   (* Read next character *)
      INC(i)
    UNTIL ch = CR;
    Y := Y - lsp;          (* Decrement y coordinate of base line *)
    X := Xleft;            (* Set x coordinate to left-hand side margin *)
    Texts.Read(R, ch);
    INC(i)
  END;
END WriteStretch;
```

In the call to *Display.CopyPattern*, invert mode is used. This is advantageous in the sense that the text will also properly be written in areas of foreground color, such as the title bar drawn in *DrawViewerFrame*.

Writing a stretch of text in this manner is typical of actions of the display manager in response to update messages. The determination of the starting position, clearing the writing area and finding the minimum extent that actually needs rewriting may be quite involved.

19.2.5   Operating directly on the pixelmap, saving the pixelmap

Using functions of module SYSTEM, it is possible to write directly into the pixelmaps, to copy portions of the video RAM to normal memory or write it to disk.

Copy pixelmap to normal memory

The following procedure copies the primary monochrome pixelmap to normal memory:

```
CONST DH = Display.Height; DW = Display.Width;

TYPE
   Bitmap = POINTER TO BitmapArray;
   BitmapArray = ARRAY DH, (DW DIV 8) OF SYSTEM.BYTE;

PROCEDURE CopyMap(S: Bitmap);
VAR A: LONGINT; D: Bitmap;
BEGIN
   A := Display.Map(Display.Left); (* Base address of map *)
   D := SYSTEM.VAL(Bitmap, A);  (* Convert A into pointer type Bitmap *)
   S↑ := D↑                     (* Copy operation *)
END CopyMap;
```

Note the dereferencing operators in the statement which copies the array. Without them, only the pointer would be assigned.

Accessing the pixelmap as array

In the current implementation of Oberon, *arrays are stored row-wise*. Knowing this, it is possible to access the pixelmap directly.

Let D denote a bitmap pointer obtained in the same way as in the foregoing example. Then, $D[i, j]$ is a byte which holds eight pixel values which have common y coordinate $y = DH - i - 1$. The pixels in $D[i, j]$ start at $x = j * 8$.

Another technique which allows the setting of individual bits directly is to define the bitmap array as an ARRAY OF SET. For this, it is necessary to know that sets are stored in 32-bit words. Thus:

```
TYPE Bitmap = ARRAY DH, (DW DIV 32) OF SET;
```

Address computation

Operations such as copying part of the pixelmap to normal memory require that the user performs explicit address computations. The function SYSTEM.VAL allows conversion of the type LONGINT to pointer types and vice versa.

Also, working on bitmaps may be computing time-intensive. Using the function SYSTEM.MOVE instead of explicit loops over arrays usually yields considerable savings.

Caution: Using the functions of module SYSTEM to avoid type rules and to perform direct address computations is machine specific and not type save. Extreme care must be exercised.

19.2.6   Design for freedom from flicker

The display strategy used in updating the screen has a crucial effect on:

- response times;
- flicker (short blanking of information already displayed.)

Flicker is quite annoying and, for optimal performance, both measures must be carefully tuned. While response time improves with advancements in hardware, flicker does not. Design for freedom of flicker really pays off as the standard text viewers amply demonstrate.
The following rules should be followed:

- Do not redraw any valid parts of the display.
- If a rectangular area shows valid data, except for its position, use a block move rather than redrawing the area.
- Generate a complex display in the secondary display map and utilize a block move on its completion.

Use of the secondary map is shown in the following over-simplified example. We draw a horizontal line, emanating at *X1, Y1* with length *L* enclosed in a rectangle *X, Y, W, H*.

```
(* Transform y coordinates to secondary map *)
Ybot := Y + Display.Ubottom;
Y1bot := Y1 + Display.Ubottom;

Display.ReplConst(bkgnd, X, Ybot, W, H, Display.replace);
   (* Clear rectangle *)
Display.ReplConst(fgnd, X1, Y1bot, L, 1, Display.replace); (* Draw line *)

(* Move viewer frame to primary map *)
Display.CopyBlock(X, Ybot, W, H, X, Y, Display.replace);
```

Note: Ubottom is negative.

19.3   Handler for a viewer

A handler intended to be installed in a viewer must process the following:

- Messages originating in modules Viewers and Oberon.
- Update messages corresponding to document types displayed by the viewer.

19.3.1   Model of a viewer handler

The following program skeleton shows the structure of a model handler. All messages of the outer core are listed in the model handler. The comments indicate what action is expected if the handler follows the recommendations of the Oberon user interface.

This handler is exported by a module which implements a viewer. This module defines the abstract data type *Viewer* which is an extension of *Viewer.Viewer*.

```
TYPE
    Viewer = POINTER TO ViewerDesc; (* The viewer type of this
                                        viewer class *)
    ViewerDesc = RECORD
        (Viewers.Viewer)
        ...                         (* Further state variables of viewer class *)
    END

PROCEDURE Handler*(V: Display.Frame; VAR: M: Display.FrameMsg);
CONST right = 0; middle = 1; left = 2; (* Mouse keys *)
VAR
    Vcopy: Viewer;          (* Used to copy viewer *)
    ...                     (* Declaration of other local variables *);
BEGIN
WITH V: Viewer DO
    IF M IS Oberon.InputMsg THEN
        (* A mouse or keyboard event occurred *)
        WITH M: Oberon.InputMsg DO
            IF M.id = Oberon.consume THEN
                (* Keyboard input occurred, M.ch contains the read character.
                Interpret the character as a command or insert it into a text or
                caption *)
                ...

            ELSIF M.id = Oberon.track THEN
                (* A mouse event occurred. The mouse coordinates are in M.X
                and M.Y. The mouse keys are contained in field M.keys *)
                Oberon.DrawCursor(Oberon.Mouse, Oberon.Arrow, M.X, M.Y);
                ...
            END
    END
```

```
            ELSIF M IS Oberon.ControlMsg THEN
              WITH M: Oberon.ControlMsg DO
                IF M.id = Oberon.defocus THEN
                  (* Focus was taken away as a result of a call to
                  Oberon.PassFocus. Remove caret *)
                  ...
                ELSIF M.id = Oberon.neutralize THEN
                  (* ESC key pressed. Remove all marks such as pointer, caret and
                  selections *)
                  ...
                ELSIF M.id = Oberon.mark THEN
                  (* SETUP key pressed, place star–shaped marker *)
                  Oberon.DrawCursor(Oberon.Mouse, Oberon.Arrow, M.X, M.Y);
                  Oberon.DrawCursor(Oberon.Pointer, Oberon.Star, M.X, M.Y)
                END
              END
            ELSIF M IS Oberon.SelectionMsg THEN
              WITH M: Oberon.SelectionMsg DO
                (* Oberon.GetSelection was called. The handler must report the
                most recent selection in the fields of the message *)
                IF ... (* There is a selection and the time of selection > M.time *)
                    THEN
                  M.text := ...;   (* The text which contains the selection *)
                  M.beg := ...;    (* Beginning of selected stretch *)
                  M.end := ...;    (* End of selected stretch *)
                  M.time := ...    (* Time of the selection *)
                END
              END
            ELSIF M IS Oberon.CopyMsg THEN
              WITH M: Oberon.CopyMsg DO
                (* A copy of the handler's viewer is requested, typically by the
                commands System.Copy and System.Grow. The state of the copy
                must be 0 (closed). The copy is returned in the field M.F of the
                message *)
                NEW(Vcopy);
                Vcopy := ...;       (* Copy structure of viewer V *)
                Vcopy.state := 0; (* Closed *)
                M.F := Vcopy
              END
            ELSIF M IS Oberon.CopyOverMsg THEN
              WITH M: Oberon.CopyOverMsg DO
                (* Insert stretch [M.beg, M.end) of text M.text at the caret location *)
                ...
              END
            ELSIF M IS Viewers.ViewerMsg THEN
              WITH M: Viewers.ViewerMsg DO
                (* The display configuration changed. The viewer manager informs
                about changes to be made. The frame of V is still the old one. The
```

message contains the nature of the change. When control returns,
the viewer manager will set V.X, V.Y, V.W and V.H to the new
values *)
IF M.id = Viewers.restore THEN
    (* An overlay track was closed or a new viewer placed on the
    display. Restore display of the viewer in its old boundary given by
    V.X, V.Y, V.W, W.H *)
    ...
ELSIF M.id = Viewers.modify THEN
    (* The frame of the viewer will be changed at the bottom. The
    message contains the new y coordinate and the new height in
    M.Y and M.H. Adjust the display at bottom of the new frame
    given by V.X, M.Y, V.W, M.H *)
    ...
ELSIF M.id = Viewers.suspend THEN
    (* The viewer will be suspended due to an overlay track
    (V.state < 0) or closed V.state = 0. Release data structure of
    display descriptors and perform possible save operations; for
    example, of a pixel map *)
    ...
    END
END
ELSIF M IS X.UpdateMsg THEN
    WITH M: X.UpdateMsg DO
    (* Process update message from module X. This viewer displays an
    instance of an abstract data type exported by X *)
    ...
    END
    ELSIF M IS Y.UpdateMsg THEN   (* Further update message types *)
    END
END   (* WITH V: Viewer *)
END Handler;

19.3.2   Example: handler of the filler viewer

From the point of view of the Oberon system, there is no mandatory
response. In fact, if a handler did nothing, other viewer classes would
still function. However, in the rectangular frame of a viewer with such
a minimalist handler, the display of viewers which previously held the
space would remain on the display and the mouse cursor would stop at
the boundary. As a minimum, therefore, the handler should blank
its frame, set the pointer and track the mouse cursor. Such a minimal handler is assigned to the filler viewers installed in tracks by
Oberon.OpenTrack. Our next and only example of a handler, intended
for a viewer, lists the program text for such a filler handler.

```
PROCEDURE FillerHandler*(V: Display.Frame;
                              VAR M: Display.FrameMsg);
CONST black = Display.black; repl = Display.replace;
BEGIN
WITH V: Viewers.Viewer DO
  IF M IS Oberon.InputMsg THEN
    WITH M: Oberon.InputMsg DO
      IF M.id = Oberon.track THEN
        (* Track mouse cursor *)
        Oberon.DrawCursor(Oberon.Mouse, Oberon.Arrow, M.X, M.Y)
      ELSIF M.id = Oberon.mark THEN
        (* Place pointer *)
        Oberon.DrawCursor(Oberon.Pointer, Oberon.Star, M.X, M.Y)
      ELSIF M.id = Oberon.neutralize THEN
        (* Remove mouse cursor and pointer *)
        Oberon.RemoveMarks(V.X, V.Y, V.W, V.H)
      END
    END
  ELSIF M IS Viewers.ViewerMsg THEN
    WITH M: Viewers.ViewerMsg DO
      IF (M.id = Viewers.modify ) & (M.Y < V.Y) THEN
        (* The frame of filler viewer will expand at the bottom, blank new
        area *)
        Oberon.RemoveMarks(V.X, V.Y, V.W, V.H);
        Display.ReplConst(black, V.X, M.Y, V.W, V.Y – M.Y, repl)
      ELSIF (M.id = Viewers.restore) & (V.H > 0) THEN
        (* The filler viewer is of height other than 0 and is restored. Blank
        viewer area *)
        Oberon.RemoveMarks(V.X, V.Y, V.W, V.H);
        Display.ReplConst(black, V.X, V.Y, V.W, V.H, repl)
      END
    END
  END
END (* WITH V: Viewers.Viewer *)
END FillerHandler;
```

19.4 Handler for a frame to be installed in a menu viewer

Module MenuViewers provides facilities which greatly ease the task of
programming a standard Oberon viewer. The client of MenuViewers
has to provide an abstract data type – typically called *Frame* – which
extends base type *Display.Frame*. Such a frame is an active object with a

handler which is similar to the handler of a viewer, except for the following:

- Messages of type *MenuViewers.ModifyMsg* supersede the viewer messages (of type *Viewers.ViewerMsg*.)

- No message of type *Oberon.ControlMsg* with *id* = *Oberon.mark* has to be processed (the pointer is set by the menu viewer.)

Like the handler for a viewer proper, the handler for a frame interprets *all* mouse and keyboard events within its frame and writes everything visible on the display.

The menu viewer is composed of two frames: the menu frame and the main frame. The menu viewer's handler and the frame handlers work in tandem as rendered in the following diagram.

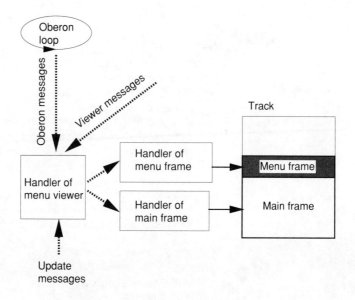

The handler of the menu viewer manages the two subframes; that is, it assigns their frame boundaries when the display configuration changes, either because the title bar is moved or because a viewer's modify message is received. For this purpose, it sends messages of type *MenuViewers.ModifyMsg* to the frame handler. Most other messages are simply passed from the viewer handler to the frame handlers.

19.4.1   Model of a frame handler

The program structure of a frame handler is similar to the structure of the viewer handler as shown in the following model. The module which exports the handler also defines the abstract data type *Frame*.

```
TYPE
    Frame = POINTER TO FrameDesc; (* The frame type of this viewer
                                                class *)
    FrameDesc = RECORD
        (Display.FrameDesc)
        ...                     (* Further state variables of viewer class *)
    END

PROCEDURE Handler*(F: Display.Frame; VAR: M: Display.FrameMsg);
CONST right = 0; middle = 1; left = 2; (* mouse keys *)
VAR
    Fcopy: Frame;      (* Used to copy frame *)
    ...                     (* Declaration of other local variables *);
BEGIN
WITH F: Frame DO
    IF M IS Oberon.InputMsg THEN
        (* A mouse or keyboard event occurred *)
        WITH M: Oberon.InputMsg DO
            IF M.id = Oberon.consume THEN
                (* Keyboard input occurred. M.ch contains the read character.
                Interpret the character as a command or insert it into a text or
                caption *)
                ...
            ELSIF M.id = Oberon.track THEN
                (* A mouse event occurred. The mouse coordinates are in M.X
                and M.Y. The mouse keys are contained in field M.keys *)
                Oberon.DrawCursor(Oberon.Mouse, Oberon.Arrow, M.X, M.Y);
                ...
            END
        END
    ELSIF M IS Oberon.ControlMsg THEN
        WITH M: Oberon.ControlMsg DO
            IF M.id = Oberon.defocus THEN
                (* Focus was taken away as a result of a call to
                Oberon.PassFocus. Remove caret *)
                ...
            ELSIF M.id = Oberon.neutralize THEN
                (* ESC key pressed. Remove all marks such as pointer, caret and
                selections *)
                ...
            END
        END
```

```
        ELSIF M IS Oberon.SelectionMsg THEN
            WITH M: Oberon.SelectionMsg DO
                (* Oberon.GetSelection was called. The handler must report the
                most recent selection in the fields of the message *)
                ...
            END
        ELSIF M IS Oberon.CopyMsg THEN
            WITH M: Oberon.CopyMsg DO
                (* A copy of the handler's frame is requested, typically by the
                commands System.Copy and System.Grow. The copy is returned in
                the field M.F of the message *)
                NEW(Fcopy);
                Fcopy := ...;  (* Copy structure of viewer V *)
                M.F := Fcopy
            END
        ELSIF M IS Oberon.CopyOverMsg THEN
            WITH M: Oberon.CopyOverMsg DO
                (* Insert stretch [M.beg, M.end) of text M.text at the caret location *)
                ...
            END
        ELSIF M IS MenuViewers.ModifyMsg THEN
            WITH M: MenuViewers.ModifyMsg DO
                (* The display configuration changed *)
                Modify(F, M)  (* See below *)
            END
        ELSIF M IS X.UpdateMsg THEN
            WITH M: X.UpdateMsg DO
                (* Process update message from module X. This viewer displays an
                instance of an abstract data type exported by X *)
                ...
            END
        ELSIF M IS Y.UpdateMsg THEN (* Further update message types *)
        END
    END                         (* WITH F: Frame *)
END Handler;
```

The frame handler interprets Oberon and updates messages to produce the desired mouse and keyboard semantics. Typically, the requirements of the Oberon interface have to be implemented.

The owning menu viewer

It is sometimes necessary to gain access to the menu viewer which manages a frame *F*. This viewer is the value of the function:

```
        Viewers.This(F.X, F.Y)
```

Typical uses are:

- To request that the focus be passed to the viewer managing the frame *F* (its ancestor) by means of:

  Oberon.PassFocus(Viewers.This(F.X, F.Y));

- To assign the field *vwr* in an Oberon parameter list *par*; that is:

  par.vwr := Viewers.This(F.X, F.Y);

Setting the caret in a text frame

If *F* is a text frame installed in a menu viewer *V*, then the caret is set at position *pos* as follows:

```
Oberon.PassFocus(Viewers.This(F.X, F.Y));
TextFrames.SetCaret(F, pos);
```

The two procedures called in this order make sure that the caret is unique within a menu viewer. To see why, we have to distinguish three cases:

(1) *V* is not the focus viewer. The first statement passes the focus to *V* and frame *F* sets the caret. Hence, the caret is unique in *F*.

(2) *V* is the focus viewer and the caret is in the other subframe. *V* receives a defocus message which is passed to both subframes. Thus, prior to *F* setting the caret, it is removed in the other subframe.

(3) *V* is the focus viewer and frame *F* has a caret set. It is removed as in step 2 prior to being set at the new position *pos*.

Following an operation which changes the text of *F*, the caret must be moved (see, for example, procedure *Write* in Section 19.3.)

Oberon copy message

When a frame, not currently visible, is to be displayed, the owning menu viewer sets its frame to height 0 and sends an appropriate extend message. It follows from this that the copy to be returned in the copy message must also be of height 0. For example, a text frame produces its copy as follows:

```
PROCEDURE CopyFrame(F: TextFrames.Frame;
                    VAR M: Oberon.CopyMsg);
VAR Fcopy: TextFrames.Frame;
BEGIN
  NEW(Fcopy);
  TextFrames.Open(Fcopy, F.handle, F.text, F.org, F.col, F.left, F.right,
                  F.top, F.bot, F.lsp);
  M.F := Fcopy
END CopyFrame;
```

The use of *TextFrames.Open* makes sure that the copy frame is of height 0 and does not possess such properties as a selection or a caret. *Fcopy* is opened with exactly the same document (*F.text*) and all other properties of *F*.

19.4.2   Processing the modify message

The only reason for the existence of module MenuViewers is to make the task of implementing standard Oberon viewers easier. For this purpose, the fields of the modify message are chosen such that a simple and standardized treatment is possible under the following assumptions:

(1) When the frame is repositioned, the objects which are already displayed keep their size and shape exactly.

(2) When the frame is repositioned, the document coordinate displayed in the upper left corner of the viewer stays fixed.

These assumptions are quite natural and are satisfied in the majority of cases. They allow a reduction of the essential procedures from four to just two – *extend at the bottom* of the frame and *reduce at the bottom* of the frame.

The following diagrams show the principle behind this reduction. *F* denotes the frame as it existed prior to the change and which is passed to the handler. The modify message has the fields *Y*, the new *y* coordinate of the lower left corner, *H*, the new height, and *dY*, a shift of the frame.

(1) An extend message with $dY = 0$ reports the basic event *extend at the bottom*. The new area is cleared and objects which will become visible in the larger area are drawn.

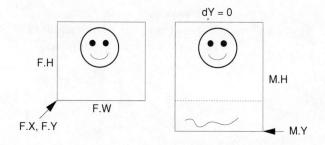

(2) A reduce message with $dY = 0$ reports the basic event *reduce at the bottom*. Objects which will only be partially visible after reduction must be either cleared or adjusted (for example, in the standard editor, a partially visible text line is deleted.)

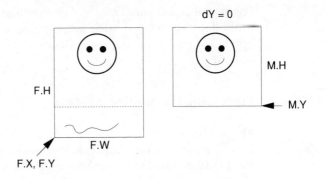

(3) An extend message with $dY > 0$ reports a shift followed by the pure *extend at the bottom*. The frame is shifted up, its y coordinate transformed and the descriptors of all visible objects are adjusted. Then, an *extend at bottom* is performed on the shifted frame.

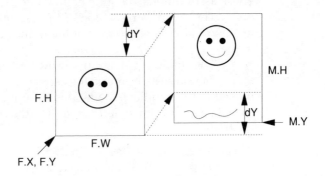

(4) A reduce message with $dY > 0$ reports a pure *reduce at the bottom* followed by a shift. First, the reduction is performed in the old frame. Then, the frame is shifted down by dY. The descriptors of the visible objects are adjusted.

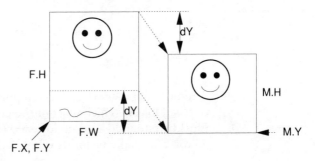

Modify

The four cases just discussed are treated by the generic procedure *Modify*, which is the same for all frame classes:

```
PROCEDURE Modify(F: Frame; VAR M: MenuViewers.ModifyMsg);
CONST repl = Display.replace;
BEGIN
  IF M.id = MenuViewers.extend THEN
    IF M.dY > 0 THEN
      (* Shift existing frame upwards *)
      Display.CopyBlock(F.X, F.Y, F.W, F.H, F.X, F.Y + M.dY, repl);
      F.Y := F.Y + M.dY;
      TransformDisplayDescriptors(F, M.dY)
    END;
    Extend(F, M.Y)
  ELSIF id = MenuViewers.reduce THEN
    Reduce(F, M.Y + M.dY);
    IF M.dY > 0 THEN
      (* Shift existing frame downwards *)
      Display.CopyBlock(F.X, M.Y + M.dY, F.W, M.H, F.X, M.Y, repl);
      TransformDisplayDescriptors(F, −M.dY);
    END
  END
END Modify;
```

Note: Block copy operations are used to shift the existing display efficiently. It is not necessary to set $F.Y$ and $F.H$; this will be done by the handler of the menu viewer.

Modify works with the following three procedures which are frame specific.

Expand

```
PROCEDURE Expand(F: Frame; newY: INTEGER);
```
Expands frame F at the bottom. The type of F is given by the frame class. The actual parameter $M.Y$ is passed to the formal parameter *newY*.

The actions of *Expand* are:

- To clear the expanded area defined by the rectangle $F.X$, $M.Y$, $F.W$, $F.Y − M.Y$.

- To draw objects which are visible in the expanded area.

Reduce

```
PROCEDURE Reduce(F: Frame; newY: INTEGER);
```
Reduces frame F at the bottom. The type of F is given by the frame class. The actual parameter $M.Y$ is passed to the formal parameter *newY*.

Normally, certain objects will no longer fit fully in the reduced frame. Three strategies may be employed:

(1) Partially visible objects are cleared from the display.

(2) Partially visible objects are adjusted such that they fit the reduced frame.

(3) Partially visible objects are inactivated but the screen is not updated.

The last strategy is the most responsive and is plagued with least flicker. However, it produces 'bodies' which have to be cleared after a while with an explicit restore command.

Transform-
Display-
Descriptors

PROCEDURE TransformDisplayDescriptors(F: Frame; dY: INTEGER);
The type of *F* is given by the frame class.

It is typical that the objects which are visible in a frame are defined through a list of display descriptors. For example, in the standard editor, each line has a line descriptor. In graphics programs, there are descriptors for lines, circles, rectangles etc.

The task of *TransformDisplayDescriptors* is to traverse the data structure of display descriptors attached to frame *F* and transform any *y* coordinate measured in absolute screen coordinates according to the statement:

$$Y := Y + dY$$

19.4.3   Reusing a frame handler

Often, a user wishes to change a viewer class only slightly. In such a case, he or she may be able to extend an existing handler. The new handler interprets the messages whose semantics have changed and calls the old handler with the rest of the messages.

For example, assume that we wish to move the caret with the arrow keys. We need to know the code which the keyboard produces when one of the arrow keys is hit. We then process the consume message with this code outside the normal handler *TextFrames.Handle*. Our modified handler is:

```
PROCEDURE MyHandler*(F: Display.Frame; VAR: M: Display.FrameMsg);
CONST
    Left = 0C4X; Right = 0C3X; Up = 0C1X; Down = 0C2X; (* see Appendix *)
VAR pos: LONGINT;
```

```
BEGIN
WITH F: TextFrames.Frame DO
    IF M IS Oberon.InputMsg THEN
        WITH M: Oberon.InputMsg DO
            IF M.id = Oberon.consume THEN
                IF F.car > 0 THEN (* A caret is set *)
                    IF M.ch = Left THEN
                        TextFrames.RemoveCaret(F);
                        TextFrames.SetCaret(F, F.carloc.pos − 1)
                    ELSIF M.ch = Right THEN
                        TextFrames.RemoveCaret(F);
                        TextFrames.SetCaret(F, F.carloc.pos + 1)
                    END
                END
            END
        END
    END;
    TextFrames.Handle(F, M); (* Call the normal handler *)
END (* WITH F: TextFrames.Frame *)
END MyHandler
```

The user also has to provide his or her own open command which will
install the modified handler.

19.5   Handling mouse events, the track message

Within the program text of the handler, processing mouse events is
usually the most complicated part. Viewer classes define a variety of
mouse commands. Recall the mouse editing commands of the standard editor which use single and interclick events and which even differ
depending on whether the mouse is in the scroll bar or in the editable
text. This section treats techniques of handling the mouse and decoding mouse commands.

When the event loop senses a mouse movement or key press, it
sends a *track message M* to the affected viewer. If it is a menu viewer,
the mouse event is further delegated to the subframe which contains
the mouse cursor (unless it is a 'reposition title bar' command.) We
recapitulate that the term *track message* means a message of type
Oberon.InputMsg with *M.id = Oberon.track*. While the mouse moves or
while a key is pressed, track messages arrive at a fast rate; that is, at the
rate at which the event loop cycles.

The first action in processing a track message *M* is always to
draw the mouse cursor using the call:

```
Oberon.DrawCursor(Oberon.Mouse, Oberon.Arrow, M.X, M.Y);
```

Note: Oberon.Arrow is the recommended cursor pattern. However, markers with other patterns may be used; for example, to indicate modes such as 'draw rectangle mode' in a graphics program.

If a key is pressed, the human operator issues a command. Two actions are typical:

(1) Clicking: The mouse is stationary and a key is pressed. On release, a specific action takes place. For example, clicking with the right key into the scroll bar scrolls to the top of the document.

(2) Dragging: The mouse moves while a key is pressed. During the move, a continuous action is visible. On release of the key, a final command is executed. There are many examples in Oberon; for example, dragging on the middle key underlines words touched with the cursor and on release the final word is executed as a command.

In both cases the action takes place on release of all mouse keys.

Oberon track messages state that, at a given time, a mouse key is either up or down. The handler must find the points in time when the key state changes.

19.5.1   The tracking loop

An elegant way to do this is as follows. At the first track message with a key-down indicator, the handler *seizes control*. A loop, called the *tracking loop*, is entered. In this loop, the mouse driver is read directly and interclick events are recorded. The loop terminates when all three keys are up again. At this point in time, the final command action is determined and executed and control reverts to the event loop. An example of such a tracking procedure is as follows:

```
PROCEDURE TrackMouse(VAR X, Y: INTEGER; VAR keysum: SET);
VAR keys: SET;
BEGIN
   keys := keysum;
   WHILE keys # { } DO
      (* There is still a key down *)
      Oberon.DrawCursor(Oberon.Mouse, Oberon.Mouse.marker, X, Y);
      ...                             (* Perform some tracking actions *)
      Input.Mouse(keys, X, Y);    (* Read mouse driver *)
      keysum := keysum + keys (* Record possible interclicks in keysum *)
   END
   (* At the exit keysum records all keys pressed *)
END TrackMouse;
```

TrackMouse is called with actual parameters $M.X$, $M.Y$ and $M.keys$, respectively (where M is the track message.)

It is noteworthy that the actual parameter indicating the marker of the mouse cursor is *Oberon.Mouse.marker*, not *Oberon.Arrow*. This is to ensure that the tracking procedure works correctly in a viewer or frame using a non-standard mouse cursor.

After a call to *TrackMouse*, the variable parameter *keysum* reports all mouse keys which were pressed during the tracking operation. Thus, inspection of *keysum* allows determination of interclick events.

Tracking a rectangle

To give a real example of a tracking loop, we span a rectangle with the mouse. Such a rectangle may define the selection or a geometrical object to be drawn. The mouse is placed at the upper left corner, a key pressed and dragged. The rectangle grows or shrinks in real time as the mouse defines the diagonal. When all keys are released, the extremal corners of the rectangle are returned and the tracked outline is removed.

Flicker avoidance

While spanning a rectangle in real time, *it is important only to redraw those line segments which change*. Otherwise, the growing rectangle flickers in an unpleasant manner. The procedure *FlipRect* shows the principle.

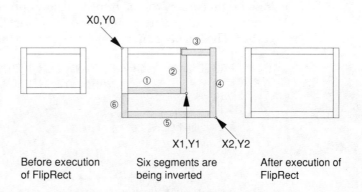

Before execution of FlipRect

Six segments are being inverted

After execution of FlipRect

In order to allow the spanned rectangle to grow and shrink, an auxiliary procedure *ReplConst* is provided, which relaxes the restriction of *Display.ReplConst* that the destination always has positive width W and height H. In the auxiliary procedure, a destination may be defined from the upper right corner X, Y, for example. In this case, W and H are negative integers.

```
PROCEDURE ReplConst(color, X, Y, W, H, mode: INTEGER);
BEGIN
  IF W < 0 THEN X := X + W; W := −W END;
  IF H < 0 THEN Y := Y + H; H := −H END;
  IF (W # 0) & (H # 0) THEN
    Display.ReplConst(color, X, Y, W, H, mode)
  END
END ReplConst;
```

Using the generalized procedure *ReplConst*, our rectangle will be
grown from the lower left corner (*X1, Y1*) to (*X2, Y2*) by inverting the
six line segments shown in the diagram:

```
PROCEDURE FlipRect(X0, Y0, X1, Y1, X2, Y2: INTEGER);
CONST fgnd = Display.white;
BEGIN
  ReplConst(fgnd, X0 + 1, Y1, X1 − X0 − 2, 1, Display.invert); (* Segment 1 *)
  ReplConst(fgnd, X1 − 1, Y1, 1, Y0 − Y1, Display.invert);     (* Segment 2 *)
  ReplConst(fgnd, X1 − 1, Y0 − 1, X2 − X1, 1, Display.invert); (* Segment 3 *)
  ReplConst(fgnd, X2 − 1, Y2, 1, Y0 − Y2, Display.invert);     (* Segment 4 *)
  ReplConst(fgnd, X0 + 1, Y2, X2 − X0 − 2, 1, Display.invert); (* Segment 5 *)
  ReplConst(fgnd, X0, Y2, 1, Y1 − Y2, Display.invert)          (* Segment 6 *)
END FlipRect;
```

The procedure *DragRect* uses the described method. The parameters
X0, Y0 define the initial upper left corner; *X1, Y2* denote the initial
lower right corner; *keysum* returns all keys pressed during the dragging
action; and *X2, Y2* are result parameters yielding the final lower right
corner. The tracking operation is confined to the frame *F*.

```
PROCEDURE DragRect(F: Display.Frame; X0, Y0, X1, Y1: INTEGER;
                   VAR X2, Y2: INTEGER; VAR keysum: SET);
VAR
  keys: SET;
  x, y: INTEGER;

BEGIN
  keys := keysum;
  (* Draw initial rectangle *)
  FlipRect(X0, Y0, X0 + 1, Y0 − 1, X1, Y1);

  WHILE keys # { } DO
    (* Track as long as any key depressed *)
    Input.Mouse(keys, x, y);
    Oberon.DrawCursor(Oberon.Mouse, Oberon.Arrow, x, y);
    keysum := keysum + keys;
    X2 := Min(Max(x, F.X), F.X + F.W);   (* Confine X2 to frame F *)
    Y2 := Min(Max(y, F.Y), F.Y + F.H);   (* Confine Y2 to frame F *)
```

```
      IF (X2 # X1) OR (Y2 # Y1) THEN
         FlipRect(X0, Y0, X1, Y1, X2, Y2);
         X1 := X2; Y1 := Y2
      END
   END;
   FlipRect(X0, Y0, X0 + 1, Y0 − 1, X1, Y1)  (* Erase spanned rectangle *)
END DragRect;
```

Note: The distinction between the mouse position, *x*, *y*, and the moving corner of the rectangle, *X2*, *Y2*, is deliberate. While the mouse cursor is allowed to move over the whole screen, the moving corner of the tracked rectangle is usually subject to restrictions. In our example, tracking is confined to the area of frame *F*.

Whether the whole rectangle being spanned is redrawn or the techniques of *FlipRect* are used makes a big difference. An unusually smooth 'rubberband-like' spanning is achieved if only those parts which actually change are erased and added.

19.5.2   Different mouse-sensitive areas

We are now in a position to elaborate the part of the handler which deals with track messages. Normally, a viewer's frame is divided into areas for which the response to mouse keys differs. In text viewers, for example, the title bar, the scroll bar and the text region are three such areas. The following program fragment provides a general framework:

```
CONST right = 0; middle = 1; left = 2;
IF M.id = Oberon.track THEN
   (* A mouse event occurred *)
   Oberon.DrawCursor(Oberon.Mouse, Oberon.Arrow, M.X, M.Y);
   IF ... (* Mouse coordinates M.X, M.Y are in area 1 *) THEN
      IF right IN M.keys THEN
         Call TrackMouseOnRightInArea1(M.X, M.Y, M.keys);
         IF (middle IN M.keys) & (left IN M.keys) THEN
            (* Mouse action cancelled *)
            RETURN
      ELSIF middle IN M.keys THEN
         ... (* Mouse command with middle key interclicked *)
      ELSIF left IN M.keys THEN
         ... (* Mouse command with left key interclicked *)
      ELSE
         ... (* Mouse command without interclicks *)
      END
```

```
            ELSIF middle IN M.keys THEN
                Call TrackMouseOnMiddleInArea1(M.X, M.Y, M.keys);
                IF (right IN M.keys) & (left IN M.keys) THEN
                    (* Mouse action cancelled *)
                    RETURN
                ELSIF right IN M.keys THEN
                    ... (* Mouse command with right key interclicked *)
                ELSIF left IN M.keys THEN
                    ... (* Mouse command with left key interclicked *)
                ELSE
                    ... (* Mouse command without interclicks *)
                END
            ELSIF left IN M.keys THEN
                Call TrackMouseOnLeftInArea1(M.X, M.Y, M.keys);
                IF (middle IN M.keys) & (right IN M.keys) THEN
                    (* Mouse action cancelled *)
                    RETURN
                ELSIF middle IN M.keys THEN
                    ... (* Mouse command with middle key interclicked *)
                ELSIF right IN M.keys THEN
                    ... (* Mouse command with right key interclicked *)
                ELSE
                    ... (* Mouse command without interclicks *)
                END
            END
        ELSIF ...  (* Mouse coordinates M.X, M.Y are in area 2 *) THEN
            ...     (* Track keys as above *)
        ELSIF ...  (* Mouse coordinates M.X, M.Y are in area 3 *) THEN
            ...     (* Track keys as above *)
        END
    END;
```

In the most general case, a tracking procedure is provided for each area and each primary key. These tracking procedures follow the example *TrackMouse* closely. In practice, the number of tracking procedures is usually less than three times the number of areas.

To prevent the handler's program text growing too big, the entire mouse tracking per area or group of areas could be encapsulated in a procedure. For the standard editor, the tracking procedure is called *TextFrames.Edit*.

Executing a command

Whenever the mouse is in an area which displays a text, the mandatory response to a middle key mouse-up event is the interpretation of the word found at the mouse location as a command. If the text is displayed in a text frame, the following program excerpt handles command execution:

```
IF middle IN M.keys THEN
    TextFrames.TrackWord(F, M.X, M.Y, pos, M.keys);
    IF ~(right IN M.keys) THEN
        TextFrames.Call(F, pos, left IN M.keys)
    END;
```

where:

```
F: TextFrames.Frame; (* The text frame containing the mouse *)
pos: LONGINT;
```

19.6   Example: handler for a text frame

19.6.1   Introduction

Since text frames are likely to be reused in many applications, we conclude this chapter by discussing the code for a handler implementing the standard editor. The handler uses the display manager of module TextFrames and is intended to be installed in frames managed by a menu viewer.

This section is a tutorial. It shows how the editor is implemented using the display manager of module TextFrames. Following the described techniques, it is easy to change or extend the editor in various ways.

The following programs are close to those employed in module TextFrames (author J. Gutknecht.) However, for tutorial reasons, the subdivision into individual procedures is different.

Recall the rules which should be observed when working with the display manager of module TextFrames:

- A caret is only allowed if the viewer which manages F is the focus viewer.
- When the focus is requested by means of a call to *Oberon.PassFocus(V)*, any caret which may be visible prior to the call is removed.
- If a caret is displayed ($F.car > 0$), it must be removed prior to using *TextFrames.SetCaret*.
- Prior to using *TextFrames.Show*, *TextFrames.Extend*, *TextFrames.Reduce*, *TextFrames.Insert*, *TextFrames.Delete* and *TextFrames.Replace*, the caret, the selection, the mouse cursor and the pointer must be removed.

- The text is changed through calls to procedures of module Texts (the data manager.) This results in a recursive call to the handler which receives an update message. After control reverts, the caret must be moved explicitly, if this is required.

19.6.2   Handler implementation

```
MODULE EditFrames;

IMPORT Texts, TextFrames, Display, Oberon, Input, MenuViewers;

CONST
    right = 0; middle = 1; left = 2; (* Mouse keys *)
    noMark = 0; positionMark = 1;
    repl = Display.replace;
VAR KeyboardWriter: Texts.Writer;
```

RemoveMarks   Removes selection and the caret from text frame F:

```
PROCEDURE RemoveMarks(F: TextFrames.Frame);
BEGIN
    TextFrames.RemoveSelection(F);
    TextFrames.RemoveCaret(F)
END RemoveMarks;
```

TrackMouse   Tracks the mouse while any key is pressed. On release of all keys, the sum of the keys pressed while tracking is reported in *keysum*. Definite command action takes place after TrackMouse, depending on the primary key and interclick keys (see Section 19.5.)

```
PROCEDURE TrackMouse(VAR x, y: INTEGER; VAR keysum: SET);
```

Scroll   Handles the mouse keys when the cursor is in the scroll bar. Note that all marks must be removed prior to a call to the procedure *Text-Frames.Show*.

Text is scrolled such that the character at *pos* will be the first one displayed where *pos* is determined according to:

$$a : H = pos : text.len, \quad a = F.Y + F.H - y \quad \text{and} \quad H = F.H$$

```
PROCEDURE Scroll(F: TextFrames.Frame; x, y: INTEGER; keysum: SET);
VAR pos: LONGINT;
BEGIN
  IF right IN keysum THEN          (* Scroll to top *)
     TrackMouse(x, y, keysum);
     IF (left IN keysum) & (middle IN keysum) THEN
        RETURN                     (* Interclick command cancelled *)
     ELSE
        RemoveMarks(F); Oberon.RemoveMarks(F.X, F.Y, F.W, F.H);
        TextFrames.Show(F, 0)
     END
  ELSIF middle IN keysum THEN (* Set position mark *)
     TrackMouse(x, y, keysum);
     IF (left IN keysum) & (middle IN keysum) THEN
        RETURN                     (* Interclick command cancelled *)
     ELSE
        pos := (F.Y + F.H − y) * (F.text.len) DIV F.H;
        RemoveMarks(F); Oberon.RemoveMarks(F.X, F.Y, F.W, F.H);
        TextFrames.Show(F, pos)
     END
  ELSIF left IN keysum THEN        (* Scroll down *)
     TextFrames.TrackLine(F, x, y, pos, keysum);
     IF (pos >= 0) & ~((left IN keysum) & (right IN keysum)) THEN
        RemoveMarks(F); Oberon.RemoveMarks(F.X, F.Y, F.W, F.H);
        TextFrames.Show(F, pos)  (* Tracked line to top *)
     END
  END
END Scroll;
```

Select key   Handles the right mouse key when the cursor is in the editable text. Note the need for the call to *Oberon.PassFocus* so that the caret can be displayed at the point where deletion took place. The caret has to be properly adjusted after each call to *Texts.Delete*. The operations on the text of frame *F* will invoke the handler of *F* recursively. The update operation will clear all marks. Hence, no explicit clearing operation is required prior to *TextFrames.SetCaret*.

```
PROCEDURE HandleRightKeyInEditArea(F: TextFrames.Frame;
                                   x, y: INTEGER; keysum: SET);
VAR
   text: Texts.Text;
   beg, end, time: LONGINT;
   M: Oberon.CopyOverMsg;
BEGIN
   TextFrames.TrackSelection(F, x, y, keysum);
```

```
              IF F.sel # 0 THEN                    (* A selection exists *)
                IF (left IN keysum) & (middle IN keysum) THEN
                  RETURN                           (* Interclick command cancelled *)
                ELSIF left IN keysum THEN          (* Delete selection *)
                  Oberon.GetSelection(text, beg, end, time);
                  Texts.Delete(text, beg, end);
                  Oberon.PassFocus(Viewers.This(F.X, F.Y));
                  TextFrames.SetCaret(F, beg)
                ELSIF middle IN keysum THEN (* Copy selection to caret *)
                  (* Send an Oberon copy over message to the focus viewer *)
                  Oberon.GetSelection(text, beg, end, time);
                  M.text := text; M.beg := beg; M.end := end;
                  Oberon.FocusViewer.handle(Oberon.FocusViewer, M)
                END
              END
            END HandleRightKeyInEditArea;
```

Execute key   Handles the middle key when the cursor is in the editable text. The
menu viewer which manages frame *F* is needed to build the parameter
list. It is the value of *Viewers.This(F.X, F.Y)*.

```
            PROCEDURE HandleMiddleKeyInEditArea(F: TextFrames.Frame;
                                                x, y: INTEGER; keysum: SET);
            VAR
              pos: LONGINT;
              par: Oberon.ParList;
              S: Texts.Scanner;
              res: INTEGER;
            BEGIN
              TextFrames.TrackWord(F, x, y, pos, keysum);
              IF (pos >= 0) & ~((left IN keysum) & (right IN keysum)) THEN
              (* A valid position found and interclick not cancelled *)
                Texts.OpenScanner(S, F.text, pos); Texts.Scan(S);
                IF S.class = Texts.Name THEN       (* A name found at mouse pos *)
                  (* Build Oberon parameter list *)
                  NEW(par);
                  par.vwr := Viewers.This(F.X, F.Y); (* The menu viewer *)
                  par.frame := F;
                  par.text := F.text;
                  par.pos := pos + S.len; (* Position immediately after cmd name *)
                  Oberon.Call(S.s, par, left IN keysum, res);
                  IF res > 1 THEN
                    LogOut.PutInt("call error", res)
                  END
                END
              END
            END HandleMiddleKeyInEditArea;
```

Point key Handles the left key when the cursor is in the editable text. After a call to *Oberon.PassFocus*, the caret will be removed. Hence, the precondition for *TextFrames.TrackCaret* is met.

The caret has to be properly adjusted after each call to *Texts.Insert*. The operations on the text of frame *F* will invoke the handler of *F* recursively. The update operation will clear all marks. Hence, no explicit clearing operation is required prior to *TextFrames.SetCaret*.

```
PROCEDURE HandleLeftKeyInEditArea(F: TextFrames.Frame;
                                  x, y: INTEGER; keysum: SET);
VAR
   B: Texts.Buffer;
   text: Texts.Text;
   beg, end, time: LONGINT;
BEGIN
   Oberon.PassFocus(Viewers.This(F.X, F.Y));
   TextFrames.TrackCaret(F, x, y, keysum);
   IF F.car # 0 THEN (* A caret is set *)
     IF (middle IN keysum) & (right IN keysum) THEN
        RETURN (* Interclick command cancelled *)
     ELSIF middle IN keysum THEN (* Copy selection to caret location *)
        Oberon.GetSelection(text, beg, end, time);
        IF time > 0 THEN (* A selection exists *)
          NEW(B); Texts.OpenBuf(B);
          Texts.Save(text, beg, end, B);
          Texts.Insert(F.text, F.carloc.pos, B);
          TextFrames.SetCaret(F, F.carloc.pos + (end − beg))
        END
     END
   END
END HandleLeftKeyInEditArea;
```

Write Writes a character from the keyboard to the caret location. Deletes character if DEL is hit.

The caret has to be properly adjusted after each call to *Texts.Insert* or *Texts.Delete*. The operations on the text of frame *F* will invoke the handler of *F* recursively. The update operation will clear all marks. Hence, no explicit clearing operation is required prior to *TextFrames.SetCaret*.

```
PROCEDURE Write(F: TextFrames.Frame; VAR M: Oberon.InputMsg);
CONST DEL = 7FX; (* The ASCII character for delete *)
```

```
            BEGIN
              IF F.car # 0 THEN (* A caret is set *)
                IF M.ch = DEL THEN
                  IF F.carloc.pos > F.org THEN (* Caret not at origin of frame *)
                    Texts.Delete(F.text, F.carloc.pos − 1, F.carloc.pos);
                    TextFrames.SetCaret(F, F.carloc.pos − 1)
                  END
                ELSE
                  Texts.Write(KeyboardWriter, M.ch);
                  Texts.Insert(F.text, F.carloc.pos, KeyboardWriter.buf);
                  TextFrames.SetCaret(F, F.carloc.pos + 1)
                END
              END
            END Write;
```

ReportSelection   Reports the selection of frame *F* in the selection message.

```
            PROCEDURE ReportSelection(F: TextFrames.Frame;
                                        VAR M: Oberon.SelectionMsg);
            BEGIN
              IF (F.sel > 0) & (F.time > M.time) THEN
                (* A selection exists and is more recent than the one contained in M *)
                M.text := F.text;
                M.beg := F.selbeg.pos;
                M.end := F.selend.pos;
                M.time := F.time
              END
            END ReportSelection;
```

CopyFrame   Produces a copy of frame *F* and reports it in the copy message (see Section 19.4.)

```
            PROCEDURE CopyFrame(F: TextFrames.Frame;
                                  VAR M: Oberon.CopyMsg);
```

CopyOver   Copies the stretch of text reported in the copyover message to the caret location. The caret has to be properly adjusted after each call to *Texts.Insert*. The operations on the text of frame *F* will invoke the handler of *F* recursively. The update operation will clear all marks. Hence, no explicit clearing operation is required prior to *TextFrames.SetCaret*.

```
            PROCEDURE CopyOver(F: TextFrames.Frame;
                                 M: Oberon.CopyOverMsg);
            VAR buf: Texts.Buffer;
```

```
                    BEGIN
                      IF F.car > 0 THEN (* A caret is set *)
                        NEW(buf); Texts.OpenBuf(buf);
                        Texts.Save(M.text, M.beg, M.end, buf);
                        Texts.Insert(F.text, F.carloc.pos, buf);
                        TextFrames.SetCaret(F, F.carloc.pos + (M.end − M.beg))
                      END
                    END CopyOver;
```

Modify   Modifies frame as directed by the MenuViewers modify message (see
                      Section 19.4.)
                          The   procedures   *TextFrames.Extend*   and   *TextFrames.Reduce*
                      use relative coordinates. Hence, no coordinate transformations are
                      required.

```
                    PROCEDURE Modify(F: TextFrames.Frame;
                                         M: MenuViewers.ModifyMsg);
                    BEGIN
                      RemoveMarks(F); Oberon.RemoveMarks(F.X, F.Y, F.W, F.H);
                      TextFrames.Mark(F, noMark);
                      IF M.id = MenuViewers.extend THEN
                        IF M.dY > 0 THEN
                          Display.CopyBlock(F.X, F.Y, F.W, F.H, F.X, F.Y + M.dY, repl);
                          F.Y := F.Y + M.dY
                        END;
                        TextFrames.Extend(F, M.Y)
                      ELSIF M.id = MenuViewers.reduce THEN
                        TextFrames.Reduce(F, M.Y + M.dY);
                        IF M.dY > 0 THEN
                          Display.CopyBlock(F.X, M.Y + M.dY, F.W, M.H, F.X, M.Y, repl)
                        END
                      END;
                      TextFrames.Mark(positionMark)
                    END Modify;
```

Update   Updates the display directed by a TextFrames update message.

```
                    PROCEDURE Update(F: TextFrames.Frame; M: TextFrames.UpdateMsg);
                    BEGIN
                      RemoveMarks(F); Oberon.RemoveMarks(F.X, F.Y, F.W, F.H);
                      IF M.id = TextFrames.replace THEN
                        TextFrames.Replace(F, M.beg, M.end)
                      ELSIF M.id = TextFrames.insert THEN
                        TextFrames.Insert(F, M.beg, M.end)
                      ELSIF M.id = TextFrames.delete THEN
                        TextFrames.Delete(F, M.beg, M.end)
                      END
                    END Update;
```

Handle   Here is the handler.

```
PROCEDURE Handle*(F: Display.Frame; VAR M: Display.FrameMsg);
BEGIN
WITH F: TextFrames.Frame DO
  IF M IS Oberon.InputMsg THEN
    WITH M: Oberon.InputMsg DO
      IF M.id = Oberon.consume THEN Write(F, M)
      ELSIF M.id = Oberon.track THEN
        Oberon.DrawCursor(Oberon.Mouse, Oberon.Arrow, M.X, M.Y);
        IF M.X < F.X + TextFrames.barW THEN (* Mouse in scroll bar *)
          Scroll(F, M.X, M.Y, M.keys)
        ELSE (* Mouse in editable text area *)
          IF right IN M.keys THEN
            HandleRightKeyInEditArea(F, M.X, M.Y, M.keys)
          ELSIF middle IN M.keys THEN
            HandleMiddleKeyInEditArea(F, M.X, M.Y, M.keys)
          ELSIF left IN M.keys THEN
            HandleLeftKeyInEditArea(F, M.X, M.Y, M.keys)
          END
        END
      END
    END
  ELSIF M IS Oberon.ControlMsg THEN
    WITH M: Oberon.ControlMsg DO
      IF M.id = Oberon.defocus THEN TextFrames.RemoveCaret(F)
      ELSIF M.id = Oberon.neutralize THEN RemoveMarks(F)
      END
    END
  ELSIF M IS Oberon.SelectionMsg THEN
    ReportSelection(F, M(Oberon.SelectionMsg))
  ELSIF M IS Oberon.CopyMsg THEN
    CopyFrame(F, M(Oberon.CopyMsg))
  ELSIF M IS Oberon.CopyOverMsg THEN
    CopyOver(F, M(Oberon.CopyOverMsg))
  ELSIF M IS MenuViewers.ModifyMsg THEN
    Modify(F, M(MenuViewers.ModifyMsg))
  ELSIF M IS TextFrames.UpdateMsg THEN
    IF F.text = M.text THEN Update(F, M(TextFrames.UpdateMsg)) END
  END
END (* WITH F: TextFrames.Frame DO *)
END Handle;
```

Open   Creates an instance of a menu viewer with a standard menu frame and
a main frame with the handler of this module installed.

```
PROCEDURE Open*;
CONST beginning = 0;
```

```
  VAR
    V: MenuViewers.Viewer;
    X, Y: INTEGER;
    editText, text: Texts.Text;
    mainF, menuF: TextFrames.Frame;
    beg, end, time: LONGINT;
    S: Texts.Scanner;
  BEGIN
    Texts.OpenScanner(S, Oberon.Par.text, Oberon.Par.pos);
    Texts.Scan(S);
    IF S.class # Texts.Name THEN
      S.s := "Edit.Text";
      IF (S.class = Texts.Char) & S.c =" ↑ ") THEN
        Oberon.GetSelection(text, beg, end, time);
        IF t > 0 THEN (* Selection exists *)
          Texts.OpenScanner(S, text, beg);
          Texts.Scan(S)
        END
      END
    END;
    editText := TextFrames.Text(S.s);
    NEW(mainF);
    TextFrames.Open(mainF, Handle, editText, beginning,
                    Display.white,
                    TextFrames.left, TextFrames.right,
                    TextFrames.top, TextFrames.bot,
                    TextFrames.lsp);
    menuF := TextFrames.NewMenu(S.s,
    "System.Close  System.Copy  System.Grow  Edit.Search  Edit.Store");
    Oberon.AllocateUserViewer(Oberon.Mouse.X, X, Y);
    V := MenuViewers.New(menuF, mainF, TextFrames.menuH, X, Y);
    TextFrames.Mark(mainF, positionMark)
  END Open;

BEGIN
  Texts.OpenWriter(KeyboardWriter);
END EditFrames.
```

19.7 Rules for well-behaved handlers

By handler, we subsequently mean the *handler proper and all procedures called by it* including those of the display manager.

- The handler is responsible for all write operations to the screen (including tracking the mouse cursor.) It typically uses procedures from module Display.

- The handler is responsible for *respecting the viewer's boundary or the frame boundary at all times* when writing to the screen. The only exception to this rule are the tracking loops in which the cursor (and possibly a figure such as a rectangle) is drawn.

- The handler *writes to the screen only if the state of the viewer is displayed* (*V.state* > 1.) *Note:* It is possible that the handler of suspended or closed viewers will still receive messages. For example, if the suspended viewer was the focus viewer before it became suspended or closed, it will continue to receive Oberon consume and defocus messages.

- The handler does *not read the keyboard directly* (through call to *Input.Read.*) Keyboard input is received through messages a character at a time.

APPENDIX A
Viewer class note board: an extended example

A.1 Introduction

Little note slips are an feature of our everyday life. Our example of a viewer class gives an electronic analog of a note board. The viewer shows portion of a board to which notes are attached.

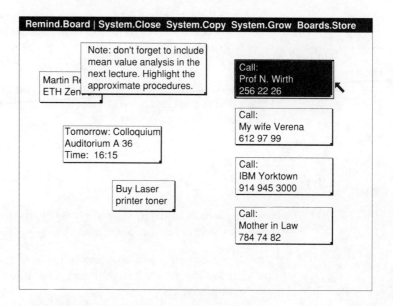

Manipulation of notes

Notes are manipulated with the mouse. Care has been taken to ensure that analogies with the standard editor are preserved:

- *Creation*: The mouse points into the board area. Dragging on the left key (the point key) spans a rectangle. On release, a note appears with the defined size.

- *Selection*: A note is selected by clicking at its border with the right key (the select key.) The selected note is highlighted in reverse video.

- *Deletion*: A note is deleted if, while selecting, the left key is interclicked (like the selection in the standard editor.)

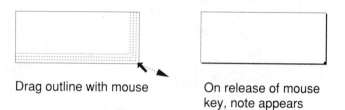

Drag outline with mouse   On release of mouse
                                  key, note appears

Scrolling   The note board may be grabbed (middle key) and moved vertically behind the window of the viewer. While the board is grabbed, the cursor shape changes to a cross.

Note board viewers can be split (*System.Copy*) or grown (*System.Grow*) as text viewers. If a viewer is copied, both viewers show the *same* note board.

Editing notes   In each note, the standard text editor functions without restrictions. Text can be entered, selected, deleted and copied. Commands may be executed as from any text.

A.1.1   Goals

The example is a tutorial. Its goal is to illustrate the design of a fully functional viewer class, in particular:

- To present an active document, the *note board*, which notifies the display whenever it is changed. The note board is similar in this respect to texts.

- To give a complete example of a handler for a frame (called *board frame*) to be installed in a menu viewer.

- To demonstrate how to reuse text frames (objects of type *TextFrames.Frame*) in a different context.

- To discuss the design aspects of a windowing system which allows for overlapping frames.

The example is fully functional and tested. However, to keep it concise, many functions which are clearly desirable are omitted, for example:

- To move notes around.
- To change the size of notes or to duplicate notes.
- To generate all kinds of prepared form notes – for calling cards, time reminders or telephone calls.
- To have calendars with automatic links to notes.
- To keep notes in different files.

Clearly, the sophistication of the viewer class is only limited by fantasy and programming man-months.

A.1.2 Module hierarchy

The module structure of board viewers is shown in the following diagram (only the major import relations are depicted.)

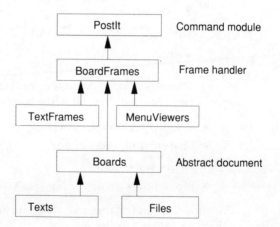

A.2 Module Boards

This module provides the document of the viewer class. The design of this module is simple. A board – an instance of the abstract data type *Board* – is an unlimited Cartesian plane which contains notes. Each note is defined by its lower left coordinate X, Y, a width W and height H. A note has an associated text. The note is itself an instance of the abstract data type *Note*.

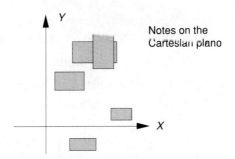

Notes on the
Cartesian plane

Notes are linked in a list with an anchor in the board descriptor. The order of the list corresponds to the *temporal order* in which notes were created (procedure *Poste*) or explicitly moved to the end of the list (procedure *ToTop*.) The latter is invoked when a note is moved to the top of a pile of overlapping notes.

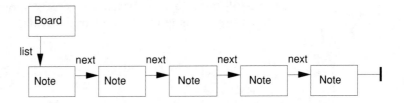

The procedures operating on notes are termed the data manager. They carry out the following functions:

- Create new notes (*PosteEmpty*.)
- Post existing notes (*Poste*.)
- Delete notes (*Delete*.)
- Move notes to top (*ToTop*.)

As with the data manger of texts, an update message is broadcasted which identifies the change.

Our module also provides procedures which initialize a board (that is, an instance of the abstract data type *Board* from a file (procedure *NewBoard*)) and stores a board to a file (procedure *Store*.)

```
Module Boards;

IMPORT TextFrames, Texts, Viewers, Files;
```

Note   The abstract data type *Note* has the properties: position, size, a text and a next note.

```
TYPE
  Note* = POINTER TO NoteDesc;
  NoteDesc* = RECORD
    X*, Y*, W*, H*: INTEGER;
    text*: Texts.Text;
    next: Note
  END;
```

Board   The abstract data type *Board* affords access to a list of notes. The notes are not visible to the client and are read using a reader.

```
TYPE
  Board* = POINTER TO BoardDesc;
  BoardDesc* = RECORD
    list: Note
  END;
```

Update message   The procedures which change a note board broadcast a message of type *Boards.UpdateMsg* to all visible viewers.

```
TYPE
  UpdateMsg* = RECORD
    (Display.FrameMsg)
    id*: INTEGER;
    board*: Board;
    note*: Note
  END;
```

Message id   The following constants define the messages in a self-explanatory manner:

```
CONST poste* = 0; discard* = 1; toTop* = 2;
```

Reader   The abstract data type *Reader* yields sequential access to notes. *Note:* The field *Note* is not visible to the client. It records the position of the reader in the list of notes.

```
TYPE
  Reader* = RECORD
    N: Note
  END;
```

Minimum size   Notes are only opened if they have minimal size:

```
VAR minW*, minH*: INTEGER;
```

File id   A note file is characterized by a two-byte tag which has value:

CONST BoardFileId = 31697;

List processing   The following procedures operate on the list of notes. Only the procedure heading is shown for brevity.

PROCEDURE Append(B: Board; N: Note);

PROCEDURE Remove(B: Board; N: Note):

PROCEDURE ToListEnd(B: Board; N: Note):

Poste   Appends a note *N* to the end of the note list and broadcasts a post message.

```
PROCEDURE Poste*(B: Board; N: Note);
VAR M: UpdateMsg;
BEGIN
  Append(B, N);
  M.id := poste; M.note := N; M.board := B; Viewers.Broadcast(M)
END Poste;
```

PosteEmpty   Creates a new note at *X, Y* with width *W* and height *H*. Posts the new note (see *Poste*.)

```
PROCEDURE PosteEmpty*(B: Board; X, Y, W, H: INTEGER);
VAR N: Note;
BEGIN
  IF (W < minW) OR (H < minH) THEN RETURN END;
  NEW(N);
  N.X := X; N.Y := Y; N.W := W; N.H := H; (* In board coordinates *)
  N.text := TextFrames.Text("");
  Poste(B, N)
END PosteEmpty;
```

Discard   Discards note *N*. Broadcasts a discard message.

```
PROCEDURE Discard*(B: Board; N: Note);
VAR M: UpdateMsg;
BEGIN
  Remove (B, N);
  M.id := discard; M.note := N; M.board := B; Viewers.Broadcast(M)
END Discard;
```

ToTop   Moves note *N* to the end of the list. When displayed, such a note will always appear at the top of a pile of overlapping notes. Broadcasts a *ToTop* message.

```
PROCEDURE ToTop*(B: Board; N: Note);
VAR M: UpdateMsg;
BEGIN
  ToListEnd(B, N);
  M.id := toTop; M.note := N; M.board := B; Viewers.Broadcast(M)
END ToTop;
```

OpenReader, Read

Sets reader to origin of list of notes of board *B*. Reads next note *N*.

```
PROCEDURE OpenReader*(VAR R: Reader; B: Board);
BEGIN
  R.N := B.list
END OpenReader;

PROCEDURE Read*(VAR R: Reader; VAR N: Note);
BEGIN
  N := R.N; IF N # NIL THEN R.N := R.N.next END
END Read;
```

Store

Stores notes of board *B* in a file *name*. The file is identified as a note board file with a two-byte tag. Behind this tag is a sequence of stored notes. Each note is represented by its descriptor followed by a text block, viz.

```
PROCEDURE Store*(B: Board; name: ARRAY OF CHAR);
VAR
    F: Files.File;
    R: Files.Rider;
    N: Note;
    pos, len: LONGINT;
    tag: INTEGER;
BEGIN
  F := Files.New(name); Files.Set(R, F, 0);
  tag := BoardFileId; Files.WriteBytes(R, tag, SIZE(INTEGER));
  N := B.list;
  WHILE N # NIL DO
    Files.WriteBytes(R, N↑, SIZE(NoteDesc));
    pos := Files.Pos(R);
    Texts.Store(N.text, F, pos, len);
    Files.Set(R, F, pos + len);
    N := N.next
  END;
  Files.Register(F)
END Store;
```

NewBoard

Returns an instance of a board which was initialized from file *name*. If no file *name* exists or if the file is not a note board file, an empty board is created.

```
PROCEDURE NewBoard*(name: ARRAY OF CHAR): Board;
VAR
  F: Files.File;
  R: Files.Rider;
  B: Board;
  N: Note;
  pos, len: LONGINT;
  tag: INTEGER;
BEGIN
  NEW(B); B.list := NIL;
  F := Files.Old(name);
  IF F# NIL THEN
    Files.Set(R, F, 0);
    Files.ReadBytes(R, tag, SIZE(INTEGER));
    IF tag = BoardFileId THEN
      NEW(N);                    (* Create instance of note *)
      Files.ReadBytes(R, N↑, SIZE(NoteDesc));
      WHILE ~R.eof DO
        NEW(N.text);            (* Create instance of text *)
        N.text.notify := TextFrames.NotifyDisplay;
        pos := Files.Pos(R) + 2; (* Note offset of 2 *)
        Texts.Load(N.text, F, pos, len);
        Files.Set(R, F, pos + len);
        Append(B, N);
        NEW(N);                  (* Create instance of note *)
        Files.ReadBytes(R, N↑, SIZE(NoteDesc))
      END
    END
  END;
  RETURN B
END NewBoard;

BEGIN
  minW := 20; minH := 15

END Boards.
```

A.3 Module BoardFrames

A.3.1 Introduction

This module provides the handler of the viewer class 'board viewers.' Of course, we will follow the Oberon user interface guidelines – hence, the use of a menu viewer is an obvious choice. The task at hand is to *program a frame*, to be installed in such a menu viewer. The duties of the handler and the use of update messages were outlined in Section 19.1.

We call the type of our frame simply *Frame*. An instance of this type is a *board frame*. Such a board frame displays exactly one board (more specifically, an instance of type *Boards.Board*.)

Display descriptors

A board frame shows those notes which are visible within its boundary. A record of these notes has to be kept by each frame. For this purpose, each displayed note is specified by a display descriptor. It is quite natural to call the type of such a descriptor *Note*. We thus deal with objects of the following type:

- *Boards.Note*: abstract note, also called 'board note.'
- *BoardFrames.Note*: display descriptor also dubbed 'frame note.'

Editor in notes

Our frame notes turn out to be rather complex objects. Within each note, the standard Oberon editor is to be provided. But notes are also allowed to overlap and form piles. Our handler has to deal with the management of such piles in addition to directing a multitude of editors.

Fortunately, objects which embody the editor in a rectangular already exist: *text frames*. If we can reuse text frames, we are home free, as far as the editor is concerned. We can easily convince ourselves that this is possible. All we have to do is to declare the type *Note* as an extension of the type *TextFrames.Frame* and take care that the right messages are forwarded to the handlers of the displayed notes.

Coordinate system

A design issue in most viewer classes is the coordinate systems used in the document and in the frame. Frame coordinates may be relative to the frame or absolute with respect to the display.

Since frame notes are extensions of text frames, absolute coordinates must be used. In order to relate display coordinates to frame coordinates, a *fixed point* is required. Our choice is the upper left corner of the frame measured in board coordinates. The upper left corner is the right choice whenever this is also the fixed point with respect to frame moves – the normal and natural choice.

Board coordinates X, Y are transformed to screen coordinates x, y according to the formulae:

$$x = X - (Xboard - F.X) \quad \text{and} \quad y = Y - (Yboard - F.Y - F.H)$$

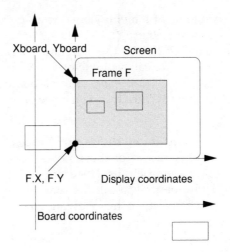

Note geometry

The geometry of a note N is shown in the diagram. The frame defined by $N.X$, $N.Y$, $N.W$ and $N.H$ is surrounded by a border of width *marg*. The wire frame is painted in that border margin.

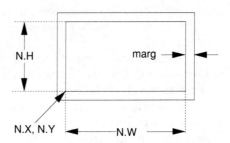

Note: It is tempting to use the text frame margins $N.left$, $N.right$, $N.top$ and $N.bot$ instead of an outer margin of width *marg*. Unfortunately, the display manager of module TextFrames sometimes clears the frame borders, hence the wire frame would also be deleted.

Types Frame and Note

We are now ready to define the abstract data types *Frame* and *Note*:

```
TYPE                                    TYPE
  Note* = POINTER TO NoteDesc;            Frame* = POINTER TO FrameDesc;
  NoteDesc* = RECORD                      FrameDesc* = RECORD
    (TextFrames.FrameDesc)                  (Display.FrameDesc)
    note*: Boards.Note;                     SelectedNote*: Note;
    flag: BOOLEAN                           board*: Boards.Board;
  END;                                      Xboard*, Yboard*: INTEGER
                                          END;
```

The properties are:

- All those inherited from *TextFrames.Frame*.
- The board note which is displayed.
- An ancillary flag.

The properties are:

- All those inherited from *Display.Frame*.
- A selected note.
- The board which is displayed.
- The coordinate fixed point.

Data structure of board viewers

Since notes are of base type *Display.Frame*, we make them descendants of the board frame *F*. Also, inspired by the viewer data structure, we use *N.next* (of a note *N*) to form a simple list of notes with anchor *F.dsc*. With these design choices, the data structure of a board viewer looks as follows:

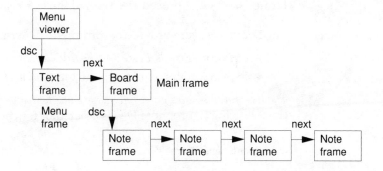

Back-to-back handlers

All objects in this data structure are active (have an installed handler.) The menu viewer is the first recipient of a message originating from viewers, Oberon or document modules. It either acts on it or else hands it over to the handler of the board frame. Again, the board frame handler either consumes a message or further relegates it to the note frames. The hand-over of messages from handler to handler observes the following rules:

- A handler may act on a message and optionally pass it to the next handler in the chain: menu viewer – board frame – frame note.
- A track message is exclusively passed to the frame which contains the mouse cursor.
- All other messages are passed to all successor handlers; that is, they are broadcast.

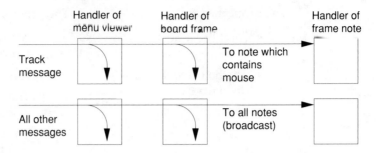

Note manager

Text frames are normally managed by a menu viewer which acts as supervisor. It assigns frame boundaries and sends modify messages. In our case, notes are extensions of text frames. However, they are now under our control. This means that the handler of a board frame creates and deletes notes, assigns their frame (X, Y, W and H) and determines their position in the list. It draws notes and finds the note corresponding to a given coordinate position. These actions are performed by a set of procedures termed the *note manager*.

Temporal order

The board notes are ordered according to increasing time of:

- Creation (*Boards.Poste* and *Boards.PosteEmpty.*)
- Explicit orders to move to the top (*Boards.ToTop.*)

The list of frame notes must reflect the same temporal order. For example, in the following figure, note D was created or touched after note A etc.

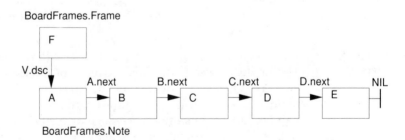

The update message mechanism provides a simple means to keep the list of board notes and display notes in step. For example, if a mouse event occurs in a note which is overlaid by other notes, that note has to be brought to the top. This means:

- The handler of the board frame calls *Boards.ToTop* to bring the board note to the end of the board list.
- An update message M with $M.id = toTop$ is broadcasted, hence also received by our handler.

- The corresponding frame note is brought to the end of the frame list and redrawn on top of its pile.

Overlapping notes

Notes in a board frame may overlap. This causes the well-known clipping problems when one of the notes is deleted or moved. The following diagram shows an example of a board frame with notes which correspond to the list shown in the previous diagram.

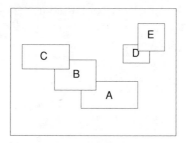

Drawing notes

If the notes are drawn in their temporal order – from the first one to the last one – then the right overlapping is always achieved. The simplest solution, therefore, is always to enact this restoration sequence when the note configuration changes.

However, initialization and display of a note is not a trivial operation. Therefore, it is vital to avoid unnecessary redrawing of notes. The result is a *better response time* paired with *less flicker*. Some sophistication is needed to reach this goal.

The trivial cases are bringing a note to the top of a pile and removing a note which does not overlap any of its peers – just draw the incriminated note without consideration for other notes.

Removing notes

The situation is complicated in all other cases. Consider the situation where a note is removed which overlaps other notes. An example is depicted in the following diagram.

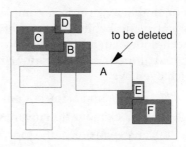

As a consequence of the removal of A, all the darkly shaded notes need restoration in the temporal order of the note list. The affected notes can be determined by a recursive procedure explained later (procedure *MarkAfterDelete*.)

Extending and reducing a frame

Similarly, when the area of the frame shrinks, those notes which overlap with the reduced area but are not fully contained in it must be removed. As a consequence, some notes, flagged by the recursive procedure mentioned earlier, may have to be redrawn even though they are fully contained in the target frame.

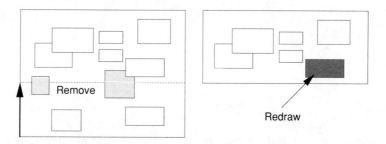

In the same vein, when the frame extends, only those notes should be drawn which are newly visible. Note that here, too, drawing such a note may lead to the need to redraw another note which is fully contained in the original frame. The same recursive method flags those notes.

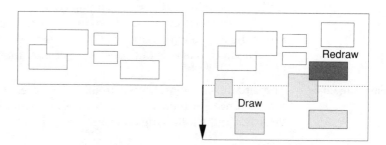

Scrolling

For simplicity, we do not implement the scroll bar but shift the document plane behind the viewer by 'grabbing' it with the mouse. The techniques already discussed can be combined with a block move to avoid unnecessary restore activity. For example, scrolling down is achieved by:

(1) a reduction at the bottom;

(2) a block move downwards;

(3) an expansion at the top.

The block move is analogous to the one discussed in Section 19.4. The following diagram shows a downward scroll. The shaded notes are redrawn.

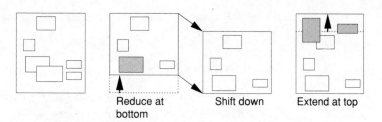

Reduce at   Shift down   Extend at top
bottom

Similarly, an upward shift of the board plane is achieved by:

(1) a reduction at the top;
(2) a block move upwards;
(3) an expansion at the bottom.

A.3.2   Declarations

```
MODULE BoardFrames;

IMPORT TextFrames, MenuViewers, Boards, Marks, Oberon, Display,
Input;
```

Note

The abstract data type *Note* is described in the introductory text. The ancillary flag is used by the procedures *MarkAfterDraw*, *MarkAfterDelete* and *DrawMarkedNotes*.

```
TYPE
  Note* = POINTER TO NoteDesc;
  NoteDesc* = RECORD
    (TextFrames.FrameDesc)
    note*: Boards.Note;
    flag: BOOLEAN
  END;
```

Frame

The abstract data type *Frame* is described in the introductory text.

```
TYPE
  Frame* = POINTER TO FrameDesc;
  FrameDesc* = RECORD
    (Display.FrameDesc)
    SelectedNote*: Note;
    board*: Boards.Board;
    Xboard*, Yboard*: INTEGER (* Upper left corner in board coordinates *)
  END;
```

```
CONST
  right = 0; middle = 1; left = 2;                    (* Mouse keys *)
  black = Display.black; white = Display.white; (* Display color *)
  repl = Display.replace;

VAR marg: INTEGER; (* Size of border around notes *)
```

A.3.3   Auxiliary procedures

```
PROCEDURE XYinRect(X, Y, RX, RY, RW, RH: INTEGER): BOOLEAN;
BEGIN (* Is point X, Y contained in rectangle R *)
    RETURN (X >= RX) & (X < RX + RW) & (Y >= RY) & (Y < RY + RH)
END XYinRect;

PROCEDURE In(BN: Boards.Note; F: Frame): BOOLEAN;
VAR X, Y, W, H: INTEGER;
BEGIN (* Is board note BN contained in frame F *)
    BoardToFrame(F, BN, X, Y, W, H);
    RETURN XYinRect(X, Y, F.X, F.Y, F.W, F.H) &
           XYinRect(X + W, Y + H, F.X, F.Y, F.W, F.H)
END In;

PROCEDURE Overlap(A, B: Display.Frame): BOOLEAN;
BEGIN (* Does frame A overlap frame B or is it contained in B *)
    RETURN
      (A.X + A.W + marg > B.X – marg) & (B.X + B.W + marg > A.X – marg) &
      (A.Y + A.H + marg > B.Y – marg) & (B.Y + B.H + marg > A.Y – marg)
END Overlap;
```

BoardToFrame   Performs address translation from board coordinates to viewer coordinates. The rectangle which corresponds to the board note is returned in the variable parameters *X, Y, W, H*.

```
PROCEDURE BoardToFrame(F: Frame; BN: Boards.Note;
                       VAR X, Y, W, H: INTEGER);
BEGIN
    W := BN.W; H := BN.H;
    X := BN.X – (F.Xboard – F.X); Y := BN.Y – (F.Yboard – F.Y – F.H)
END BoardToFrame;
```

A.3.4   Draw notes

DrawNoteFrame   Draws the wire frame of a note *N*. The little handle at the lower right corner is intended for resizing the note. This function is not part of the tutorial.

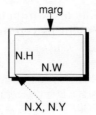

```
PROCEDURE DrawNoteFrame(N: Display.Frame);
VAR X, Y, W, H: INTEGER;
BEGIN
  X := N.X − marg; Y := N.Y − marg; W := N.W + 2* marg;
  H := N.H + 2*marg;
  Oberon.RemoveMarks(X, Y, W, H);
  Display.ReplConst(black, X, Y, W, H, repl);                    (* Clear frame *)
  Display.ReplConst(white, X, Y + 1, 1, H − 1, repl);                 (* Left *)
  Display.ReplConst(white, X + W − 2, Y + 1, 1, H − 1, repl);        (* Right *)
  Display.ReplConst(white, X + W − 1, Y, 1, H − 1, repl);
  Display.ReplConst(white, X + 1, Y + 1, W − 3, 1, repl);           (* Bottom *)
  Display.ReplConst(white, X + 1, Y, W − 2, 1, repl);
  Display.ReplConst(white, X + 1, Y + H − 1, W − 3, 1, repl);          (* Top *)
  Display.ReplConst(white, X + W − marg, Y, marg, marg, repl)   (* Handle *)
END DrawNoteFrame;
```

ClearNoteFrame   Clears the rectangle of note *N*.

```
PROCEDURE ClearNoteFrame(N: Display.Frame);
VAR X, Y, W, H: INTEGER;
BEGIN
  X := N.X − marg; Y := N.Y − marg; W := N.W + 2* marg;
  H := N.H + 2*marg;
  Oberon.RemoveMarks(X, Y, W, H );
  Display.ReplConst(black, X, Y, W, H, repl)
END ClearNoteFrame;
```

DrawNote   Draws the note frame and restores the note text.

```
PROCEDURE DrawNote*(N: Note);
BEGIN
  DrawNoteFrame(N);
  TextFrames.Restore(N)
END DrawNote;
```

DrawMarked-
Notes

Draws all notes *N* from the list of notes with *N.flag* = TRUE. These are the notes which were marked by the procedure *MarkAfterDraw* and *MarkeAfterDelete*.

```
PROCEDURE DrawMarkedNotes(F: Frame);
VAR Q: Display.Frame;
BEGIN
  Q := F.dsc;
  WHILE Q# NIL DO
    IF Q(Note).flag THEN
      DrawNote(Q(Note)); Q(Note).flag := FALSE
    END;
    Q := Q.next
  END
END DrawMarkedNotes;
```

A.3.5   Tracking procedures

TrackMouse

Keeps control in a loop by reading the mouse directly as long as a key is pressed. Returns final position and keys which were interclicked.

```
PROCEDURE TrackMouse(Marker: Oberon.Marker; VAR X, Y: INTEGER;
                             VARkeysum: SET);
VAR keys: SET;
BEGIN
  keys := keysum;
  WHILE keys # { } DO
    Oberon.DrawCursor(Oberon.Mouse, Marker, X, Y);
    Input.Mouse(keys, X, Y); keysum := keysum + keys;
  END
END TrackMouse;
```

DragRect

Spans a rectangle with the mouse (see Section 19.2.) The initial rectangle is defined by the diagonal points *X0, Y0* and *X1, Y1*. The final lower left point is returned in *X2, Y2*.

```
PROCEDURE DragRect(F: Display.Frame; X0, Y0, X1, Y1: INTEGER;
                           VARX2,Y2:INTEGER; VARkeysum: SET);
```

A.3.6   The note manager

This

Returns the topmost note which contains the point *X, Y*; NIL if *X, Y* does not designate a note.

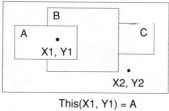

This(X1, Y1) = A
This(X2, Y2) = NIL

```
PROCEDURE This*(F: Frame; X, Y: INTEGER): Display.Frame;
VAR Q, DF: Display.Frame;
BEGIN
  Q := F.dsc; DF := NIL;
  WHILE Q # NIL DO
    IF XYinRect(X, Y, Q.X − marg, Q.Y − marg, Q.W + 2*marg, Q.H +
            2*marg) THEN
      DF := Q
    END;
    Q := Q.next
  END;
  RETURN DF
END This;
```

List processing

The following procedures operate on the list of notes. Only the procedure heading is shown for brevity.

```
PROCEDURE Append(F: Frame; DF: Display.Frame);
```
```
PROCEDURE Remove(F: Frame; DF: Display.Frame);
```
```
PROCEDURE ToListEnd(F: Frame; DF: Display.Frame);
```
```
PROCEDURE Locate*(F: Frame; BN: Boards.Note): Display.Frame;
```

IsTop

Returns TRUE if *DF* is on top; that is, not overlapped by any other note frame. *Note:* It is not necessary that *DF* is at the end of the list of notes.

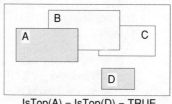

IsTop(A) = IsTop(D) = TRUE

```
PROCEDURE IsTop*(DF: Display.Frame): BOOLEAN;
VAR res: BOOLEAN; Q: Display.Frame;
BEGIN
  Q := DF.next; res := TRUE;
  WHILE Q # NIL DO
    res := res & ~Overlap(Q, DF);
    Q := Q.next
  END;
  RETURN res
END IsTop;
```

Broadcast   Broadcasts message *M* to all note frames in the list.

```
PROCEDURE Broadcast*(F: Frame; VAR M: Display.FrameMsg);
VAR Q: Display.Frame;
BEGIN
  Q := F.dsc;
  WHILE Q # NIL DO
    Q.handle(Q, M); Q := Q.next
  END
END Broadcast;
```

MarkAfterDraw   All notes which need restoration as a consequence of the redrawing of *N* are flagged. Only notes which follow *N* in the list need to be searched. *Note: E* is not flagged. Procedure *MarkAfterDraw* works recursively.

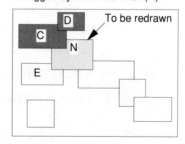

Flagged by MarkAfterDraw(N)

To be redrawn

```
PROCEDURE MarkAfterDraw(N: Display.Frame);
VAR Q: Display.Frame;
BEGIN (* All flags FALSE *)
  N(Note).flag := TRUE;
  Q := N.next;
  WHILE Q # NIL DO
    IF ~Q(Note).flag & Overlap(Q, N) THEN
      Q(Note).flag := TRUE;
      MarkAfterDraw(Q)
    END;
```

```
            Q := Q.next
        END
    END MarkAfterDraw;
```

MarkAfterDelete   Note *N* will be deleted. All notes which need restoration as a consequence are flagged. Procedure *MarkAfterDelete* invokes *MarkAfterDraw*
for all notes which overlap with it.

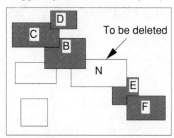

Flagged by MarkAfterDelete(F, N)

```
PROCEDURE MarkAfterDelete(F: Frame; N: Display.Frame);
VAR Q: Display.Frame;
BEGIN (* All flags FALSE *)
    Q := F.dsc;
    WHILE Q # NIL DO
        IF ~Q(Note).flag & Overlap(Q, N) & Q # N THEN
            MarkAfterDraw(Q)
        END;
        Q := Q.next
    END
END MarkAfterDelete;
```

OpenNote   Opens frame note *N* from board note *BN*.

```
PROCEDURE OpenNote*(F: Frame; N: Note; BN: Boards.Note);
VAR X, Y, W, H: INTEGER;
BEGIN
    BoardToFrame(F, BN, X, Y, W, H);
    N.X := X + marg; N.Y := Y + marg;
    N.W := W + 2 * marg; N.H := H + 2 * marg;
    TextFrames.Open(N, TextFrames.Handle, BN.text, 0, black, 5, 0, 0, 0,
                    TextFrames.lsp);
    N.next := NIL;
    N.note := BN;
    N.flag := FALSE
END OpenNote;
```

NewNote   Creates an instance of a new frame note *N* from board note *BN*.

```
PROCEDURE NewNote*(F: Frame; BN: Boards.Note): Note;
VAR N: Note;
BEGIN
   NEW(N); OpenNote(F, N, BN); Append(F, N);
   RETURN N
END NewNote;
```

A.3.7   Response to Oberon messages

Neutralize   If a note is selected, removes that selection. Also, removes all text
                     selections in notes, the caret and the pointer.

```
PROCEDURE Neutralize*(F: Frame);
VAR M: Oberon.ControlMsg;
BEGIN
   Oberon.RemoveMarks(F.X, F.Y, F.W, F.H);
   M.id := Oberon.neutralize; Broadcast(F, M);
   Deselect(F)
END Neutralize;
```

CopyFrame   Produces a copy of frame *F*. The frame must be of height 0, thus the list
                     of notes is empty. The function New produces such a frame.

```
PROCEDURE CopyFrame*(F: Frame; VAR M: Oberon.CopyMsg);
BEGIN
   M.F := New(F.board, F.Xboard, F.Yboard);
END CopyFrame;
```

ShiftBoard   Shifts the board vertically under the direction of the mouse. The mouse
                     cursor takes the shape of a cross-hair to indicate 'grabbing mode' (see
                     Chapter 19.) Dragging the mouse defines a translation vector dY. The
                     frame is scrolled upwards ($dY > 0$) or downwards ($dY < 0$.) The
                     method discussed in the introduction is used (a call of *Reduce*), fol-
                     lowed by a shift followed by execution of *Expand*.

```
PROCEDURE ShiftBoard*(F: Frame; VAR X, Y: INTEGER;
                                VAR keysum: SET);
VAR dY, Y0: INTEGER;
BEGIN
   Y0 := Y;
   TrackMouse(Marks.Cross, X, Y, keysum);
   Neutralize(F);
   dY := Y − Y0; (* The translation vector *)
```

```
        IF dY < 0 THEN (* Scroll downwards *)
            Reduce(F, F.Y + F.H, F.Y − dY); (* Reduce at bottom *)
            Display.CopyBlock(F.X, F.Y, F.W, F.H, F.X, F.Y + dY, replace); (* Shift *)
            TransformDisplayDescriptors(F, dY); F.Y := F.Y + dY;
                (* Transform coord. *)
            Extend(F, F.Y + F.H − dY, F.Y); (* Extend at top *)
            F.Yboard := F.Yboard − dY (* Adjust coord. of upper left corner of F *)
        ELSIF dY > 0 THEN (* Scroll upwards *)
            Reduce(F, F.Y + F.H − dY, F.Y); (* Reduce at top *)
            F.Yboard := F.Yboard − dY;
            Display.CopyBlock(F.X, F.Y, F.W, F.H, F.X, F.Y + dY, replace); (* Shift *)
            TransformDisplayDescriptors(F, dY); F.Y := F.Y + dY;
                (* Transform coord. *)
            Extend(F, F.Y + F.H, F.Y − dY) (* Expand at bottom *)
        END
    END ShiftBoard;
```

Deselect   Removes the selection from a selected note, if one exists.

```
        PROCEDURE Deselect*(F: Frame);
        VAR N: Note;
        BEGIN
            IF F.SelectedNote # NIL THEN
                N := F.SelectedNote; F.SelectedNote := NIL;
                Display.ReplConst(white, N.X − marg, N.Y − marg, N.W + 2 * marg,
                                N.H + 2 * marg, Display.invert);
            END
        END Deselect;
```

Select   Selects note N and displays it in reverse video. If while the select key remains pressed the left key is interclicked, then note N is deleted.

```
        PROCEDURE Select*(F: Frame; N: Note; keysum: SET);
        VAR X, Y: INTEGER;
        BEGIN
            Neutralize(F);
            Display.ReplConst(white, N.X − marg, N.Y − marg,
                                N.W + 2 * marg, N.H + 2 * marg, Display.invert);
            TrackMouse(Oberon.Arrow, X, Y, keysum);
            F.SelectedNote := N;
            IF (left IN keysum) & ~((middle IN keysum) & (right IN keysum)) THEN
                Boards.Discard(F.board, N.note)
            END
        END Select;
```

A.3.8   Response to boards update messages

Poste   Board note *BN* was posted. If it is visible in *F,* creates a corresponding frame note (the display descriptor) and appends it to the end of the list of notes.

```
PROCEDURE Poste*(F: Frame; BN: Boards.Note);
VAR N: Note;
BEGIN
  IF In(BN, F) THEN
     N := NewNote(F, BN); Neutralize(F); DrawNote(N)
  END
END Poste;
```

ToTop   Board note *BN* was moved to top (to the end of the list of board notes.) Moves the corresponding frame note to top. If it is overlapped, it is redrawn.

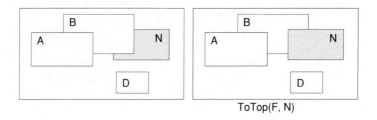

ToTop(F, N)

```
PROCEDURE ToTop*(F: Frame; BN: Boards.Note);
VAR N: Display.Frame;
BEGIN
  IF In(BN, F) THEN
     N := Locate(F, BN);
     IF ~IsTop(N) THEN
        Neutralize(F); DrawNote(N(Note))
     END;
     ToListEnd(F, N)
  END
END ToTop;
```

Discard   Board note *BN* was discarded. Removes corresponding frame note and redraws notes which overlapped with the discarded note.

```
PROCEDURE Discard*(F: Frame; BN: Boards.Note);
VAR N: Display.Frame;
```

```
        BEGIN
          IF In(BN, F) THEN
            N := Locate(F, BN);
            Neutralize(F);
            MarkAfterDelete(F, N);
            ClearNoteFrame(N);
            Remove(F, N);
            DrawMarkedNotes(F)
          END
        END Discard;
```

A.3.9   Response to menu viewer's messages

Extend

Extends frame F such that the new top edge has y coordinate $Ytop$ and the new bottom edge has y coordinate $Ybot$. All notes visible in the extended area will be drawn at completion of *Extend*. An attempt is made to draw only newly visible notes. However, due to overlapping conditions, some notes contained in the original frame may have to be restored. The temporal order of the frame notes and board notes is strictly preserved. The values of $F.Y$ and $F.H$ are adjusted to reflect the new size of F.

```
        PROCEDURE Extend(F: Frame; Ytop, Ybot: INTEGER);
        VAR
          BN: Boards.Note;
          R: Boards.Reader;
          N: Note;
          A, Q: Display.Frame;
          X, Y, W, H: INTEGER;
        BEGIN (* Ytop > F.Y + F.H and Ybot < F.Y *)
          (* Clear enlarged area *)
          IF F.Y − Ybot > 0 THEN
            Display.ReplConst(black, F.X, Ybot, F.W, F.Y − Ybot, repl)
          END;
          IF Ytop − F.Y − F.H > 0 THEN
            Display.ReplConst(black, F.X, F.Y + F.H, F.W, Ytop − F.Y − F.H, repl)
          END;
          (* Phase 1: Read all board notes sequentially and test whether they are
          displayed. If one is found that is not, an instance of a frame note is created
          and inserted in the list of notes such that the temporal order is preserved *)
          Boards.OpenReader(R, F.board);
          Boards.Read(R, BN);                (* Read first board note *)
          NEW(A); A.next := F.dsc; Q := A; (* Auxiliary list element *)
```

```
WHILE BN # NIL DO
   BoardToFrame(F, BN, X, Y, W, H);
   IF (X >= F.X) & (X + W < F.X + F.W) & (Y >= Ybot) & (Y + H < Ytop)
   THEN
      (* Board note is contained in the enlarged area *)
      IF Q.next = NIL THEN
         (* Board note BN is not displayed. Create a new note and append it
         to the list *)
         NEW(N); OpenNote(F, N, BN); Q.next := N; Q := N
      ELSIF Q.next(Note).note = BN THEN
         (* Board note BN is already displayed *)
         Q := Q.next
      ELSE
         (* Board note BN is not displayed. Create a new note and insert it
         into the list after auxiliary note Q *)
         NEW(N); OpenNote(F, N, BN);
         N.next := Q.next; Q.next := N; Q := N
      END
   END;
   Boards.Read(R, BN)                 (* Read next board note *)
END;
F.dsc := A.next;
(* Phase 2: Mark all notes which were newly created and draw the marked
notes *)
Q := F.dsc;
WHILE Q # NIL DO
   IF ~In(Q(Note).note, F) THEN      (* Note is newly created *)
      MarkAfterDraw(F, Q); Q(Note).flag := TRUE
   END;
   Q := Q.next
END;
DrawMarkedNotes(F);
F.Y := Ybot; F.H := Ytop − Ybot    (* Adjust frame *)
END Extend;
```

Reduce   Reduces frame F such that the new top edge has y coordinate *Ytop* and
the new bottom edge has y coordinate *Ybot*. All notes which overlap
with the reduced area but are not fully contained in it are removed
from the display. Some notes may have to be restored due to removal
of overlapping frames. The values of $F.Y$ and $F.H$ are adjusted to reflect
the new size of F.

```
PROCEDURE Reduce(F: Frame; Ytop, Ybot: INTEGER);
VAR Q: Display.Frame;
```

```
              BEGIN (* Ytop < F.X + F.H, Ybot > F.Y *)
                Q := F.dsc;
                WHILE Q # NIL DO
                  IF (Q.Y − marg < Ybot) OR (Q.Y + Q.H + marg >= Ytop) THEN
                    Remove(F, Q);
                    ClearNoteFrame(Q);
                    MarkAfterDelete(F, Q)        (* Mark frames for restoration *)
                  END;
                  Q := Q.next
                END;
                DrawMarkedNotes(F);
                F.Y := Ybot; F.H := Ytop − Ybot  (* Adjust frame *)
              END Reduce;
```

Modify   Modifies frame *F* as directed by the menu viewer's modify message *M*
                    (see Section 19.4.)

```
              PROCEDURE TransformDisplayDescriptors(F: Frame; dY: INTEGER);
              VAR Q: Display.Frame;
              BEGIN
                Q := F.dsc;
                WHILE Q # NIL DO
                  Q.Y := Q.Y + dY;
                  Q := Q.next
                END
              END TransformDisplayDescriptors;

              PROCEDURE Modify(F: Frame; M: MenuViewers.ModifyMsg);
              BEGIN
                Neutralize(F);
                IF M.id = MenuViewers.extend THEN
                  IF M.dY > 0 THEN
                    Display.CopyBlock(F.X, F.Y, F.W, F.H, F.X, F.Y + M.dY, repl);
                    F.Y := F.Y + M.dY;
                    TransformDisplayDescriptors(F, M.dY)
                  END;
                  Extend(F, F.Y + F.H, M.Y)
                ELSIF M.id = MenuViewers.reduce THEN
                  Reduce(F, F.Y + F.H, M.Y + M.dY);
                  IF M.dY > 0 THEN
                    Display.CopyBlock(F.X, M.Y + M.dY, F.W, M.H, F.X, M.Y, repl);
                    TransformDisplayDescriptors(F, −M.dY)
                  END
                END
              END Modify;
```

A.3.10 The handler

The handler uses the preceding procedures as components.

```
PROCEDURE Handler* (F: Display.Frame; VAR M: Display.FrameMsg);
VAR
  N: Display.Frame;
  X, Y: INTEGER;
BEGIN
WITH F: Frame DO
  IF M IS Oberon.InputMsg THEN
    WITH M: Oberon.InputMsg DO
      IF M.id = Oberon.track THEN (* Mouse event *)
        Oberon.DrawCursor(Oberon.Mouse, Oberon.Arrow, M.X, M.Y);
        N : = This(F, M.X, M.Y);     (* Note which contains mouse *)
        IF N = NIL THEN              (* Mouse in board area *)
          IF left IN M.keys THEN
            DragRect(F, M.X, M.Y, M.X + 2, M.Y − 2, X, Y, M.keys);
            Boards.PosteEmpty(F.board, F.Xboard + M.X − F.X, F.Yboard
                            + Y − F.Y − F.H, X − M.X, M.Y − Y)
          ELSIF middle IN M.keys THEN
            ShiftBoard(F, M.X, M.Y, M.keys)
          END
        ELSE                        (* Mouse in note frame *)
          IF M.keys # {} THEN
            IF ~IsTop(N) THEN        (* Bring note to top *)
              Boards.ToTop(F.board, N(Note).note)
            END;
            IF XYinRect(M.X, M.Y, N.X, N.Y, N.W, N.H) THEN
              (* Mouse is in the text area of N *)
              IF N(Note) # F.SelectedNote THEN
                N.handle(N, M)     (* Pass track message to note N *)
              END
            ELSE
              IF right IN M.keys THEN Select(F, N(Note), M.keys) END
            END
          END
        END
      ELSE
        Broadcast(F, M)            (* Pass input message M to all notes *)
      END
    END
  ELSIF M IS Oberon.ControlMsg THEN
    IF M(Oberon.ControlMsg).id = Oberon.neutralize THEN
      Neutralize(F)
    ELSE
      Broadcast(F, M)
    END
```

```
        ELSIF M IS Oberon.CopyMsg THEN
          CopyFrame(F, M(Oberon.CopyMsg);
        ELSIF M IS MenuViewers.ModifyMsg THEN
          Modify(F, M(MenuViewers.ModifyMsg))
        ELSIF M IS Boards.UpdateMsg THEN
          WITH M: Boards.UpdateMsg DO
            IF M.board = F.board THEN
              IF M.id = Boards.poste THEN
                Poste(F, M.note)
              ELSIF M.id = Boards.toTop THEN
                ToTop(F, M.note)
              ELSIF M.id = Boards.discard THEN
                Discard(F, M.note)
              END
            END
          END
        ELSE
          Broadcast(F, M)              (* Pass message M to all notes *)
        END
    END                                (* WITH F: Frame DO *)
    END Handler;
```

A.3.11   Creating an instance of frame

NewViewer   Creates an instance of the abstract data type *Frame* displaying board *B*.

```
        PROCEDURE New*(B: Boards.Board; Xboard, Yboard: INTEGER): Frame;
        VAR F: Frame;
        BEGIN
          NEW(F); F.handle := Handler;
          F.board := B;
          F.Xboard := Xboard; F.Yboard := Yboard; F.SelectedNote := NIL;
          RETURN F
        END New;

        BEGIN
          marg := 5;

        END BoardFrames.
```

A.4   Module PostIt (command module)

The module *PostIt* is the command module of the viewer class board viewers. We will keep it as simple as possible.

```
        Module PostIt;

        IMPORT TextFrames, Boards, Files, Texts, Oberon, Viewers, BoardFrames,
        MenuViewers, LogOut;
```

Open   Opens a note board. The command functions in the same way as
                    Edit.Open. If a name follows *PostIt.Open*, then a viewer with that name
                    is opened. If *PostIt.Open* is followed by '↑', then the selection is
                    searched. If both methods do not yield a name, the default
                    'Boards.Board' is applied.

```
PROCEDURE Open*;
VAR
   S: Texts.Scanner;
   V: MenuViewers.Viewer;
   X, Y: INTEGER;
   menuF: TextFrames.Frame; mainF: BoardFrames.Frame;
   text: Texts.Text; beg, end, time: LONGINT;
BEGIN
   Texts.OpenScanner(S, Oberon.Par.text, Oberon.Par.pos); Texts.Scan(S);
   IF S.class # Texts.Name THEN
      S.s := "Boards.Board";
      IF (S.class = Texts.Char) & (S.c = " ↑ ") THEN
         Oberon.GetSelection(text, beg, end, time);
         IF time >= 0 THEN (* Selection exists *)
            Texts.OpenScanner(S, text, beg); Texts.Scan(S);
         END
      END
   END;
   menuF := TextFrames.NewMenu(S.s,
            "System.Close  System.Copy  System.Grow  PostIt.Store");
   mainF := BoardFrames.New(Boards.NewBoard(S.s), 0, 0);
   Oberon.AllocateUserViewer(Oberon.Mouse.X, X, Y);
   V := MenuViewers.New(menuF, mainF, TextFrames.menuH, X, Y)
END Open;
```

Store   If executed from the menu frame, the board of that viewer is stored. If
                    executed from another text, typically a tool, the marked viewer is
                    stored under a given name. The name is derived as in *Open*. Procedure
                    Backup is elaborated in Section 8.7.2.

```
PROCEDURE Store*;
VAR
   V: Viewers.Viewer; S: Texts.Scanner; text: Texts.Text;
   beg, end, time: LONGINT; res: INTEGER;
BEGIN
   V := Oberon.Par.vwr;
   IF Oberon.Par.frame = V.dsc THEN
      (* Command executed from the menu frame *)
```

```
      IF (V.dsc # NIL) & (V.dsc.next IS BoardFrames.Frame) THEN
        (* A board frame exists *)
        Texts.OpenScanner(S, Oberon.Par.text, 0);
        Texts.Scan(S); (* Read the name of the viewer *)
        IF S.class = Texts.Name THEN
          Backup(S.s, bak);
          Files.Rename(S.s, bak, res);
          Boards.Store(V.dsc.next(BoardFrames.Frame).board, S.s);
          LogOut.PutString("PostIt.Store "); LogOut.PutString(S.s)
        ELSE
          LogOut.PutString("PostIt.Store illegal name")
        END
      ELSE LogOut.PutString("PostIt.Store not a board viewer")
      END
    ELSE
      (* Command executed from a text other than the menu *)
      V := Oberon.MarkedViewer( );
      IF (V.dsc # NIL) & (V.dsc.next IS BoardFrames.Frame) THEN
        (* A board frame exists *)
        Texts.OpenScanner(S, Oberon.Par.text, Oberon.Par.pos);
        Texts.Scan(S);
        IF S.class # Texts.Name THEN
          S.s := "Boards.Board";
          IF (S.class = Texts.Char) & (S.c = " ↑ ") THEN
            Oberon.GetSelection(text, beg, end, time);
            IF time >= 0 THEN (* Selection exists *)
              Texts.OpenScanner(S, text, beg); Texts.Scan(S);
            END
          END
        END;
        Backup(S.s);
        Files.Rename(S.s, bak, res);
        Boards.Store(V.dsc.next(BoardFrames.Frame).board, S.s);
        LogOut.PutString("PostIt.Store "); LogOut.PutString(S.s)
      ELSE
        LogOut.PutString("PostIt.Store not a board viewer")
      END
    END
  END Store;
```

APPENDIX B
Keyboard and ASCII characters

Ceres features a standard ASCII keyboard, as depicted in the following diagram. A numeric keypad is present but not shown.

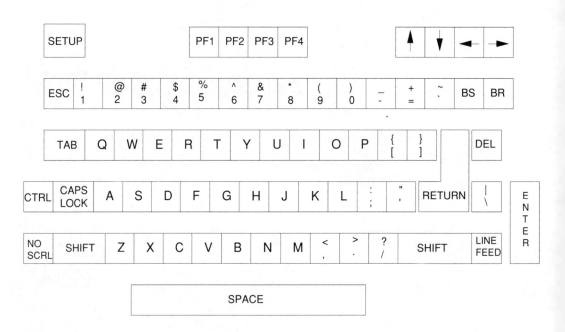

Dec	Hex	Char	Key[1]		Dec	Hex	Char	Key[1]
0	0X	NUL			41	29X	)	
1	1X	SOH	CTRL–A		42	2AX	*	
2	2X	STX	CTRL–B		43	2BX	+	
3	3X	ETX	CTRL–C		44	2CX	,	
4	4X	EOT	CTRL–D		45	2DX	-	
5	5X	ENQ	CTRL–E		46	2EX	.	
6	6X	ACK	CTRL–F		47	2FX	/	
7	7X	BEL	CTRL–G		48	30X	0	
8	8X	BS	CTRL–H		49	31X	1	
9	9X	HT	CTRL–I | TAB		50	32X	2	
10	0AX	LF	CTRL–J | LINE FEED		51	33X	3	
11	0BX	VT	CTRL–K		52	34X	4	
12	0CX	FF	CTRL–L		53	35X	5	
13	0DX	CR	CTRL–M | RETURN		54	36X	6	
14	0EX	SO	CTRL–N		55	37X	7	
15	0FX	SI	CTRL–O		56	38X	8	
16	10X	DLE	CTRL–P		57	39X	9	
17	11X	DC1	CTRL–Q		58	3AX	:	
18	12X	DC2	CTRL–R		59	3BX	;	
19	13X	DC3	CTRL–S		60	3CX	<	
20	14X	DC4	CTRL–T		61	3DX	=	
21	15X	NAK	CTRL–U		62	3EX	>	
22	16X	SYN	CTRL–V		63	3FX	?	
23	17X	ETB	CTRL–W		64	40X	@	
24	18X	CAN	CTRL–X		65	41X	A	
25	19X	EM	CTRL–Y		66	42X	B	
26	1AX	SUB	CTRL–Z		67	43X	C	
27	1BX	ESC	CTRL–[| ESC		68	44X	D	
28	1CX	FS	CTRL–\		69	45X	E	
29	1DX	GS	CTRL–]		70	46X	F	
30	1EX	RS	CTRL–6		71	47X	G	
31	1FX	US	CTRL–- (hyphen)		72	48X	H	
32	20X	SP	SPACE[2]		73	49X	I	
33	21X	!			74	4AX	J	
34	22X	"			75	4BX	K	
35	23X	#			76	4CX	L	
36	24X	$			77	4DX	M	
37	25X	%			78	4EX	N	
38	26X	&			79	4FX	O	
39	27X	'			80	50X	P	
40	28X	(			81	51X	Q	

[1] Ceres-3 keyboard. Most ASCII keyboards are similar.
[2] Between 20X and 7FX lies the standard ASCII characters. They are produced with the respective labelled keys, including the use of SHIFT.

Dec	Hex	Char	Key[1]	Dec	Hex	Char	Key[1]
82	52X	R		126	7EX	~	
83	53X	S		127	7FX	DEL	DEL
84	54X	T		128	80X	Ä[4]	— (CTRL–SHIFT–A)[5]
85	55X	U		129	81X	Ö	CTRL–SHIFT–A
86	56X	V					(CTRL–SHIFT–O)[5]
87	57X	W		130	82X	Ü	CTRL–SHIFT–B
88	58X	X					(CTRL–SHIFT–U)[5]
89	59X	Y		131	83X	ä	CTRL–SHIFT–C (CTRL–a)[5]
90	5AX	Z		132	84X	ö	CTRL–SHIFT–D (CTRL–o)[5]
91	5BX	[		133	85X	ü	CTRL–SHIFT–E (CTRL–u)[5]
92	5CX	\		134	86X	â	CTRL–SHIFT–F
93	5DX	]		135	87X	ê	CTRL–SHIFT–G
94	5EX	^[3]		136	88X	î	CTRL–SHIFT–H
95	5FX	_		137	89X	ô	CTRL–SHIFT–I
96	60X	`		138	8AX	û	CTRL–SHIFT–J
97	61X	a		139	8BX	à	CTRL–SHIFT–K
98	62X	b		140	8CX	è	CTRL–SHIFT–L
99	63X	c		141	8DX	ì	CTRL–SHIFT–M
100	64X	d		142	8EX	ò	CTRL–SHIFT–N
101	65X	e		143	8FX	ù	CTRL–SHIFT–O
102	66X	f		144	90X	é	CTRL–SHIFT–P
103	67X	g		145	91X	ë	CTRL–SHIFT–Q |
104	68X	h					NO SCRL
105	69X	i		146	92X	ï	CTRL–SHIFT–R
106	6AX	j		147	93X	ç	CTRL–SHIFT–S |
107	6BX	k					CTRL–NO SCRL
108	6CX	l		148	94X	á	CTRL–SHIFT–T
109	6DX	m		149	95X	ñ	CTRL–SHIFT–U
110	6EX	n		150	96X		CTRL–SHIFT–V
111	6FX	o		151	97X		CTRL–SHIFT–W
112	70X	p		152	98X		CTRL–SHIFT–X
113	71X	q		153	99X		CTRL–SHIFT–Y
114	72X	r		154	9AX		CTRL–SHIFT–Z
115	73X	s		155	9BX	–[6]	CTRL–SHIFT–[
116	74X	t		156	9CX		CTRL–SHIFT–\
117	75X	u		157	9DX		CTRL–SHIFT–]
118	76X	v		158	9EX		CTRL–SHIFT–6
119	77X	w		159	9FX		CTRL–SHIFT–– (hyphen)
120	78X	x		160	0A0X		
121	79X	y		161	0A1X		
122	7AX	z		162	0A2X		
123	7BX	{		163	0A3X		
124	7CX	|		164	0A4X		SETUP
125	7DX	}		165	0A5X		SHIFT–SETUP

[3] Oberon fonts print an upward arrow '↑' instead of the caret '^'.
[4] Special language symbols as defined in the Syntax family fonts.
[5] Translation by Oberon loop (that is, 81X is substituted for 8FX) to make national language characters accessible with simple key combinations.
[6] En-dash.

Dec	Hex	Char	Key[1]	Dec	Hex	Char	Key[1]
166	0A6X		CTRL SETUP	211	0D3X		
167	0A7X		CTRL–SHIFT–SETUP	212	0D4X		
168	0A8X			213	0D5X		
169	0A9X			214	0D6X		
170	0AAX			215	0D7X		
171	0ABX			216	0D8X		
172	0ACX		BREAK	217	0D9X		
173	0ADX		SHIFT–BREAK	218	0DAX		
174	0AEX		CTRL–BREAK	219	0DBX		
175	0AFX		CTRL–SHIFT–BREAK	220	0DCX		
176	0B0X			221	0DDX		
177	0B1X			222	0DEX		
178	0B2X			223	0DFX		
179	0B3X			224	0E0X		
180	0B4X			225	0E1X		
181	0B5X			226	0E2X		
182	0B6X			227	0E3X		
183	0B7X			228	0E4X		
184	0B8X			229	0E5X		
185	0B9X			230	0E6X		
186	0BAX			231	0E7X		
187	0BBX			232	0E8X		CTRL–SHIFT–BS
188	0BCX			233	0E9X		CTRL–SHIFT–TAB
189	0BDX			234	0EAX		CTRL–SHIFT–LINE FEED
190	0BEX			235	0EBX		
191	0BFX			236	0ECX		
192	0C0X			237	0EDX		CTRL–SHIFT–RETURN
193	0C1X		UP ARROW	238	0EEX		
194	0C2X		DOWN ARROW	239	0EFX		
195	0C3X		RIGHT ARROW	240	0F0X		
196	0C4X		LEFT ARROW	241	0F1X		PF1
197	0C5X			242	0F2X		PF2
198	0C6X			243	0F3X		PF3
199	0C7X			244	0F4X		PF4
200	0C8X			245	0F5X		
201	0C9X			246	0F6X		
202	0CAX			247	0F7X		
203	0CBX			248	0F8X		
204	0CCX			249	0F9X		
205	0CDX		ENTER	250	0FAX		
206	0CEX			251	0FBX		
207	0CFX			252	0FCX		
208	0D0X			253	0FDX		
209	0D1X			254	0FEX		
210	0D2X			255	0FFX		CTRL–SHIFT–DEL

Remarks:

(1) Only the code points 00X to 7FX are standardized (ASCII code.)

(2) The assignment of special language characters to code points 80X ≤ *ch* ≤ 95X is a property of the fonts of the Syntax family.

(3) The creation of codes outside the printable characters (20X ≤ *ch* ≤ 7FX) by means of the CTRL and CTRL–SHIFT modifier keys is particular for the keyboard of Ceres-3. It is, however, typical for many ASCII keyboards. With different equipment, the user needs to consult the hardware documentation.

(4) The procedure *Oberon.Loop* substitutes the code points for the *umlaut characters* to the following key combinations: CTRL–A = ä, CTRL–O = ö, CTRL–U = ü, CTRL–SHIFT–A = Ä, CTRL–SHIFT-O = Ö and CTRL–SHIFT–U = Ü. If this substitution is not desired, *Oberon.Loop* needs to be modified.

(5) Except for the substitution of point 4, the event loop transfers all codes in the consume message.

(6) Text viewers, however, accept only standard ASCII characters (that is, 20X ≤ *ch* ≤ 7FX) and the umlaut characters ä, ö, ü, Ä, Ö and Ü. If other codes generated by the keyboard should be inserted in texts, the procedure *TextFrames.Write* has to be modified (or a different procedure called in a customized handler.)

APPENDIX C
MS/DOS files

File compatibility between Oberon and MS/DOS systems can be achieved on the level of ASCII files. If an Oberon text is to be displayed by a DOS (ASCII) editor, the character attributes (font, color and vertical offset) must be first eliminated and the textual representation stored in a file. The command *Miscellaneous.Cleanup* may be used for this purpose.

However, DOS differs from Oberon in the way line breaks and the end of a file are marked:

	Oberon	MS/DOS
Line break	CR (0DX)	CR–LF (0DX–0AX)
End of file	—	CR–LF–SUB (0DX–0AX–1AX)

The following procedure transforms a text into a file which may be properly viewed in a DOS ASCII editor:

```
PROCEDURE TextToDOSFile(text: Texts.Text; file: Files.File);

CONST
    CR = 0DX;
    LF = 0AX;
    SUB = 1AX;

VAR
    Reader: Texts.Reader;
    Rider: Files.Rider;
    ch: CHAR;

BEGIN
    Texts.OpenReader(Reader, text, 0);
    Files.Set(Rider, file, 0);
    Texts.Read(Reader, ch);
```

```
        WHILE ~Reader.eot DO
          Files.Write(Rider, ch);
          IF ch = CR THEN
            Files Write(Rider, LF)
          END;
          Texts.Read(Reader, ch)
        END;
        Files Write(Rider, CR); Files Write(Rider, LF); Files Write(Rider, SUB)
      END TextToDOSFile;
```

Note: Procedure *TextToDOSFile* performs the elimination of character attributes. Unlike *Miscellaneous.Cleanup*, however, it does not eliminate non-printable characters. If this is desired, an appropriate test which filters out characters in the range $ch < 20X$ and $ch > 7FX$ should be added.

The translation from DOS to Oberon is similarly achieved:

```
PROCEDURE DOSFileToText(file: Files.File): Texts.Text;

CONST
  LF = 0AX;
  SUB = 1AX;

VAR
  text: Texts.Text;
  Writer: Texts.Writer;
  Rider: Files.Rider;
  ch: CHAR;
BEGIN
  Texts.OpenWriter(Writer);
  Files.Set(Rider, file, 0);
  Files.Read(Rider, ch);
  WHILE ~Rider.eof DO
    IF (ch # LF) & (ch # SUB) THEN
      Texts.Write(W, ch)
    END;
    Files.Read(Rider, ch)
  END;
  NEW(text); text.notify := TextFrames.NotifyDisplay;
  Texts.Open(text, ""); Texts.Append(text, W.buf);
  RETURN text
END DOSFileToText
```

If a file is transferred to a DOS machine through a diskette, the user must not forget to transform the diskette directory using *Miscellaneous.ConvertToMSDOS*. Similarly, *Miscellaneous.ConvertFrom-MSDOS* is needed when a diskette is transferred from DOS to Oberon.

Bibliography

Oberon language

The Oberon language is described in the following papers and reports:

Wirth N. (1987). Type extensions. *ACM Transactions on Prog. Languages and Systems*, **10**, 204–14

Wirth N. (1988). The programming language Oberon. *Software – Practice and Experience*, **18**, 671–90

Wirth N. (1988). From Modula to Oberon. *Software – Practice and Experience*, **18**, 661–70

Gutknecht J. (1989). Variations on the role of module interfaces. *Structured Programming*, **10**, 40–6

Mössenböck H. and Templ J. (1989). Object Oberon – a modest object-oriented language. *Structured Programming*, **10**(4), 199–207

Reiser M. and Wirth N. The Oberon language – steps beyond Pascal and Modula. To be published.

Ceres workstation

Architecture and implementation of the Ceres workstation is the object of:

Eberle H. (1987). Development and analysis of a workstation computer. PhD thesis, ETH Nr 8431

Heeb H. (1988). *Design of the Processor Board for the Ceres-2 Workstation*. Technical Report 93, Institut für Informatik, ETH

Wirth N. (1989). *Ceres-Net: A Low-Cost Computer Network and Extending Ceres-Net by a Mail Service*. Technical Report 112, Institut für Informatik, ETH

Oberon operating system

Goal and structure of the Oberon operating system is discussed in:

Wirth N. (1988). Oberon: A system for workstations, *Microprocessing and Microprogramming*, **24**, 3–8. North-Holland

Wirth N. (1989). Designing a system from scratch. *Structured Programming*, **1**, 10–18

Wirth N. and Gutknecht J. (1989). The Oberon system. *Software – Practice and Experience*, **19**(9), 857–93

Gutknecht J. (1989). *The Oberon Guide*. Technical Report 119, Institut für Informatik, ETH

Wirth N. and Gutknecht J. The Oberon system. To be published.

Oberon implementa- tions

Templ J. (1990). *SPARC–Oberon, User's Guide and Implementation*, Report 133, Institut für Informatik, ETH

Franz M. (1990). *The Implementation of MacOberon*, Technical Report 141, Institut für Informatik, ETH

Franz M. (1990). *MacOberon Reference Manual*, Technical Report 142, Institut für Informatik, ETH

Glossary

Arrow mark An arrow shown at the bottom left corner of a viewer indicating that a command is executed from that viewer which takes noticeable time (for example, more than about a tenth of a second.)

Bitmap A special area of the computer's memory which is dedicated to the display hardware. Each point on the display, called a *pixel*, corresponds to a number of bits which hold a *pixel value*, which determines the color of the pixel. For a monochrome display, the pixel value is 0 (black) or 1 (white) which may be stored in one bit. The bitmap is also called pixelmap.

Caret A mark in texts designating the point receiving characters from the keyboard or from copied selections.

Clicking Pressing and releasing a mouse key.

Color number The pixel value which defines the color of a point on the display.

Color palette A set of registers which define 16 hues out of 256 shades of blue, red and green.

Command (1) Informal definition: A system action initiated by clicking at the command name in a text with the execute key. (2) Technical definition: Any parameterless Oberon procedure exported by a module.

Command module A module which only exports commands, which can be executed from texts typically displayed in tool viewers.

Cooperative process multitasking A multitasking system where the overall functioning depends on well-behavedness of the individual commands (or tasks.) Oberon, for example, recognizes the procedure (or command) as an indivisible unit and therefore assumes its run-time to be short.

Cursor (1) Informal definition: A pattern moving over the display under mouse direction and used to point at objects. The mouse cursor is typically a left pointing arrow. (2) Technical definition: An object which fades and draws patterns on a trail.

Directory A table on the disk which allows access to the file data by a file name.

Display manager A set of procedures which draw the portion of a document which fits the area of a viewer. Example: Module TextFrames contains the display manager of the standard editor.

Dragging Moving the mouse while one of the keys remains pressed.

Driver A system routine dealing with hardware registers or interrupts; for example, module Input reads special registers which hold mouse and keyboard information.

Dynamic loading   The modules (or the procedures in a module) are only loaded into memory on demand.

Event loop   *see* Loop.

Execute key   The middle mouse key used to execute commands from texts.

File   (1) Data stored on fixed disk or on diskette. The abstraction of contiguous bytes is constructed from (possibly) non-contiguous disk sectors. (2) An Oberon object which provides access to the disk sectors holding the data.

File server   A machine on the network enabled to receive or deliver files. Note that any station may be put into a file server mode.

Filler viewer   A viewer which represents empty areas in a track (either the track is empty or the top most viewer is dragged down with the mouse.) With the filler viewer, the display is exhaustively tiled with a non-overlapping rectangular viewer.

Focus   The viewer which receives keyboard input. It typically contains a caret. Typed characters or copied selections are inserted at the caret.

Font   (1) The set of characters of a given design and size. (2) Abstract data type which yields access to font data, loaded from disk files. The type Font is exported by modules Display and Font.

Frame   An Oberon object which describes a rectangular area of the screen. It has provisions to install a handler and affords pointer type fields which allow frames to form a hierarchical data structure. The type Frame (exported by module Display) is extended to the types Viewers.Viewer, MenuViewers.Viewer and TextFrames.Frame. Other viewer classes may add further extensions.

Handler   Command interpreter of a viewer (or viewer class.) The handler is a procedure which is assigned to the field *handle* of the viewer descriptor. The handler is called on system events such as mouse and keyboard input, change in the viewer configuration etc. The parameters for the handler are passed in a record termed a *message*.

Inner core   Set of modules of the Oberon system providing basic operating system functions such as storage management, module loading, file directory functions and file access.

Interclicking   Clicking a mouse key while another key (the primary key) remains pressed.

Logical display   A display organized into tracks and viewers within tracks which tile the screen area exhaustively. Allows for overlay tracks.

Loop   A procedure in module Oberon which contains the idle loop. When nothing else happens, the loop continuously polls mouse, keyboard and possibly the network drivers. Besides the drivers, the garbage collector is periodically invoked. The user may install procedures, called tasks, in the loop. These tasks will periodically execute.

Mail server   A dedicated machine maintaining mailboxes for each user participating in electronic mail.

Main frame   The second subframe of a menu viewer. It is an active frame which embodies the specialized function of the viewer. If the main frame is a text frame, the menu viewer is a text viewer.

Map Short for bitmap (*see* Bitmap.) Oberon knows three maps: (1) The primary monochrome map; (2) The secondary monochrome map; (3) The color map.

Mark A pattern overlaid over the display which will be removed again and which does not change the displayed contents. For example, the mouse cursor, the star-shaped pointer, the selection mark or the caret.

Marker An abstract data type to draw and fade the pattern of a cursor. For example, Oberon.Arrow and Oberon.Star.

Menu command A command listed in the title bar of a viewer. It usually operates on its viewer.

Menu frame The first subframe of a menu viewer. It typically is a text frame which displays the viewer's title bar (*see* Title bar.)

Menu viewer A viewer which supports two (active) subframes. A menu viewer can be repositioned with the mouse. Typically, the first subframe (menu frame) is a text frame displaying the viewer's name and the menu commands. If both frames are text frames, the viewer is a text viewer.

Message A record variable of a given message type which holds parameters for handlers of viewers. The fields of the message are first filled and then the message is passed as an actual parameter when the handler is called. This sequence is termed 'sending a message.'

Message identifier An integer field which differentiates variants of a message type; for example, the message type Oberon.InputMsg has variants: consume = 0 and track = 1. In short, one speaks of an Oberon track message and means a message of type Oberon.InputMsg with id = track.

Module hierarchy The partial ordering of modules defined by the relation module A imports module B.

Multiple views Two (or more) viewers showing the *same* document which may be individually scrolled in each viewer.

Name A sequence of name parts delimited by periods. A name part is a word starting with a letter. Examples: Edit.Open, Syntax10.Scn.Fnt.

Network name A name under which an Oberon server on the network knows the users. The network name is linked to the user name by the network administrator.

Notifier A procedure invoked by texts when they are changed. The notifier is installed in a text descriptor; that is, it is assigned to the descriptor's procedure field *notify*.

Oberon (1) A programming language which simplifies and generalizes Modula-2. (2) An operating system for a personal workstation.

Object An instance of an abstract data type. It is described by a record variable which is accessed through a pointer. Typically, the pointer type has the name of the object and the record is called the object descriptor. If the object possesses a procedure field (to which a procedure is actually assigned), then it is called an *active object*. Examples of active objects: Viewers.Viewer, TextFrames.Frame.

Outer core Set of modules of the Oberon system managing display, keyboard and mouse (modules: Input, Display, Fonts, Texts, Viewers, Oberon, MenuViewers and TextFrames.)

Parameter Information for commands executed with the mouse (must be distinguished from the formal and actual parameters of Oberon procedures.) The parameter sources are (1) The text from which the command is executed; (2) The selection; (3) The marked viewer.

Parameter list   (1) A list of parameters following the command name in the text from where the command was executed. Typically, the parameter list consists of names and is terminated by a special symbol, usually "~." (2) A variable of type Oberon.ParList which transfers information about the environment from which the command was executed to the invoked procedure.

Password   A secret string of characters used to secure network access. The password is registered with the command *System.SetUser* and stored in encoded form in the variable Oberon.Password.

Pattern   An array of bytes which stores a pattern of (monochrome) pixels to be transferred to the display maps through procedures performing raster operations. Typically, a pattern holds a screen font or a cursor shape.

Pixel   A raster point on the display specified through its display coordinates or an address in the bitmap.

Pixelmap   *see* Bitmap.

Point key   The right mouse key used, for example, to set or track the caret.

Pointer   A star-shaped mark placed on the display with the SETUP key which designates a point or a viewer. The coordinates of the pointer or the marked viewer may be parameters of commands. Technically, the pointer is a cursor (*see* Cursor.)

Polymorphic command   A command which admits various parameter sources depending on context.

Position mark   A beam perpendicular to the scroll bar which shows the relative position of the viewer in the document (in proportions of the scroll bar height or width.)

Pressing   Holding down a mouse key while the mouse remains stationary.

Print server   A dedicated machine managing a (electrophotographic) printer on a network.

Reader   (1) An abstract data type exported by module Texts which affords sequential access to the characters in an associated text (spelled upper case.) (2) An instance of the abstract data type (spelled lower case.)

Rider   (1) An abstract data type exported by module Files which affords sequential read/write access to the characters in an associated file (spelled upper case.) (2) An instance of the abstract data type (spelled lower case.)

Scanner   (1) An abstract data type exported by module Texts which affords sequential access to tokens such as integers, reals, names etc. in an associated text (spelled upper case.) (2) An instance of the abstract data type (spelled lower case.)

Scroll bar   A stripe at the left (optionally on top) of viewer frames serving for mouse-based scrolling commands.

Scrolling   Positioning the viewer frame in a document whose size exceeds the viewer.

Select key   The right mouse key used to select objects (for example, stretches of text.)

Selection   Objects marked for subsequent actions or as parameters for commands. The selection of objects is performed with the right mouse key. Selected objects are marked, typically displayed in reverse video.

Sending a message   *see* Message.

Server   A special machine running a dedicated file, print or mail service over a network.

Stretch   Part of a text defined by the starting character position and by the position of the first character not included in the stretch.

System log   A global text into which commands report progress and completion messages. The system log is displayed in a text viewer named System.Log. The system log is open on the start-up display.

System tool   A tool listing frequently used commands from modules System, Edit and Compiler. The system tool is open on the start-up display.

System track   *see* Track.

Task   A parameterless procedure which is called at each cycle of the loop.

Text   An abstract data type describing a sequence of characters together with their properties. Texts are active objects exported by module Texts.

Text display manager   A set of procedures exported by module TextFrames which display texts in text frames.

Text frame   A frame specialized to display texts for editing with the standard editor. A text frame is an (active) object exported by module TextFrames which embodies the standard editor.

Text viewer   (1) The viewer class which embodies the standard Oberon text editor. (2) An active Oberon object which is or type MenuViewers.Viewer and has two text frames installed.

Title bar   A bar at the top of viewer frames which is displayed in reverse video. The title bar has the viewer title and, optionally, a set of commands (also termed menu commands) which operate on the viewer. The title bar is also used to drag the viewer under mouse control.

Tool   A text displayed in a text viewer which lists commands ready for execution with the mouse. Parameters may be typed in first. The notion of tool supplants the menu of standard system designs.

Track   A vertically oriented stripe on the display in which viewers are stacked contiguously. A standard Oberon display features two tracks: a wide user track and a narrower system track.

Trap   A run-time error leads to abnormal program termination which is reported in a trap viewer.

Up-call   A procedure call where the parameters are not fully specified at compile time. This is the case for a call to a procedure whose source code is in a module which is *not* imported by the caller.

User identification   *see* Password and User name.

User name   Name under which a station is known to the network. The user name is normally a short; for example, the user's initial. The user name is set with the command System.SetUser.

User track   *see* Track.

Viewer   (1) A rectangular area of the display together with its semantics which is defined by the viewer's command interpreter (or handler.) Typically, a viewer displays a document, such as a text or a graphic, and provides an editor for that document. (2) An active Oberon object which defines a viewer. The base type Viewers.Viewer is exported by module Viewers and is normally extended in the modules comprising a viewer class.

Viewer class   A specialized viewer together with a command module which, among other commands, provides an Open command to create instances of the viewer. A viewer class is typically comprised of a viewer type, an abstract document manager, a display manager and a handler.

Viewer manager   The set of procedures which manages the hierarchical data structure of tracks and viewers. These procedures are exported by module Viewers. They send viewer messages to handlers.

Writer   (1) An abstract data type exported by module Texts which adds character or textual representations of integers, reals and strings to the end of an associated buffer (spelled upper case.) (2) An instance of the abstract data type (spelled lower case.)

Index